INDUSTRIAL RELATIONS RESEARCH
ASSOCIATION SERIES

The Comparative Political Economy of Industrial Relations

EDITED BY

Kirsten S. Wever and Lowell Turner

First edition

Library of Congress Catalog Card Number: 50-13564

ISBN 0-913447-64-1

PRICE $22.95

INDUSTRIAL RELATIONS RESEARCH ASSOCIATION SERIES
    Proceedings of the Annual Meeting
    Proceedings of the Spring Meeting
    Annual Research Volume
    Membership Directory (every fourth year)
IRRA Newsletter (published quarterly)
IRRA Dialogues (published periodically)

Inquiries and other communications regarding membership, meetings, publications, and general affairs of the Association, as well as notice of address changes, should be addressed to the IRRA national office.

INDUSTRIAL RELATIONS RESEARCH ASSOCIATION
4233 Social Science Building, University of Wisconsin—Madison
1180 Observatory Drive, Madison, WI 53706-1393 U.S.A.
Telephone: 608/262-2762   Fax: 608/265-4591

CONTENTS

iii

PREFACE

For too long, comparative industrial relations has been treated as a subfield of industrial relations in the U.S. and has remained relatively isolated from the empirical contributions and theoretical insights of related fields, such as political sociology and comparative political economy. Many of the best works in our field have reached into other disciplines to try to make sense of the rapidly changing and often all too discouraging industrial relations scene both in the U.S. and worldwide. But few have done so self-consciously and with a view to picking out industrial relations trends that unify the experiences—and can illuminate new strategic directions—of labor movements throughout the world. This is the ambitious task that we undertook—as political scientists who have chosen to make our homes in the field of industrial relations—in pulling together the current volume on the comparative political economy of industrial relations.

As the reader will see, the chapters in this volume cover a wide and seemingly disparate range of countries and themes from Southeast Asian economic development strategies to Polish political culture. Yet we were surprised as we surveyed the evidence and arguments of the different pieces of this volume at the clarity of themes that unify them. The particulars are laid out in the individual chapters and pulled together in the conclusion. A set of common strategic challenges emerge for labor movements across developed and newly industrializing countries alike. We suggest, therefore, that broad comparative analyses of domestic and international political economies can illuminate both basic theoretical issues and the critical industrial relations problems and challenges facing employers, labor, and governments.

We would like to thank Tom Kochan and Bob McKersie for their early encouragement and suggestions regarding the need for this volume. John Burton and George Strauss both made helpful comments at the outset, and we especially want to thank them for urging us to include more that the "usual suspects" of the advanced industrial countries for our comparisons. Thanks are due, of course, to all of the chapter authors for their penetrating and highly complementary contributions and to

v

Michael Fichter of the Freie Universität in Berlin for his comments on several early chapter drafts. Finally, we are extremely grateful for the patience, good humor, and efficiency of Kay Hutchison at the IRRA in Madison. What a job!

KIRSTEN WEVER
LOWELL TURNER

A Wide-Angle Lens for a Global Marketplace

KIRSTEN S. WEVER
Radcliffe Public Policy Institute

LOWELL TURNER
Cornell University

In the United States, comparative industrial relations has generally been treated as a subfield of industrial relations proper. Moreover, American IR has traditionally been viewed in isolation from industrial relations in the rest of the world. Comparison has not appeared to be of central concern, and the notion of American "exceptionalism" has remained essentially unchallenged. Moreover, most comparative works are organized around country cases, leaving scholars and practitioners wondering what, if anything, different countries have in common or what they suggest about an overarching theory of industrial relations that could be relevant throughout the advanced industrial world and possibly in the industrializing world.[1]

We undertook to pull together this volume in the belief that our field can no longer afford to see comparative industrial relations as a secondary pursuit. The U.S. experience alone makes this clear, with its high degree of diversity in terms of pressures on different industrial and employment relationships, varieties of regional and local influences on those relationships, alternative strategic responses (or nonresponses) on the part of management, labor and other socioeconomic and political actors, and a broad range of very different kinds of outcomes. Everywhere we see similar kinds of economic and technological pressures working themselves out in very different ways. The differences and similarities that emerge force us to reevaluate traditional categories. They illuminate distinctions not just across national systems but also across regions within countries and even across localities and workplaces. They also draw our attention to interesting parallels in the most unlikely places. For instance, as will become apparent in this volume, on some dimensions the Polish and Australian labor movements have much in common with each other (see the chapters by Marc Weinstein and Margaret Gardner). Auto plants worldwide appear increasingly similar in some ways, while they become more and more different in others (see John Paul MacDuffie's chapter). National economic patterns in Southeast Asia constrain organized labor in ways that recall some of the problems of the U.S. labor movement in the 1980s and 1990s (see the chapter by Sarosh Kuruvilla). This volume reveals an odd and counterintuitive conjunction of distinctions and parallels. Indeed, comparative IR seems at first glance to interweave too many kinds of factors to allow for the kind of elegant theorizing we associate with social science models of the first several post-World War II decades. Nevertheless, the eclectic view through a wide-angle lens that we offer in this volume reveals new and important insights.

In *Industrial Relations Theory*, Dunlop (1958) characterized the IR "system" as a "subsystem" of the "economic system," which in turn he viewed as being analytically separable from the "political system." Kerr et al. (1960), in *Industrialism and Industrial Man*, argued for the inevitability of significant convergence across IR systems in the direction of the pattern Dunlop maps out. If nothing else, this approach no longer matches empirical reality. All of the chapters in this volume are instructive as to the many linkages between the "economic" and the "political," and between actors, events, and dynamics at the micro (company or local), meso (industry or regional), and macro (national or economy-wide) levels of analysis and activity. Each chapter shows in different ways how the very diverse array of contexts within which labor-management relations at the point of production takes place is importantly linked to the bargains, deals, and relationships that are adopted, adapted, or even considered. Likewise, each explores ways in which events at the lowest level of analysis—the point of production— call on governments, business communities, and employee representative organizations to redefine basic roles and functions. As such, this volume explores and challenges, both empirically and theoretically, the conventionally separated fields of industrial relations (subfield, comparative industrial relations) and political science (subfield, comparative political economy, which itself overlaps with sociology, industrial relations, and economics), drawing on the strengths of each in the interest of building on both.

The Chapters

The chapters in this volume show how common underlying trends and pressures—all stemming directly or indirectly from the much-discussed globalization of markets—do evoke a pattern of responses, shedding light on historical influences, political vagaries, economic and technical particulars, strategic inclinations, and institutional constraints. In one way or another, each shows the continuing importance of the institutions of employment and industrial relations in shaping outcomes—both positively and negatively—and in influencing the strategies adopted by actors as they grapple with common and particular pressures. These difficult and changing relationships across levels and between structures and strategies is the necessarily messy organizing theme for our volume.

The first chapter by Richard Locke begins with an overview of industrial relations and human resource management (HRM) policies that are changing across industrial relations systems and settings. Locke discusses developments in eleven advanced industrial economies (Australia, Great Britain, Canada, France, Germany, Italy, Japan, Norway, Sweden, Spain, and the United States), illustrating the importance of different local configurations of interest and power that influence how labor, business, and government navigate the increasingly complex terrain of "leaner" and "meaner" workplace relations. His argument questions the notion of industrial relations convergence, pointing instead to the very different ways in which pressures common to all the advanced industrial countries are interpreted and played out and the high degree of variation in the "valence" of those pressures and their manifestations in workplace practice.

The chapter by Margaret Gardner (Chapter 2) compares labor movement responses to common international pressures in Australia, New Zealand, and the United States. Gardner draws attention to the importance of a unified and politically powerful national labor movement in the development and implementation of effective strategies for meeting employer pressures for decentralization and flexibilization. Thus the Australian Confederation of Trade Unions (ACTU—labor's umbrella organization) fared better in the 1980s and 1990s than its counterparts in New Zealand and the U.S. The critical role of institutions in structuring IR is illustrated by the case of New Zealand, where sweeping deregulation of labor markets in the early 1990s profoundly weakened organized labor's influence at all levels of the economy. Gardner also notes the paradoxical outcome in the Australian case, where the ACTU's success in pushing through its economic restructuring agenda may ultimately weaken the very bases of the movement's political power. This chapter highlights the continuing importance of centralizing institutions that allow for a measure of economy-wide standardization of conditions and practices. However, Gardner's caveat concerning the emerging problems of the Australian unions also evokes Locke's argument about the increasing salience of local dynamics.

The third chapter in this volume, by John Paul MacDuffie, broadens the focus back to a wider range of countries, taking as the point of departure recent developments in the international auto industry. MacDuffie's chapter analyzes data on work and production organization in the auto plants of a variety of companies operating in a range of countries (Japan, Australia, the United States, Canada, as well as several western European and newly industrializing countries). This chapter concludes that trends toward convergence—in particular, the diffusion of lean production models—are visible across countries. Nonetheless, within countries—across and even within companies and plants—widespread divergence can also be seen: for instance, with regard to company strategies for meeting market challenges and organizing the labor-management relationship. Among other things, MacDuffie thus argues for the importance of "best practice" (i.e., lean production) and—unlike Locke—sees important aspects of international convergence. At the same time, his empirical analysis emphasizes the continuing importance of company strategy in determining workplace policies and thus in shaping workplace-level labor-management relations.

In his chapter on Malaysia and the Philippines (the fourth in this volume), Sarosh Kuruvilla calls attention to the close links between industrialization strategies (e.g., import-substitution versus export-led), on the one hand, and the structures and processes of industrial relations systems, on the other. This chapter elaborates the close interconnections between economic structures and the political processes of industrial relations. Kuruvilla also argues that the confluence of the prevailing industrializing strategy and industrial relations system in a given country at a given point in time has specific implications for local workplace and IR practices. He offers an intriguing comparison of how two economies that are quite similar in comparative perspective, facing first similar but later diverging industrialization challenges, find these challenges translated into very different local labor-management outcomes.

Finally, Marc Weinstein's chapter on the dramatic decline of Solidarity in Poland (Chapter 5) emphasizes the powerful influence of an

Anglo-American version of "free market ideology" on the thinking, strategy, and ultimately the strength (that is, relative weakness) of Polish labor. Weinstein shows how Solidarity's emphasis on the rapid free marketization of the Polish economy paradoxically undermined the union's power at the level of the workplace and at the same time weakened its influence in national politics. In this regard, the Polish case recalls the Australian: in both cases labor's bold and proactive strategic calculations, emphasizing fundamental changes as against tried and true structural positions and sources of power, appear to have produced negative effects for the unions and to have strengthened employers. Weinstein's chapter raises the important question of why Polish labor made the choices it made, especially in view of Solidarity's apparently unassailable social and economic standing in the 1980s and in light of the very different strategies pursued by labor in other eastern European countries. This chapter concludes the empirical body of our volume with a reminder of the importance of actor strategies as well as the undeniably powerful influence of the *international* institutions of free-market capitalism.

The last, concluding chapter explores the theoretical implications of this catholic collection of data and arguments. Surprisingly, there appears to be a great deal of theoretical coherence in this apparently disparate collection of essays. Combined, they point to six related themes. First, industrial relations developments must be analyzed in the context of a changing global economy and in particular of the broader "competitiveness" pressures and debates that have taken center stage on national political and economic agendas. Second, apparent everywhere are simultaneous pressures for decentralization and for a realignment of the division of labor between local and central decision making and activities. Third, existing institutions continue to be very important in shaping industrial relations outcomes. Fourth, actor strategies, too, are increasingly important in shaping outcomes and influencing how institutions are used. Fifth, if the benefits of economic growth and competitiveness are to be widely diffused throughout an economy, labor must be included as a key partner in political economic negotiations. Sixth, a model of industrial competitiveness that excludes labor, whose benefits accrue primarily to isolated segments of the economy, remains entirely viable.

In addition, the following three main implications emerge from this collective effort at comparative analysis. First, key actors in advanced and developing economies alike are linking industrial relations structures and strategies into broader economic and social policies, as well as establishing linkages across the different levels at which production and industrial relations take place. Second, labor's strength and adept strategizing are not sufficient to ensure these kinds of linkages. Finally, labor—as a unified actor—is not necessarily involved at all at the intersection between industrial and employment relations, on the one hand, and industrial growth and adjustment, on the other.

Conclusion

We hope in this volume to accomplish three things. First, we hope to meet the wide and growing demand in the IR community for a better understanding of industrial relations developments abroad. That is, we would like to help lift comparative IR out of its secondary status to a more prominent position within the field as well as reaffirm its centrality to other fields, such as comparative political economy and political sociology. Secondly, we aim to shed light on the specific comparison between other advanced industrial economies and industrializing countries, on the one hand, and the U.S., on the other. Since employee representation in the U.S. is experiencing a crisis more profound than in many, if not most, other countries, we believe that the effort to draw as many lessons as possible from other cases is well timed. Finally, we hope to move the field forward in its effort to specify a theory of industrial relations that can update the "New Deal Model." Recently industrial relations scholars have been reaching toward higher levels of analysis to balance the field's traditional shopfloor focus and explain events that the country-centered framework cannot capture (see, for example, Kochan and Osterman 1995). Likewise, after decades of focusing on macro-level variables, comparative political economists (such as ourselves) are increasingly interested in trying to understand shopfloor industrial relations (Thelen 1991; Turner 1991; Wever 1995). We hope this work will aid in these endeavors.

Endnote

[1] For some of the best of these country-based collections, see, for example, Bamber and Lansbury 1993; Windmuller, et al. 1987; Ferner and Hyman 1992; Gourevich, et al. 1984; Rogers and Streeck 1994. Exceptions organized around comparative analysis include Bean 1994; and Adams 1995.

References

Adams, Roy, J. 1995. *Industrial Relations Under Liberal Democracy*. Columbia, SC: University of South Caroline Press.

Bamber, Greg. J., and Russell D. Lansbury. 1993. *International and Comparative Industrial Relations*, 2nd ed. London: Routledge.

Bean, Ron. 1994. *Comparative Industrial Relations: An Introduction to Cross-National Perspectives*. London: Routledge.

Dunlop, John. 1958. *Industrial Relations Systems*, Carbondale, IL: Southern Illinois University Press.

Ferner, Anthony and Richard Hyman, eds., *Industrial Relations in the New Europe* (Oxford: Basil Blackwell, 1992).

Gourevich, Peter, Andrew Martin, George Ross, Stephen Bornstein, Andrei Markovits, and Christopher Allen. 1984. *Unions and Economic Crisis: Britain, West Germany and Sweden*. London: George Allen and Unwin.

Kerr, Clark, John Dunlop, Frederick Harbison, and Charles Meyers. 1960. *Industrialism and Industrial Man*, Cambridge: Harvard University Press.

Kochan, Thomas, and Paul Osterman. 1995. *Mutual Gains Enterprise: Setting the Agenda for Workplace Innovations*. Boston: Harvard Business School Press.

Rogers, Joel, and Wolfgang Streeck. 1994. *Works Councils: Consultation, Representation, Cooperation*. Chicago: University of Chicago Press and NBER.

Thelen, Kathleen. 1991. *Union of Parts: Labor Politics in Postwar Germany*. Ithaca, NY: Cornell University Press.

Turner, Lowell. 1991. *Democracy at Work; Changing World Markets and the Future of Labor Unions*. Ithaca, NY: Cornell University Press.

Wever, Kirsten. 1995. *Negotiating Competitiveness: Employment Relations and Organizational Innovation in Germany and the United States*. Boston: Harvard Business School Press.

Windmuller, John P., et al. 1987. *Collective Bargaining in Industrialized Market Economies: A Reappraisal*. Geneva: International Labor Organization.

CHAPTER 1

The Transformation of Industrial Relations? A Cross-National Review

RICHARD M. LOCKE

Massachusetts Institute of Technology

Much of comparative industrial relations theory rests on the premise that there exist different "national models" of industrial relations, each associated with distinct institutional arrangements governing employment relations within national borders.

Underlying this premise are three basic but interrelated assumptions: that national borders are synonymous with the scope of markets, that differences across nation-states are more pronounced and salient than variations within national economies, and that certain national institutional arrangements are more effective than others at adapting to changing political-economic circumstances. Based on these assumptions, comparative industrial relations research has traditionally treated "national systems" as the basic unit of analysis and focused on macro-institutional features as the key dimensions to use in constructing comparative typologies of industrial relations.

Yet the simultaneous globalization and fragmentation of markets, along with technological innovations, have led to a proliferation of diverse employment relations within and not simply across nations (Locke 1992). In just about every advanced industrial nation, enterprises are experimenting with a variety of new strategies that test and/or transcend traditional industrial relations practices. Whereas in some firms new productivity coalitions among workers, unions, and employers have emerged; elsewhere relations between labor and management have become polarized as managers have sought to reduce costs by "re-engineering" their operations and squeezing their workforce. These developments have not simply challenged established patterns of labor-management relations but also much of industrial relations theory. In other words, given these recent micro-level developments, does it still make sense to speak of distinctive national systems of industrial relations when there appears to be as much variation within different countries in terms of employment practices as there exists across them? Are changes observed in employment relations throughout the advanced industrial nations being driven by differences in the competitive strategies of firms (Kochan, Katz, and McKersie 1986) or by differences in national institutional arrangements, public policies, and long-term historical/cultural traditions (Maurice, Sellier, and Silvestre 1986)? Who are the relevant actors driving the change process, and at what level of the political economy and industrial relations system do they interact? What role do these national institutions play in an increasingly global economy? How do they interact with micro-level actors to shape and/or restrict the range of strategic choices of individual firms and unions?

In an effort to address these questions and consider their implications for comparative industrial relations research and theory, this essay will summarize the initial findings of an eleven-country study on recent developments in employment relations in the advanced economies.[1] The countries in this study include the United States, United Kingdom, Australia, Spain, Italy, France, Germany, Sweden, Norway, Japan, and Canada. This cross-national study focused on four common firm-level employment practices:

1. Changes in the organization of work due to new technologies and altered competitive strategies (i.e., decentralization, team systems of work organization, etc.). Linked to this are shifts in work rules and changing patterns of employee participation within the firm.

2. New compensation schemes affecting the level, structure, and forms of compensation of both blue-collar and white-collar workers.

3. Changing patterns of skill formation and training to match the altered needs of the firms. Related to this is another set of questions regarding the shifting balance between the public and private provision of not just education and training but a whole array of other social welfare benefits and services.

4. Issues of staffing, employment security, and job mobility. How are entry and exit regulated in the various nations? How do individual firms and industries adjust their labor force when faced with cyclical and long-term or structural declines in product demand?

Although these four practices do not constitute an exhaustive list of industrial relations arrangements, they can serve as windows on recent developments in employment relations in a variety of different countries. In other words, by examining a representative set of observable employment practices and how these practices are unfolding in different national and industrial settings, we hoped to assess the degree of change in industrial relations arrangements that have occurred in recent years and determine for each nation what forces and/or actors were driving these changes and at what level of the political economy these decisions/debates were taking place.

The remainder of this chapter is divided into three parts. The first section reviews common patterns emerging across the eleven advanced industrial nations covered in the study. The following section then analyzes divergent patterns of change both across and within countries and shows how both institutional and strategic factors drive these divergent outcomes. The final section concludes by identifying three themes or tensions that may allow us to push forward future research and theorizing in comparative industrial relations.[2]

What's Changing in Industrial Relations? Evidence from the Country Studies

The evidence presented in the eleven-country study, which constitutes the first phase of this research project,[3] documents that many individual firms and even entire industries in different countries are indeed adapting their employment practices to the new terms of international competition. Yet this process of adaptation is neither universal nor uniform. In some firms, the new competitive strategies build on a variety of industrial relations and human resource practices which enhance the skill base and flexibility of the workplace and promote greater communication, trust, and coordination among the firm's various stakeholders. Yet other firms have sought to adjust to increased competition by subcontracting work to lower-wage workers and firms, downsizing, and seeking to compete on the traditional basis of cost and price competition. Still other companies have combined both strategies, adapting "high-trust" practices for their more skilled and valued employees while simultaneously sweating other groups of workers employed in other divisions or areas of the firm. In other words, although a new approach to employment relations has emerged in *all* the advanced industrial nations included in our research, the particular forms it has taken and the extent to which it has diffused vary considerably both within nations—across firms, industries and regions—as well as across countries with different institutional arrangements and historical traditions. Closer examination of both these commonalities and differences illuminates the nature and extent of change in comparative industrial relations.

Common Patterns

The evidence provided in the various country studies suggest that several general patterns are indeed emerging across the advanced industrial states.

An Enterprise Focus

In all countries covered in this study, the individual enterprise has emerged as an increasingly important locus of human resource and industrial relations decision making and strategy. This, in turn, implies that managers (sometimes in collaboration with local unions or works councils) have been the driving force for introducing changes in employment practices in recent years. This was not always the case. In the past in most European countries and in Australia, national or industry-level union-management bargaining or even tripartite negotiations with government established the basic wage benefits and conditions of employment. Even in the United States with its highly decentralized industrial relations system, industrywide pattern bargaining arrangements in industries such as coal, steel, rubber tire, and transportation existed for much of the postwar era. Both in these sectors and in others where these arrangements did not exist, labor unions were the driving force behind improvements in wages and benefits while management reacted to (or sought to insulate itself from) union initiatives. All of this has changed in recent years.

Sweden represents the most visible case in point. There employers have led efforts to break out of national and even industry-level collective bargaining structures in order to allow individual firms to negotiate terms and conditions of employment that best fit their particular circumstances. Australia's highly centralized system of national arbitration awards has also been reformed in order to promote enterprise bargaining and wage adjustments in return for efficiency enhancing changes in work practices. Individual employers must now take the lead in proposing the specific changes necessary to improve productivity in their operations in order to justify wage increases. Similar decentralizing trends are visible in Italy, where the national wage escalator (*scala mobile*) was recently abolished and where a reconfiguration of bargaining arrangements toward the local level is taking place, and in Japan, where a debate is beginning to emerge over whether the national Spring Wage Offensive is still workable, given the pressures on labor costs resulting from the fallen yen/dollar ratio. More subtle but comparable signs of decentralization are visible in Germany, where it is reported that works councils are taking on a greater role vis-à-vis industrywide collective bargaining as the "qualitative issues" related to training, new technology, work organization, and employment adjustment grow in importance. Decentralization occurred throughout the 1980s in the U.S. with the decline of industry-wide pattern bargaining and was also reinforced in the U.K. through various government policies (i.e., privatization) and managerial strategies.

Increased Flexibility

Decentralization was accompanied by the search for greater flexibility in how work is organized and labor is deployed. In just about every country covered in this study, various government regulations and norms governing hiring, firing, layoffs, and the use of labor have been relaxed or modified so as to give individual employers greater discretion. For example, in Italy regulations requiring that employers seeking new hires give priority to workers who have waited longest on the government unemployment agency's lists have been modified so that employers can hire the specific individuals they want. In Germany the CDU-led government also promoted a limited deregulation of the labor market which permitted temporary work contracts and simplified the regulation of part-time jobs. Similar modifications took place throughout the advanced industrial nations. As a result, youth, part-time, and/or temporary employment contracts exploded in number in Italy, Spain, Norway, the United Kingdom, the United States, Germany, and Japan. Swedish employers are pushing for analogous changes in their country's regulatory framework.

Linked to these changes in external labor market practices are a series of related efforts on the shopfloor and in the internal labor markets of firms. The essence of these initiatives is to draw out the discretionary effort and creative potential of workers at all levels of the organization by providing work arrangements that delegate decision-making authority to the source of the problem, encourage teamwork, promote problem identification and resolution, and enhance coordination across functional boundaries. In the United States, for example, Paul Osterman (1994) has reported that 64% of the establishments covered in his nationally representative survey have introduced innovations such as employee problem-solving groups, work teams, total quality management, and job rotation. In a survey of industrial enterprises in Lombardia, Italy's most industrial region, 56% of the companies claimed to have introduced new job rotation arrangements. Flexible work hours were reported to be even more widespread. Job rotation, flexible job arrangements, quality circles, and small group activity are reported to be widely diffused in a number of Japanese industries, including the iron and steel, automobile, chemical, and machinery industries. Even in the United Kingdom, the Third Workplace Industrial Relations Survey reported that 20% of all large enterprises covered in the study had problem-solving groups and/or quality circles.

Growing Importance of Skill Development

Another common pattern we are observing across these countries is the premium that the labor market places on the skills of the workforce. Because the pressures for continuous improvements in productivity and quality are intensifying and because effective use of new technologies require increased analytical and behavioral skills, both firms and governments in most of the advanced industrial nations covered in this study are increasing their investments in training and skill development. For example, the federal government of Canada has sought to support training efforts by earmarking $800 million a year to finance these efforts. The Australian and French governments have both established compulsory levies on companies in order to fund expanded training programs. The British, Spanish, Norwegian, and Swedish governments have all promoted a series of major institutional reforms aimed at enhancing the quality of vocational training in their respective states. The reform of the apprenticeship and vocational training systems are hotly debated issues in the U.S. and Italy as well.

Associated with the greater attention to skill development and training is an increase in performance- and/or skill-related pay systems. Thirty-nine percent of Australian workplaces with five or more employees have performance-related compensation schemes. The 1992 Workplace Industrial Relations Survey in Britain reported that 20% of both skilled manual and nonmanual workers received some form of merit pay, and a recent survey of company-level negotiations in Italy found that between 1984 and 1989, 130 agreements covering 700,000 employees had introduced different forms of performance-based pay arrangements. Similar developments were reported in the U.S. and Japan.

Union Membership Declines

A fourth common finding is that unions are experiencing major challenges in all countries as the pace of restructuring intensifies, the workforce becomes more diverse, and as the average size of enterprises declines. In an era of rapid organizational and industrial restructuring, the ability to recruit new members or retain existing members when they move across jobs, organizations, or in and out of employed status becomes crucial for unions. Managerial ideology and the degree of legitimacy unions enjoy in the broader society also influence the ability of unions to adapt to the changes underway. Thus countries in which unions have a difficult time recruiting or retaining members and/or where the role of unions in society or in specific enterprises meets with the strongest ideological resistance from business and/or government leaders experienced the largest losses in union membership and the greatest challenges to shift their basic role and patterns of worker representation. Not surprisingly, unions in the U.S., Britain, and France experienced especially difficult times and steep membership declines over the course of the past decade. But similar (although less pronounced) declines in union membership are visible in Japan, Australia, Italy, and in the private sector in Canada. Moreover, in several countries (i.e., Italy, the U.K., and Norway) new kinds of unions or employee associations have emerged to challenge the organizational dominance of the more established unions.

As this quick survey of common trends suggests, it does appear that a general process of change or transformation of employment relations is indeed taking place throughout the advanced industrial world. Everywhere unions are in decline and management is resurgent. In all countries we can identify firms engaged in new forms of work organization and more flexible use of labor. And a greater appreciation for and investment in skill formation and training is manifest in all the countries covered in this study. Yet common trends can sometimes be deceiving, given that not all countries began at the same starting point and that seemingly similar practices and arrangements can have significantly different meanings in different national contexts. For example, employer efforts to reorganize work on the shopfloor are sometimes strongly resisted by unions in the United States since they undermine narrow job definitions with their related wage, seniority, and security provisions—practices that represent the institutional anchors for American labor's rights within the firm. In Germany, however, where employment security and union strength are not dependent upon shopfloor practices like job control, workers and their unions have welcomed similar changes that upgrade their skills and enhance their autonomy. Conversely, American employers have traditionally enjoyed substantial flexibility both in the determination of wages and in the hiring, firing, and laying off of workers. But the drive for employment flexibility in Germany and for wage flexibility in Sweden have produced major new conflicts between labor and management since the late 1970s.

The point is that while employers' "search for flexibility" (Boyer 1988) may be a general phenomenon emanating from international pressures that are common to all the advanced industrial nations, different institutional arrangements filter these common pressures differently, so that the valence of particular issues is quite varied in the different national contexts. Thus equally interesting to analyze are the variations in patterns of adaptation observed across different nation states.[4] We now turn to a discussion of these issues.

Cross-National and Cross-Firm Variations

Work Organization

As noted above, flexibility in work organization is becoming a key source of competitive advantage for firms across all the advanced industrialized nations we are studying. Experiments with greater teamwork, employee participation in problem solving and productivity improvements, quality circles and the use of total quality management tools were documented in all the countries covered in our study. But diffusion of these practices remains uneven. In some countries, such as Japan and Germany, these flexible and team-oriented work systems were relatively common already, while in others they represent such fundamental changes in culture and practice that they tend to be adopted slowly and meet with strong resistance from supervisors, managers, and in some cases union leaders. For example, in the United Kingdom, no more than 2% of all establishments with more than 25 workers have quality circles or problem-solving groups. Team work and major alterations in job content are even more rare. In the United States, recent survey research suggests that no more than one-third of American workplaces have introduced more flexible work systems covering a majority of their employees. And the majority of these were introduced within the past five years and, therefore, remain subject to the challenge of skeptics that they are just another management fad that will not withstand the test of time. Canada appears to have experienced only a handful of cases (predominantly in large companies) where large scale innovations in work organization have taken place.

In contrast, quality circles, team-based work, job rotation, and flexible jobs appear to be extensive and diffused widely throughout Japanese industry. Research by the SOFI Institute of Göttingen also suggests that new forms of work organization are widespread in the German automobile, machine tool, and chemical industries. The diffusion of new forms of work based on more flexible and autonomous teams of workers was also documented in several case studies on the Italian petrochemical, telecommunications, personal computer, machine tool, and automobile industries (Regini and Sabel 1989). Elsewhere in Spain, Norway, and Sweden, for example, work reorganization has also taken place but primarily within large, "leading edge" or, in the case of Spain, multinational companies.

These observed differences in patterns of work reorganization suggest that those countries that come from a tradition of job control—the United States, Australia, Britain, and Canada—in which work was traditionally organized along more rigid Taylorist lines and where union strategy sought to regulate rather than transform work practices have experienced the greatest pressures to transform their work organization arrangements. In contrast, those national systems of industrial relations that were never completely Taylorist and/or where they already had workplace practices that promote flexibility and communication such as Japan, Germany, and to some degree Italy, seem to have been able to accommodate more easily the need for these new workplace practices through incremental adaptations of their existing arrangements.

Interestingly enough, variation in the adaptation of new forms of work organization exists not simply across but also within most of the countries covered in this study. Within all of these countries (even the ones that appear to be most advanced in new forms of work organization), the most profound departures from traditional practices are manifest in settings where (1) a new "greenfield" plant or worksite is established (e.g., Volvo's Kalmar and Udevalla plants, Opel's Eisenach and Volkswagen's Mosel plant in eastern Germany); (2) major technological changes are introduced and employees or their representatives have some voice in that process (e.g., many of the large Japanese firms in the automobile, steel, and electronics industries); (3) the pressures of international competition have been strongest (such industries as autos, steel, electronics and related high technology sectors); and (4) new union-management partnerships have been created such as in the Japanese transplants in the U.K. or Saturn Corporation in the U.S. In Germany, for instance, where new forms of work organization are reported to be widespread, differences in the extent and modalities of workplace change nonetheless exist across sectors or between new and older plants within the same industry. As one indicator of this variation, take, for example, the emergence of new kinds of more broadly trained, highly skilled workers. Recent research by the SOFI Institute of

Göttingen revealed that these so-called "system regulators" made up only 5% of the total workforce in the automobile industry but 33% of the chemical industry's labor force. Likewise, in Japan tremendous variation in the use of teams, quality circles, and job enrichment programs exists between large and small enterprises within the same industries. In short, even within countries there appears to be significant variation in the extent and modality of change, and these differences seem to be linked to the particular characteristics of individual establishments, firms, and industries and not merely the institutional environment in which they are embedded.

Clearly, many of these workplace innovations remain in a fragile or vulnerable state and face a number of obstacles that limit their sustainability and diffusion. Among these obstacles, the most serious appear to be the lack of an adequate rate of economic growth needed to absorb the jobs lost to increases in productivity. This reinforces the already strong pressures to downsize or "reengineer" organizations in ways that produce short-term cost savings but that, in the long run, may destroy the trust and mutual commitment needed to sustain work organization innovations and flexibility.

Some countries also suffer from a lack of strong government support for innovation. With the possible exception of Australia, there are no national institutions that approach the significance of the Japan Productivity Center for sharing information and promoting adoption of ideas and practices that promise long-term gains to firms and their employees. Some countries also continue to suffer from highly adversarial labor-management relations and declining membership, power, and security of unions. This makes it difficult to develop sustained partnerships between labor and management at the macro level of these economies or at the industry level that are needed to provide a supportive institutional umbrella for labor-management cooperation and innovation in specific enterprises and workplaces. Although the relative importance of these obstacles vary across these countries, our prediction is that those countries that are able to overcome them will be the ones where innovations in work organization are likely to diffuse most widely in the future.

Job Mobility, Staffing, and Employment Security

One of the most widely accepted propositions in our field is that innovations in work practices or other forms of worker-management cooperation or productivity improvement are not likely to be sustained over time when workers fear that by increasing productivity they will work themselves out of their jobs. Unfortunately, the past decade has been a time when the demand for change and innovation has been strong while job security generally declined in nearly all of the countries included in our study. But again, there has been tremendous variation among countries. In the U.K., for example, one-half of all workplaces in manufacturing and one-third in private services resorted to compulsory redundancy as a means of reducing the size of their workforces. In Canada only about 20% of workers employed in large establishments enjoyed any kind of employment and/or income guarantees. The situation was even more precarious for workers in smaller firms. Even in Japan many companies promoted "voluntary severance" (de facto forced layoffs with severance pay) as a way of drastically reducing their labor forces. In contrast, in Norway and Sweden a combination of laws and collective bargaining agreements provided relatively high job security for workers, while in Italy laid-off workers received income maintenance payments and benefits until they were either hired back by their employers or paid a severance bonus. German workers also enjoyed considerable employment security and extensive benefits during layoffs.

A quick review of these differences illustrates clearly the important role institutional arrangements play in providing workers with various forms of job and/or income security. Notwithstanding various efforts to roll back state intervention in the Italian, French, and German economies or the setbacks Social Democratic regimes in northern Europe have suffered in recent years, most of these countries continue to possess an array of institutional arrangements (e.g., retraining programs, *cassa integrazione guadagni*, active labor market policies, etc.) aimed at protecting workers from the consequences of job loss. Yet here, too, we see significant variation within countries as well. For example, employees in small Japanese and Italian companies do not enjoy the same kinds of benefits, security, and possibilities for transfer as workers in larger establishments. Likewise, in the U.K., employment security (insecurity) is as much a sectoral and status issue as a national phenomenon. Although manual workers in the private sector enjoy little, if any, job security—they can be dismissed with a week's notice—in the public sector, both manual and nonmanual workers are so well protected that they enjoy de facto lifelong employment.

Nonetheless, the problem of job security is one that all parties who seek to promote innovations must face. Unfortunately, there are no easy answers to this dilemma. As recent experiences by leading high-tech firms in the U.S. or large manufacturing companies in Japan have illustrated, few, if any, individual firms can credibly guarantee lifetime employment security. Negotiating or offering job transfers, early retirements, severance payments, and other adjustment assistance is and has been used as part of the way out of this dilemma. But in the longer run, perhaps the greatest employment security a firm can offer is to provide employees continuous training and development opportunities while employed so that if and when the time comes for employees to reenter the external labor market, they will possess the skills necessary to secure another job.

Unfortunately, it is not clear that many firms are thinking this way at the moment. Instead, there has been an explosion in the use of part-time and temporary employees or short-term employment contracts in many countries. This builds on a trend that was first introduced with "guest workers" in Germany and other northern European countries during periods of labor shortages in the 1960s and 1970s. These contingent or flexible employment relationships pose difficult problems for managers, public policy officials, and unions, since the traditional lines of authority and responsibility for management often get blurred, and the training, benefits, and other human resource practices needed to promote a highly skilled, committed, and productive workforce are less likely to be found in contingent employment relationships. Sometimes mixing regular and contingent workers also introduces new social tensions in the workplace and in the larger society. Women, minorities, and immigrants are particularly vulnerable and over-represented in these situations. The U.S., for example, has experienced major debates and conflicts between labor and management over the increasing trend to "contract out" work that was previously performed by full-time career employees. In Japan the role of immigrant workers has become a significant political and social issue as well. Clearly, a major development in recent years has been the increase in the diversity of the labor force and the types of employment relationships found within these economies. Whether these are managed in ways that promote mutual gains through new opportunities for new classes of workers or whether they degenerate into two classes of employment—a small and shrinking core of well-paid and secure employees surrounded by a large number of lower-paid, less secure, less loyal, and less well-trained employees—remains to be seen.

Japan faces an especially acute employment adjustment crisis, particularly in the service sector of its economy. Pressures from U.S. trade negotiators to open Japanese markets to foreign competitors are likely to uncover considerable overstaffing and inefficiencies in this sector. Some of our colleagues in Japan are now openly questioning whether the "lifetime employment system" commonly found in large firms will survive.

Compensation

The worldwide slowdown in economic growth and productivity along with the recessions of the early 1980s and again in the early 1990s held back real wage growth in most advanced industrialized countries of the world. Real wages were most stagnant in the U.S., however, and grew moderately in Japan, Germany, and several other European countries. Inequality in income also grew within most of the countries included in this study but, again, to the greatest extent in the U.S. In contrast, income inequality remained stable or grew only slightly in Germany, Norway, and Japan (Freeman and Katz 1994). In these countries their centralized wage-setting structures and traditions continued to hold down expansion of wage differentials, while in Italy and Sweden the longstanding solidaristic wage policies followed through most of the 1970s gave way somewhat as business pushed hard to decentralize bargaining structures and lower labor costs. Once again we see that in countries lacking strong national or sectoral bargaining arrangements (e.g., the U.S. and U.K.), wage differentials and income inequality grew the most. Nonetheless, in all countries there was a resurgence of inequalities either in income or employment opportunities. This threatens not only to polarize these societies into "haves" and "have nots" but also to undermine the solidaristic principles around which labor movements have traditionally organized.

These varying wage developments are closely related to other features of the employment relationships examined in this research. For example, the growth in inequality is, in part, a function of the increased demand for skilled blue-collar, technical, and professional workers with advanced analytical and problem-solving skills needed to effectively use new technologies. In the U.S. where training institutions that other countries use to produce new employees with these skills are relatively weak and where the unions that traditionally supported development of these skills have declined precipitously, the supply of workers with the requisite skills also declined. This combination of shifting supply and demand accompanied by the institutional differences in wage setting helps explain why the U.S. is such a deviant case (Freeman and Katz 1994).

Human Resources and Firm Governance

Some believe that a strategy for adjusting to the changing environment of employment relations that achieve mutual gains for firms and their employees will only be chosen and sustained over time if employee interests and human resource considerations are strongly represented in the top strategic level and governance processes of corporations. This representation might be direct and formal—through worker representatives on supervisory or corporate boards of directors, or indirect and/or informal—through the role of the top human resource management professional and/or union-management consultations and information sharing. Yet we observe wide variation in the extent to which human resources has gained this strategic position in corporations around the world.

Although we have seen a good deal of debate and some experimentation with new ways to engage human resource issues in corporate strategy and governance processes, the general view from our country teams is that relatively little has changed over the course of the past decade. Those countries that had strong formal institutional arrangements, such as Germany and Norway, continued them or strengthened them in marginal ways. As noted earlier, in Germany the evidence suggests that the role of works councils increased relative to the role of unions as "qualitative" issues, such as the introduction of new technologies, training, work reorganization, etc., gained in importance. In Japan, informal labor-management consultation continued and perhaps was strengthened somewhat as firms and union representatives sought to cope with the aftermath of the two oil shocks of the 1970s. There has also been a variety of experiments with greater information sharing, union-management consultation, and worker representation on corporate boards in the U.S., Britain, and Australia, but these experiences have so far been quite limited.

Tentative Conclusions and Questions for Future Research

The cross-national review of recent changes in employment relations presented above suggests that there is indeed a significant transformation of industrial relations practices taking place in the advanced industrial nations. But the extent of this transformation and the modalities it takes on vary significantly both across and within national industrial relations systems. Certainly, national institutions and traditions continue to be important in shaping employment relations. The above review illustrated clearly the continued importance they played in shaping divergent patterns of, say, work organization or staffing arrangements. But at the same time, notwithstanding these national divergences, significant subnational variation in just about all employment practices was visible as well. This suggests that perhaps cross-national research in industrial relations needs to move beyond simple macro-institutional analysis and focus on developments as well.

One possible way of moving future research in this direction is by studying common themes or tensions found in all countries and how they are affecting both the strategic choices of micro-level actors and the traditional institutional arrangements of various countries. What follows are three suggestions for future research based on three sets of tensions observed in our multi-country study.

Coexistence of Cost-based and Value-added Strategies

Within all the countries we studied we see the uneasy coexistence of cost-based and differentiation high-value-added competitive strategies. These two polar opposites do not divide up along national lines, although the distribution of the two may vary within different countries. Value-added-based strategies are expected to lead to the most fundamental transformations in employment relations and have the best chance of producing outcomes of mutual benefit to firms and their employees. Cost-based strategies, on the other hand, are expected to lead to a downward spiral of wages, working conditions, and labor standards and to reinforce adversarial relations at the workplace. Given the values we hold for industrial relations, a strong preference is expressed for the value-added strategies.

The data provided in the various national studies included in our research suggest that firms are indeed struggling with these choices, but few firms can be clearly identified as pure adopters of either option. Instead we observe most firms engaging in both strategies, sometimes simultaneously, but often sequentially. The dramatic changes in Fiat's strategy over the course of the 1980s and early 1990s illustrate the point most vividly. After an intensive period of labor conflict initiated by the company's decision to restructure and lay off 20,000 workers in the early 1980s in order to reduce its costs and weaken the unions, Fiat has engaged in a gradual process of rebuilding its relationships with its workforce and unions in order to pursue its current strategy of rapid product development, extensive use of state-of-the-art technologies, and production of high-quality products (Locke 1995; Camuffo and Volpato 1995). Countless similar examples can be found in the U.S. where the initial round of concession bargaining of the early 1980s in industries as varied as airlines, autos, steel, and paper (Cappelli 1983) were followed by efforts to engage employees and their union representatives in partnerships to improve quality, productivity, and labor-management relations. The case of AT&T in telecommunications is especially instructive, since this company and its union representatives experienced a tumultuous decade of continuous downsizing and restructuring in the face of emerging new competition. Yet even as the downsizing continued, by the 1990s this company and its union were developing one of the more advanced models of labor-management partnership and employee participation found in the U.S. today (e.g., the "Workplace of the Future").

However, a reverse trend can be observed as well. For example, in the United States a number of the high-technology firms long known for their commitment to state-of-the-art human resource practices, such as IBM and Digital Equipment Corporation, have taken the reverse path in the 1990s as markets for their hardware products declined forcing them to downsize and cut labor costs dramatically. Volvo in Sweden presents another example of the reverse scenario. After developing one of the world's boldest efforts to reorganize work in its Kalmar and Udevalla auto assembly plants, the company decided to restructure by closing these innovative operations in favor of its larger and more traditionally organized facilities in Göteburg. In the United Kingdom the mixture of traditional and new human resource practices observed in many industries has led to a debate over whether or not anything was changing at all.

The low-cost response to market pressures and changes appears to be most frequent in countries with weak institutions, low levels of unionization, decentralized bargaining structures, and a limited government role in labor market affairs. Again the U.S. is the extreme case, followed closely by Britain. Cost-based strategies may give firms a comparative advantage over value-added firms in the short run. However, they exert a perverse externality on society as a whole by making it riskier for competing firms to make the long-term investments needed to upgrade skills and change their organizational practices to get the benefits of these investments. Thus to the extent that cost-based strategies dominate in a country, the nation risks getting caught in a low-wage/low-skill equilibrium. Nations that lack strong institutions that constrain the choice of the low-wage option are particularly vulnerable to this problem. The U.S. may be suffering from this phenomenon at the moment.

Although there is less flexibility for individual firms to choose the low-cost option in countries such as Germany, Japan, Sweden, and

Norway, even in these countries firms have experienced increasing pressures to restructure in ways that reduce their labor cost disadvantages. Thus while strong industrial relations institutions can moderate the tendency of firms to adjust by controlling labor costs, firms working within these institutional contexts nonetheless experience increasing pressures from competitors in other countries. Whether negotiated adjustments will occur through traditional institutional mechanisms or whether we observe a general weakening of these previously strong institutional arrangements is an issue that needs to be followed closely by future comparative research. An equally important question is whether a negotiated or gradual adjustment strategy involving worker representation produces outcomes that better balance the interests of all the stakeholders involved than the now unilateral management-driven approach observed in countries with weaker and more decentralized unions and industrial relations institutions. A good experiment to watch carefully on this point is the "managed decentralization" strategy presently being pursued in Australia.

The Flexibility/Polarization Nexus

A second tension that appears to be arising from the drive for increased flexibility in work organization and the related employment practices is the potential for polarization of employment opportunities between those with access to jobs with innovative practices and those without. Inequality in income, temporary or other forms of contingent work, differential access to training and career opportunities that build the human capital necessary to be competitive in external labor markets—all of these are the product of the type of partial diffusion of the workplace innovations. This not only makes it more difficult to sustain commitment to value-added strategies at the micro level but also exacerbates the divisions among different groups within society. The potential for polarization is again the greatest in situations where the decisions about how to structure employment relations are left to individual employers unmediated by strong institutions that represent the interests of workers. Yet strong institutions alone are not enough. The evidence suggests that worker representatives and/or government regulatory agencies need to have strategies of their own that both support the innovative efforts of individual firms and *complement* these strategies by extending access to these innovations and their benefits to those work groups in which individual firms have no self-interest in investing. In contrast, strong worker institutions that lack this type of complementary strategy are likely to simply resist these innovations for fear of undermining their traditional roles and approaches to representing or protecting workers. In this case, the result is increased conflict over the innovations themselves that further limits their diffusion.

Again, the U.S. provides the clearest example. The U.S. petrochemical industry has experienced a growth in contract workers in recent years as firms in that industry have sought to increase their flexibility, lower their labor costs, and substitute unionized workers with non-union contract employees (Kochan, Smith, Wells, and Rebitzer 1994). One of the consequences of this development is that the influx of less experienced and less trained workers has led to increased rates of accidents and personal injuries among those doing the most high-risk work in this industry. Despite the vocal opposition of the unions representing petrochemical workers, and despite the understanding of these trends and their effects by the government agencies responsible for enforcing safety regulations, little has yet been done to deal with the consequences of this search for flexibility by individual employers. Only recently have some local unions and employers and some local employer associations acting on their own begun to address these issues by forming regional partnerships to train the contract workers and upgrade the labor standards under which these employees work.

Examples of this same phenomenon can be observed in other countries as well. In Europe the general debate over "insiders" versus "outsiders" in the labor market is a macro-level manifestation of this issue. In Japan the general exclusion of women from the lifetime employment system and the debates about whether those working in the smaller subcontracting firms that lie outside the interlocking networks of large firms enjoy benefits and labor standards similar to those inside these networks are likewise manifestations of this issue.

Variations in wages, working conditions, and labor market outcomes will be found in any employment relations system reflecting differences in individual human capital and a host of other well-documented organizational and institutional factors. Thus it should not be surprising that a gap exists on these dimensions between those with access to workplace innovations and those left out. The question that begs for more micro-level research is whether this gap is larger or smaller than those found in traditional employment systems. If it is found to be larger, the question then might well turn to what institutional responses on the part of unions, industry-level associations, and government can best cope with the consequences of this disparity by extending access to these innovations rather than by policies that seek to return to the more traditional modes of employment relations and regulation.

Voice Versus the Decline of Traditional Unions

It is ironic that just as unions in many countries around the world have been declining in influence and membership, the need for a strong role for employee voice in corporate decision making, industry-level interactions, and national policymaking is growing. Yet there is little evidence that human resource issues have gained increased influence in corporate decision making in any of the advanced industrial nations. If anything, they are losing what little voice they previously possessed. Even in Germany where the law institutionalizes employee representation in corporate governance through establishment-level works councils and codetermination, unions now appear on the defensive, and relations between works councils and unions are strained. Moreover, the decentralizing trend observed in most countries is leading to a weakening of industry-level bargaining and other forms of union-management interaction in some but not all countries. And in some countries national-level tripartite or corporatist structures have been in decline for a number of years (Swenson 1989).

Yet as the above discussion of polarization suggests, a simple reconstruction of union membership and union power exerted around traditional strategies is not only unlikely to occur in many countries, but also, given the forces that have led to union decline, such a mirror image rebound would not effectively serve the interests of workers in coping with the forces affecting their vital interests in an international economy. The question, therefore, is what new or modified voice mechanisms can effectively represent worker interests in the current environment?

Several examples from different countries suggest some tentative answers or hypotheses that need to be tested in future micro-level analyses. In Germany, works councils appear to be increasingly important because they deal with "qualitative" issues such as training, new technology, work organization, and adjustments to restructuring. Moreover, they do so by representing all of the workers in an establishment, not just union members or blue-collar workers. Works councils also represent workers while operating under a "peace obligation." By their design, works councils are expected to be integrative rather than distributive institutions. Likewise, IG Metall has initiated its own strategy for promoting "groupwork," its version of the type of teamwork employers in the automobile and many other manufacturing industries are seeking as part of their agenda for workplace innovation and transformation. It is not surprising, therefore, that there is growing interest and debate over how to achieve the functional equivalent of the German works council system in the U.S. and Canada (Wever 1995; Adams 1985; Freeman and Rogers 1993; Rogers and Streeck 1995; Kochan and Osterman 1994; Weiler 1990).

The Australian case illustrates an effort to reform national institutions and to decentralize industrial relations decision making to the enterprise while attending to some of the potential negative side effects of decentralization and work reform within individual enterprises. In Australia "managed decentralism," a strategy that evolved, in part, out of policy debates initiated by the labor movement and the labor government, has been developing in interesting ways. Included in the decentralizing program in Australia are efforts to restructure the trade union movement along industry lines and to promote industrywide training and occupational standards. In the auto industry a Trade Union Training Authority (TUTA) helps oversee these standards and to support training on an industrywide basis. Although it is too early to tell whether this managed decentralism strategy will obtain the changes in employment practices and institutions needed to improve the competitiveness of Australian industry while simultaneously safeguarding employment standards, it does provide an interesting model for other countries to observe and one that needs to be tested in future research.

New forms of employee representation have emerged recently in Italy as well. After years of debate, the moribund factory councils have been replaced by the RSU—plant-level bodies open to all workers, regardless of union affiliation. Linked to this are other organizational reforms that have enhanced the internal democracy, representation, and, hence, vibrancy of the Italian unions.

Thus a final line of research would focus on alternative forms of employee voice and their consequences for both workers and firms. Linked to this is a second concern focusing on attempts by the unions to reform their structures and strategies as they seek to aggregate and represent an increasingly heterogeneous workforce.

New research in comparative industrial relations needs to investigate the determinants of these diverse patterns and tensions manifest both across and within different national systems. In the same way that traditional comparative research sought to identify the key institutional variables shaping patterns of industrial relations across different countries, we could begin comparing seemingly analogous subnational models or patterns across nations in order to better grasp the underlying political, economic, and social factors shaping these divergent patterns *within* each nation.

Once we better understand the determinants and consequences of each of these micro-level patterns, we can begin to analyze the different mixes or distributions of these subnational models *across* nations. Only if one or a particular set of models emerges as dominant in a given country should we return to the convention of comparing industrial relations systems in terms of national models. If such a model or set of models is indeed identified, we will be on our way toward reconstructing national models that highlight rather than obscure the dynamic relationship that exists between macro-level practices and national regulatory institutions. If not, we must construct completely new typologies, based perhaps on a more local or micro-level patterns of employment relations, to guide future comparative research and theorizing. Only time and a lot more comparative work will allow us to decide.

Endnotes

[1] See Locke, Kochan, and Piore (1995a). The countries in this study include the United States, United Kingdom, Australia, Spain, Italy, France, Germany, Sweden, Norway, Japan, and Canada.

[2] This chapter draws heavily on Locke, Kochan, and Piore (1995b).

[3] A second phase of cross-national industry-specific studies is currently underway. Industries under examination include automobiles, financial services, steel, and telecommunications.

[4] For more on this theme, see Locke and Thelen (1995).

References

Adams, Roy. 1985. "Should Works Councils Be Used as Industrial Relations Policy?" *Monthly Labor Review*, Vol. 108, no. 7, pp. 25-9.

Boyer, Robert. 1988. "The Search for New Wage/Labor Relations." In Robert Boyer, ed., *The Search for Labor Management Flexibility*. Oxford: Clarendon Press.

Camuffo, Arnaldo, and Giuseppe Volpato. 1995. "Labor Relations Heritage and Lean Manufacturing at Fiat." Paper presented at the 10th World Congress of the International Industrial Relations Research Association, Washington DC.

Cappelli, Peter. 1983. "Concession Bargaining and the National Economy." In *Proceedings of the Thirty-fifth Annual Meeting of the Industrial Relations Research Association*, New-York, Dec. 28-30, 1982. Madison, WI: Industrial Relations Research Association, pp. 362-71.

Chaykowski, Richard, and Anil Verma, eds. 1992. *Industrial Relations in Canadian Industry*. Toronto: Holt Reinhart and Winston.

Dunlop, John T. 1958. *Industrial Relations Systems*. New York: Holt.

Dore, Ronald. 1973. *British Factory Japanese Factory.* Berkeley: University of California Press.

Edwards, Paul K., and Keith Sisson. 1990. "Industrial Relations in the UK: Change in the 1980s, ESRC Research Briefing." University of Warwick.

Freeman, Richard B., and Larry Katz. 1994. "Rising Wage Inequality: The United States Versus Other Countries." In Richard B. Freeman, ed., *Working Under Different Rules.* New York: Russell Sage.

Freeman, Richard B., and Joel Rogers. 1993. "Who Speaks for Us?" In Bruce E. Kaufman and Morris M. Kleiner, eds., *Employee Representation: Alternatives and Future Directions.* Madison, WI: Industrial Relations Research Association, pp. 13-80.

Kerr, Clark, John T. Dunlop, Frederick Harbison, and Charles Myers. 1960. *Industrialism and Industrial Man.* Cambridge: Harvard University Press.

Kern, Horst, and Michael Schumann. 1984. *Das Ende der Arbeitsteilung?* Frankfurt: Campus Verlag.

Kochan, Thomas A., Harry Katz, and Robert B. McKersie. 1986. *The Transformation of American Industrial Relations.* New York: Basic Books.

Kochan, Thomas A., and Paul Osterman. 1994. *The Mutual Gains Enterprise.* Boston: Harvard Business School Press.

Kochan, Thomas A., Michael Smith, John C. Wells, and James B. Rebitzer. 1994. "Human Resource Strategies and Contingent Workers: The Case of Safety and Health in the Petrochemical Industry." *Human Resource Management,* Vol. 33, pp. 55-78.

Locke, Richard. 1992. "The Demise of the National Union in Italy: Lessons for Comparative Industrial Relations Theory." *Industrial and Labor Relations Review,* Vol. 45, no. 2 (January), pp. 229-49.

_____. 1995. *Remaking the Italian Economy.* Ithaca: Cornell University Press.

Locke, Richard, Thomas Kochan, and Michael Piore, eds. 1995a. *Employment Relations in a Changing World Economy.* Cambridge, MA: MIT Press.

_____. 1995b. "Reconceptualizing Comparative Industrial Relations: Lessons from International Research." *International Labor Review,* Vol. 134, no. 2, pp. 139-62.

Locke, Richard, and Kathleen Thelen. 1995. "Apples and Oranges Revisited: Contextualized Comparisons and the Study of Comparative Labor Politics." *Politics & Society,* Vol. 23, no. 3 (September), pp. 337-67.

Marginson, Paul, et al. 1988. *Beyond the Workplace: Managing Industrial Relations in the Multi-establishment Enterprise.* London: Basil Blackwell.

Mathews, John. 1989. *Tools of Change.* Sydney: Pluto Press.

Maurice, Marc, Francois Sellier, and Jean-Jacques Silvestre. 1986. *The Social Foundations of Industrial Power.* Cambridge: MIT Press.

Osterman, Paul. 1988. *Employment Futures.* New York: Oxford University Press.

_____. 1994. "How Common is Workplace Transformation and Who Adopts It?" *Industrial and Labor Relations Review,* Vol. 47, pp. 173-84.

Piore, Michael, and Charles Sabel. 1984. *The Second Industrial Divide.* New York: Basic Books.

Regini, Marino, and Charles Sabel, eds. 1989. *Strattegie di riaggiustamento industriale.* Bologna: Il Mulino.

Rogers, Joel, and Wolfgang Streeck, eds. 1995. *Works Councils*. Chicago: University of Chicago Press.

Shirai, Taishiro, ed. 1983. *Contemporary Industrial Relations in Japan*. Madison: University of Wisconsin Press.

Sisson, Keith. 1990. "Strategy, Structure and Choice in Industrial Relations: A Comparison of U.S. and U.K. Research and its Implications." Working Paper, Industrial Research Unit, University of Warwick.

Streeck, Wolfgang. 1991. "The Federal Republic of Germany." In John Niland and Oliver Clarke, eds., *Agenda for Change*. Sydney: Allen and Unwin.

Swenson, Peter. 1989. *Fair Shares: Unions, Pay and Politics in Sweden and Germany*. Ithaca, NY: Cornell University Press.

Verma, Anil, Thomas A. Kochan, and Russell D. Lansbury. 1995. *Employment Relations in Asian Economies*. London: Routledge.

Weiler, Paul. 1990. *Governing the Workplace*. Cambridge: Harvard University Press.

Wever, Kirsten. 1995. *Negotiating Competitiveness: Employment Relations and Organizational Innovation in Germany and the United States*. Boston: Harvard Business School Press.

Wood, Stephen. 1990. "Comparing Survey and Case Study Interpretations of Change in Industrial Relations." Draft manuscript, London School of Economics.

Chapter 2

Labor Movements and Industrial Restructuring in Australia, New Zealand and the United States

Margaret Gardner
Griffith University, Australia

Most Western nations have undergone significant economic change in the last twenty years which has created pressure for transformation in industrial relations structures and practices. There are many aspects to the industrial relations changes contemplated or occurring. Of major importance is the role of unions and their response to economic restructuring. For while trade union influence varies, unions still represent one of the major sites for collective response by workers to major economic change.

Concern with economic restructuring and industrial relations has produced a significant literature, much of which attempts to place national experience in comparative perspective (Gourevitch et al. 1984; Juris, Thompson, and Daniels 1985; Frenkel and Clarke 1990; Niland and Clarke 1991; Turner 1991; Golden and Pontusson 1992; Bray and Haworth 1993). All these comparative studies examine the nature of recent economic restructuring and are concerned, among other things, with union strategic responses to it. This chapter examines the variations in national trade union response in three economies: Australia, New Zealand, and the United States. It argues this national response matters because it affects the degree of diffusion of industry and workplace reform and, thus, national responses to economic restructuring generally. Unions are not only affected by economic restructuring but are part of the context within which it occurs. Differences in structure and strategy affect their ability to influence this context.

The argument in this chapter has three components. First, how union movements respond at the national level affects the possibilities for industry and workplace action. Recent experience in Australia, New

Zealand, and the United States indicates the greater effectiveness of inclusive national union movements in diffusing a coherent response to economic restructuring. Second, it reveals as well the continuing importance of national political movements and contingencies in constraining union strategies and effectiveness. Third, this comparison also highlights the paradoxical outcomes of the greater "flexibility" demanded by economic restructuring for national trade union movements.

The three countries chosen provide interesting insights into the effects of national trade union movements on the way industry and enterprise responses to economic restructuring have been shaped. Australia and New Zealand are both small open economies with a similar industrial relations history, being at one time two examples of the arbitral model of national industrial relations. Until the late 1980s they were good examples of similar cases for comparative investigation.[1] From that point the divergences in their experience point us to the limited number of factors that really make a difference to industrial relations.

The U.S. has a very different industrial relations system and development from Australia and New Zealand, and yet recent New Zealand experience is closer to that of the U.S. than to Australia. Moreover, in the 1990s Australia has also chosen to borrow aspects of U.S. collective bargaining law in introducing a decentralized industrial relations system. In this three-way comparison of the way national trade union movements respond to economic restructuring, there is a prospect of reducing the "noise" of history in national experience and suggesting the factors that seemed to make a difference in this period of profound dislocation. Before proceeding to the empirical evidence, however, some comparative frameworks are analyzed to highlight the features of national trade union movements that are salient for this type of comparison.

Comparative Frameworks

Of the many possible comparative frameworks, one of the most common is to consider the extent of divergence or convergence among a selected group of countries. In the recent literature on economic restructuring and trade unions, Frenkel and Clarke (1990) provides explicit discussion of the merits of these explanations in terms of the extent of dualism or fragmentation of industrial relations in Western nations. This is an important way of examining changing industrial relations, and one which is salient for this comparison with the recent changes in Australia and New Zealand, borrowing, in part, from the U.S. My concern, however, is limited to national trade union movements rather than industrial relations as a whole. The three frameworks discussed below differentiate national union movements. They all share one concern: to divide union movements in terms of their espoused goals or approaches, although they all do this in different ways. In particular, the first concentrates on trade union goals; the second on trade union relationships to political parties; and the third, internal structural features of trade unions. Although in each the significant categorizing feature is different, the actual distinctions drawn between national movements are remarkably similar. The frameworks that point to the importance of the relationship to political parties or to internal structural features of movements are, in part, explanations of the differences in goal and strategy observed.

Trade Union Goals

There is a traditional duality used to characterize national trade union movements. This centers on the divide between the political and the economic, and despite argument, this duality has remained tenacious. It arose as part of the American "exceptionalism" arguments that seek to contrast the U.S. labor movement to that of other countries. This divide between economic and political unionism can be found in Hoxie's (1919) work and then permeates a range of other comparative analyses of unionism (Goodrich 1928; Kassalow 1969; Kendall 1975; Gallie 1978; Hibbs 1978). A recent use of this divide to explain trade union activity is Murray and Reshef's (1988) typology, identifying the differences between a political and economic paradigm driving trade union action. They see union action as being driven by internally consistent paradigms. These paradigms or union organizational cultures are differentiated by their goals and assumptions (Murray and Reshef 1990). Thus a political paradigm is one in which unions are concerned with influencing national policy and legislation in contrast to an economic paradigm in which unions concentrate on directly influencing employers.

The broad outlines of economic or job control unionism versus political unionism share a number of features. First, it is usually assumed that broad goals or purpose vary: that is, that economic unionism concentrates on the conditions and benefits for union members, while political unionism turns its attention to broader goals for wage earners or wider "societal interests" (Murray and Reshef 1988:616). While unions may use a mix of methods in economic unionism, collective bargaining predominates, and any political activity, such as lobbying, is subsidiary. Conversely, political unionism is characterized by a variety of actions, but usually collective bargaining is secondary and strike action greatly reduced or suppressed. Murray and Reshef (1988:617) also contend that economic unionism is a "high risk/high payoff strategy, whereas the political . . . seeks more modest, yet durable, gains for the union member." Typically the U.S., Canada, and sometimes the U.K. are seen as examples of economic unionism, with union movements in Europe and Scandinavia such as the French, Italian, German, and Swedish regarded as political.

There is argument (Martin 1989; Jacobs 1990; Ofori-Dankwa 1993) about whether this division is appropriate and whether "pure" forms of economic and political unionism exist,[2] nevertheless, the main distinction remains. The reasons for this divide in goals between political and economic unionism is sought typically in the historical circumstances of union development.

Relationship to Political Parties

Martin (1989) advances another typology revolving around the degree of autonomy of the trade union movement, that is, the nature of its relationship with political parties and the state. He notes three situations: unions may be dominated (the ancillary position), they may dominate (the surrogate position), or they may be autonomous. This produces five categories, since unions may be dominated by parties or the state and so on. In practice, however, most trade union movements are in one of three positions: dominated by the state, dominated by political parties, or autonomous. With the collapse of Communist regimes in Eastern Europe, trade union movements dominated by the state are largely to be found in Africa, the Middle East, Asia, and Latin America. Trade union movements dominated by political parties are to be found throughout Western Europe and are also of significance in the Americas and Asia. The autonomous movements are in English-speaking countries as well as Scandinavia and Germany.

Martin (1989) contends that the relationship of trade unions to political parties and the state is shaped by the political system in which they develop. He cites, in particular, the existence of a polarizing party. The polarizing party is one with substantial political representation, an "extreme" political ideology, and an interest in trade unionism. The polarizing party creates competition in terms of political action within the trade union movement and so leads to a fragmentation where trade unions compete politically through party identification. The effect of the polarizing political party is to create competing trade union programs.

In concluding his discussion of the effects of union autonomy versus union domination by a political party, Martin (1989:239) argues that the autonomous movements rely heavily on collective bargaining as a method and correspondingly "an overriding concern with a narrow range of issues." In this, at least Martin's conclusions reproduce the duality between economic and political unionism described above. However, the union movements labeled as autonomous are not the same as those commonly seen as falling within the economic unionism group. In particular, the Swedish and German trade union movements are grouped with the U.S., U.K., Canadian, Australian, and New Zealand movements as autonomous. This appears to be because Martin's typology separates political goals and actions that are the result of party domination from other political goals and action. His arguments about autonomous union movements would imply that the political actions of the Swedish and German trade union movements are in pursuit of economic or collective bargaining goals, although nowhere does he make this argument explicitly.

In this typology the division between European and American union movements is redrawn. Autonomy breeds diversity, Martin suggests, and the only relevant relationship is whether the trade union movement is dominated by the state or a political party or not. As Martin (1989) notes Millen, Davies, and Cella and Treu have all developed typologies revolving around the relationship of unions to the state or political parties. These other typologies also emphasize the relationship with a political party (Millen 1963) or relationship with the state (Davies 1966) or some combination (Cella and Treu 1982). All these taxonomies of national union movements turn the duality between economic and political unionism into a spectrum in which shades of political unionism reflect the nature of the relationship between union movement and political party or union movement and the state.

Trade Union Structures

The third framework is that of Visser (1990).[3] This is concerned largely with internal structural features of national trade union movements. From these features Visser creates a measure of a union movement's degree of inclusiveness and distinguishes among national trade union movements on this basis. The features of importance he outlines are the degree to which a union movement encompasses all possible members, the degree of horizontal integration or unity of the movement, and the degree of vertical integration or centralization of decision making within the movement.

Visser's concern is with the degree of inclusiveness, because he argues this has a direct impact on the goals and actions of trade union movements. Inclusive union movements tend to "embrace a wide range of interests" (Visser 1990:95) and are more flexible and resilient in the face of change and economic restructuring. Many of his measures of union inclusiveness are, as he notes, consistent with the institutional factors identified by Schmitter as the basis for neo-corporatism.

The notion of inclusive unionism shares something with Murray and Reshef's ideas of political unionism by explaining the way the structural features of unionism may support broad goals or the recognition and internalization of societal interests. Murray and Reshef note the limited but more durable payoffs from political unionism. Visser's argument about inclusive unionism provides an explanation for that observation. He suggests that although inclusive union movements may have significant power, they rarely exploit this fully, restricting their demands and actions because they "'internalize' contrasting demands and pressures within their own ranks" (Visser 1990:189).

The measures of inclusiveness of a union movement that Visser uses are threefold. First is the representativeness or the coverage of the union movement. The second is horizontal integration or unity, which is the proportion of unions in the largest confederation, the degree of confederation unity, organizational concentration, and political factionalism. The third, called vertical integration or authority, relates to the resources of the confederation. Strike funds, finances, staff, the level of involvement of the confederation in collective bargaining, as well as the degree of centralization of wage bargaining and the degree of inequality among affiliates,[4] are the measures for this dimension.

Using these measures to compare European trade union movements, Scandinavian movements such as the Swedish, Norwegian, and Danish, along with the Austrian and German, are classified as much more inclusive than the French and Swiss movements.

Visser also notes that the degree of political mobilization or the stability of links to social democratic political parties in and out of government is linked to the level of union representativeness. Indeed, measuring political influence through the proportion of "left" votes and level of representation in government indicates the same rank ordering of European countries as that identified for their trade union movements in terms of inclusiveness. The more inclusive the trade union movement, the more political influence of "left" parties is observed.

It is then not surprising that those union movements identified by Visser as inclusive are also those that are some of the exemplars of political unionism. But again, there is a difference since Visser's typology differentiates among "political" union movements, with some (such as France) regarded as sectoral or fragmented, while others (such as Sweden) are inclusive.[5]

Comparing Frameworks

These three frameworks all categorize the differences between national trade union movements in terms of their goals and actions and broadly agree on the implications of these differences for union responses. The first general conclusion they all provide is there is a broad duality in union goals and strategy between union movements. Inclusive or political unionism tends to embrace broad political programs and political action as an important part of the repertoire of methods. This type of unionism works closely with other institutions whether it be the state or political parties. Conversely, economic or noninclusive unionism tends to concentrate on a comparatively narrow range of collective bargaining issues and to treat political action as a minor part of trade union methods. Generally, there is concern for a substantial degree of independence from other institutions, such as the state or political parties.[6] While this duality appears in various forms in all the taxonomies considered above, only Martin and Visser provide a way of identifying from various features of trade union movements when they might be classified as economic or political in general orientation.

Where the explanations differ is in the nature and extent of their reasons for differences in union movement strategy. Some locate these differences in the national circumstances and history within which union movements developed; that is, differences in strategy are the result of historical contingencies. Martin concentrates on the structural features of the political system as a source of opportunities and constraints that shape strategy, while Visser regards the internal organizational features of the union movement as the constraining factor affecting strategy. But even here the broad form of argument of the last two explanations is consistent with a second identifiable proposition that strategy follows from structure.

From these frameworks then we can identify differences between national trade union movements in terms of their goals and strategies, broadly between the economic and the political. To divide national union movements into these two categories, we examine their degree of inclusiveness and their relationship to political parties or the state. From this, our third proposition would be that political or inclusive unionism will be more strongly associated with broad and moderate demands and greater flexibility in response to economic restructuring.

Comparing Union Movements

Australia and New Zealand have not loomed large in many of the taxonomies of union movements, including the ones discussed above, while the U.S. forms the end of a spectrum or an "exceptional" case in most of them. However, where consideration has been given to all three, they have been classified together within the broad ambit of the economic or noninclusive category. This categorization usually groups Australia and New Zealand with the U.K. (from whose union movement they borrowed much) and Canada and the U.S., even if the North American case is seen as being a more extreme version. In this chapter, however, the focus is on these union movements in the contemporary period of economic restructuring. In the case of Australia and New Zealand, there has been considerable change in the national context in which union movements find themselves. The judgments made below relate to their positions in the last two decades.

Australia

The Australian Union Movement: Toward Inclusiveness? In the mid-1980s the Australian trade union movement consciously embarked on a program of structural and strategic change. This change in strategy, along with the election of a Labor government at the national level in 1983,[7] led to a series of internal structural changes in the trade union movement as well as changed policy focus. Despite the changes, Australia, along with many other trade union movements, has faced significant decline in union representation through the 1980s and 1990s. In Australia, union density was 49.5% in 1982, 40.5% in 1990 (ABS 1990), and 37.6% in 1992 (ABS 1993).[8] Nevertheless, in international comparative terms, the Australian union movement has a reasonably strong level of union representation of the working population.

A number of features point to an increasing level of unity or horizontal integration of the Australian trade union movement over the period. Australia has one confederation, though the Australian Council of Trade Unions (ACTU) became the single national trade union confederation only in the 1980s, bringing both private and public sector unions under the one umbrella. With some 72 trade union affiliates in 1993[9] (assembled for representative purposes inside the ACTU in 21 "industry" groups) the ACTU represents almost all Australian unions.[10] The ACTU affiliates represent about 87% of all unionists (Griffin 1994). As a result of the rapid process of union amalgamations instigated by the ACTU, the degree of concentration of Australian unionism has grown, with a declining number of unions[11] and an increase in the number of large unions. The Secretary of the ACTU, Bill Kelty, estimated (optimistically) that by 1994 over 90% of the unionized workforce would belong to around twenty unions—and by that time the majority of unionists belonged to less than forty. All of these structural changes have increased the apparent cohesion of the union movement by focusing the national union movement within a smaller number of unions in a single representative confederation.

Accompanying and indeed encouraging many of these changes has been a reduction in the degree of overt political factionalism exhibited within the ACTU and the trade union movement over much of the period. This followed a greater coincidence in the views of "left" and "right" unions over many policies (particularly wage policy) in the 1980s. However, the divisions, if muted for some time in national policy debates of the union movement, remained, and new policy splits began opening in the 1990s. These divisions, however, do not seem to be tightly related to the old political factions.[12] In sum then, the ACTU developed more cohesion over the period.

The level of authority of the ACTU with the state, employers, and its affiliates also grew during the period. The ACTU from its inception has represented unions in national industrial negotiations and industrial disputes and, as a result, exercised considerable authority over its affiliates (Martin 1966). In the 1990s there was a major transformation in wage policy with an ACTU-endorsed shift to decentralized (or enterprise) bargaining in Australia. This followed a period of highly centralized wage bargaining through the 1980s (Gardner 1990). Although enterprise bargaining devolves much of the earlier control exercised by the ACTU to unions at the workplace level, the ACTU currently remains a major force shaping the directions of bargaining. Over the period the ACTU, through the renegotiation of the accord[13] with the Labor government, exercised tight control of wage policy and outcomes, as well as the behavior of affiliates.

The organizational resources through which the ACTU exercises its central authority are comparatively scarce, however. For example, unlike some European movements, there is no provision for strike funds to support unions in industrial action, and the council's overall resources and staff, while having increased rapidly during the period, are still comparatively modest. The authority of the ACTU is thus based almost exclusively on its role in industrial and political negotiations.

In part, the increase in authority of the ACTU followed from its long-term links with a social-democratic party, the Australian Labor party (ALP).[14] A significant number of Australian unions are affiliated with the Labor party providing a substantial proportion of the ALP's finances and other organizational support. The union movement generally retains strong formal and informal links with the ALP. As a result of the negotiation of the accord with the Labor party in 1983, those links were given a much tighter focus and form. Throughout the period the union movement has wielded greater political influence than in earlier periods of labor in government. This has proven a substantial resource for the authority of the ACTU and the union movement generally.[15]

Over the 1980s and 1990s the Australian trade union movement's increase in cohesion and authority, both with its own affiliates and with the state, came despite declining levels of representation. Moreover, for much of the period the union movement coalesced around a clearly articulated national agenda related to economic and industry restructuring, given shape by the ACTU and effect through unions at the national industry and workplace level. It was only in the 1990s that unease in parts of the union movement with aspects of this agenda became apparent. This unease has not yet translated into major splits and divergences in the union movement, although implementation of the national agenda has become more uneven.

Australian Union Policy and Economic Restructuring: National Agendas. The Accord, an agreement between the ACTU and the Australian Labor party (and subsequently the federal Labor government), has proved remarkably flexible and continues to the present as the negotiating framework for changing union and government priorities in a variety of areas concerning economic and social policy.

The Australian union movement began with an approach to economic policy and restructuring that emphasized continuous consultation over a whole range of matters, from the unambiguously industrial through other areas of redistributive policy, such as education, health and welfare, to issues such as industry policy and investment.

Not only did the union movement push for involvement in a wide range of national policy matters, but it pursued a particular set of policies which revolved around the creation of full employment: a wage policy of centralized wage fixation with cost-of-living compensation; improvement of the social wage (government spending on health, education, and welfare); industry policy which involved active state intervention; and a comprehensive policy on training and retraining, among other things. So a range of industrial relations and other economic policies were constructed as part of a package negotiated with government. This involved direct negotiations between the ACTU and the Labor government, as well as the involvement of union representatives in a range of tripartite fora, including industry planning bodies and training boards.

Originally, the thrust of the agenda was at the national policy level, with some industry matters included such as training and industry restructuring policy. Yet increasingly, the Accord framework, through successive bargains, came to focus on microeconomic reform and the way unions and management could change workplace practices and increase productivity.

Many elements of the package retained union movement support in the period. However, national wage policy set and implemented for much of the period at the national and industry level was the main area of activity. In this the union movement, through the ACTU, bargained for much of the period directly with the federal government. Espoused union wage policy and the eventual outcome through the national arbitration system were relatively similar through the 1980s. The initial thrust of that wage policy was the maintenance of real wages over time: that is, that wages would be adjusted in line with prices and that this would be the major single source of wage increases gained by the wage earners. There was continuing focus on wage outcomes for the low paid, with national wage increases designed to minimize the effect of wage restraint on this group. By the mid-1980s this policy was elaborated to allow for deferred wage increases in the form of employer contributions to superannuation.[16]

By the late 1980s the union movement had modified its wage policy strategy and eventually in the 1990s (after successive Accord deals) abandoned its commitment to centralized wage fixation and embraced enterprise bargaining. This was presented as a logical extension of national wage policy, which from the mid-1980s was used as an instrument of microeconomic reform. This microeconomic reform was accomplished initially through tying national wage increases to changes in work practices and modernization of awards and then through revision of whole job classification structures and the introduction of competency-based standards in training and skill acquisition. The microeconomic reform aspects of wage policy meant the national framework dictated the bargaining agenda and outcomes at the workplace and industry level. One major outcome was a decline in real wages over the period. Unfortunately, although a major focus of the accord was employment creation, unemployment grew to about 10% by the early 1990s and did not begin to decline until 1994. There was, however, high growth in employment also during the period.

There is a clear relationship between the increased organizational cohesion and authority of the ACTU and the development and prosecution of national union objectives and strategies for economic restructuring. These objectives and strategies were achieved largely through bargaining with the federal government. Moreover, the influence of union movement demands on national social and economic policy relied on union ability to control national wage policy.

Australian Unions and Industry Plans. Part of the initial national agenda was a plan for increased union involvement in industry restructuring. In Australia in 1987 a joint ACTU government task force produced *Australia Reconstructed* (ACTU/TDC 1987), a blueprint for economic restructuring which articulated a union perspective for and role in trade and industry policy and labor market programs including training and education. Of the many recommendations of this report, union and employer involvement is a key finding that has been implemented at the industry level in the development of training agendas. Industry training advisory boards (ITABs) have developed competency-based training systems linked to newly emerging career paths in a number of areas previously without industry specific training.

Unions were also involved in a series of tripartite industry councils overseeing the restructuring of a number of key Australian industries including heavy engineering, steel, textile, clothing and footwear, and vehicle. There is skepticism about their effectiveness in these fora, with some arguing that economic rationalism prevailed over the industry planning approach of the unions (Ewer et al. 1991). While many hopes for industry policy were not realized, some tripartite industry bodies did facilitate restructuring in the manufacturing industry, in particular in the textile, clothing and footwear, and automobile industries.

Australian Unions and Workplace Reform. By the mid-1980s the national agendas of unions was to encourage workplace reform as part of a strategy to build a stronger union presence at the workplace level. The microeconomic reforms linked to national wage increases were the first examples of this focus. The second tier (or restructuring and efficiency) and the structural efficiency principles articulated in national wage policy provided that wage increases could not be gained without demonstration at the workplace level of increased flexibility and efficiency in work organization and work practices.

In an Australian-wide survey of over 2,000 workplaces conducted in 1989 and 1990, around one-third indicated they had undertaken major restructuring of how work was done and had introduced new technology in the previous two years[17] (Callus et al. 1991:186-87). Indeed, close to half of all workplaces employing more than 500 employees had been involved with these two areas of workplace reform. Of particular significance, the analysis revealed that those workplaces with active unions and bargaining relationships reported twice the level of work restructuring of other workplaces. The evidence also revealed that a considerable proportion of the changes undertaken were directly the result of the reforms identified as part of the 1987 restructuring and efficiency national wage case. This included matters from changes to work practices, through changes to job classifications, career paths, and working time arrangements (p. 198).

Following the reforms introduced at the workplace level as a result of national wage policy changes in 1987 and 1989, the union movement in Australia, partly in strategic response to a concerted campaign by some employer associations and a potential change of government, embraced "enterprise bargaining." The legislative changes in 1993, which followed from broad agreement by unions, employers, and government on the desirability of removing the centralized bargaining and arbitral arrangements of the 1980s, embedded requirements for workplace bargaining.[18] This workplace bargaining was hailed as a way to improve flexibility and efficiency at the workplace level and as the linchpin of effective workplace reform.

Such a radical change in structural bargaining arrangements produced very slow and uneven responses at the workplace level. By early 1995 just over half of workers previously covered by federal awards were now covered by enterprise bargaining agreements. The research evidence has yet to reveal conclusively the significance of these agreements in the process of workplace reform. Many have suggested that they add little to the existing award arrangements and so have not advanced workplace reform. There is also evidence that enterprise bargaining is leading to widening disparities in pay between groups, including men and women workers.[19]

When the workplace reform agenda was driven by national wage policy, then union involvement directly in workplaces or indirectly through shaping that agenda for workplaces was significant. The available evidence indicates that it was large workplaces and those with high union activity that engaged most vigorously in this reform, but it affected in lesser degree a considerable proportion of other workplaces. Recent data on the outcomes of a national program to encourage the best practice in Australian manufacturing and service industries also points to the critical role of the unions and their involvement in broad and effective workplace reform (Rimmer and MacNeil 1995).

Since the advent of decentralized bargaining, union involvement in workplace reform is more tightly circumscribed. Union influence on this process is concentrated increasingly on those workplaces with effective union representation. There is no direct policy mechanism to take union agendas to other workplaces. It is not coincidental that in 1995 the ACTU has announced a major campaign to increase the number of job delegates in workplaces across the nation.

In the late 1980s the union movement's agenda for workplace reform was to agree to increased flexibility in work organization through reductions in demarcations in jobs, increased multiskilling, and more flexibility in working time arrangements among other things. They insisted this flexibility would also mean the introduction of career paths for more workers and the recognition of skills in many occupations through the development of competency-based training systems linked to these career paths. The unions tied a flexibility agenda to long-term development of worker skills and enhancement of their jobs. The underpinning for this agenda was put in place at the national and workplace level through the late 1980s and early 1990s. In the mid-1990s decentralized bargaining makes the implementation of such grand schemes more difficult. The outcomes remain uncertain, but the mechanisms for union influence of workplaces without significant union presence do not exist.

Inclusive Unionism with Decentralized Bargaining. Policy debate in Australia about enhancing workplace reform through increased flexibility and efficiency emphasized the importance of decentralizing bargaining to facilitate a workplace focus. The union movement (perhaps reluctantly) was drawn into this "consensus." Legislation has now undermined the centralized arbitral framework used so creatively in the 1980s. While the Australian union movement has operated through times of largely decentralized (but usually industry) bargaining as well as times of highly centralized national bargaining, the legislation for enterprise bargaining limits union ability to use arbitration to centralize and diffuse gains.

The Australian experience is thus a paradox. In the 1980s, circumstances and a coherent strategy brought together increased cohesion and authority for the national union movement and a commitment by that union movement to national economic restructuring. As part of the union movement's move to a more inclusive or political unionism, it embraced (as the argument would predict) a broad political program that was developed and given effect in concert with the ALP government. The program focused on measures to enhance the efficiency of the Australian economy as a means to increase employment and general living standards but also emphasized the importance of equity measures including increases in the social wage. In embracing this program, the union movement showed great flexibility. It ameliorated a commitment to protecting workers' real wages to embrace productivity-based increases; it abandoned long entrenched demarcations in favor of multiskilling; it reorganized traditional union boundaries and representation; and finally, it endorsed a move to decentralized workplace bargaining away from the centralized arbitral framework. In all these matters, the observation that the Australian union movement had become more inclusive is accompanied by behaviors consistent with this type of unionism.

The paradox lies in the possibility that its flexible response to economic restructuring may have removed the preconditions for remaining an inclusive union movement. Enterprise bargaining does not provide the mechanism for national union influence and cohesion presented by centralized wage bargaining. A small number of large unions may promote cohesion, but only in circumstances where the national union movement has authority over these affiliates. In the Australian case, ACTU authority has been derived from national political and industrial bargains. Such political influence is in part dependent on the party in power at the national level and in part on the level of industrial authority wielded by the ACTU. Where national wage bargaining is insignificant, that industrial authority is diminished. Splits in strategy emerged in the national union movement by the mid-1990s. Individual unions are now large enough, and bargaining is situated at a level where they can pursue their own strategies without reference to national position if they so choose. The high point of national union cohesion and authority in Australia may have already passed.

New Zealand

The New Zealand Union Movement: Forced Restructuring. Major changes in the legislative regime of labor relations in New Zealand have led to significant shifts in union movement organization. Union representation in New Zealand was estimated at approximately 66% in 1985 (Harbridge and Hince 1993:226) and remained very high until the introduction of the Employment Contracts Act (ECA) in 1991, following the defeat of a longstanding Labor government. The introduction of the Employment Contracts Act was a watershed in New Zealand industrial relations, removing the remains of the arbitral framework and promoting decentralized industrial relations through individual and collective contracts. Most importantly, the act repealed all statutory rights and privileges for trade unions (Mitchell and Wilson 1993).

Since then, membership of trade unions has declined dramatically, particularly in the private sector.[20] Government statistics are no longer available, but recent estimates suggest that union density fell from 65% to 56% in the six months from the introduction of the ECA in 1991 (Harbridge, Hince, and Honeybone 1993:231). The most recent estimates suggest that union density in 1993 was 43% (Harbridge et al. 1993:175).[21] In general, New Zealand has experienced the decline in union representativeness that has affected other countries, but the decline has been precipitous following the change in legislation.

Unlike the Australian case, the program of union amalgamations in New Zealand was not engineered by the NZCTU but followed legislative changes that required a minimum size for trade unions and then abolished union registration and compulsory unionism. As a result, the average size of New Zealand unions has increased, and the number of unions declined from 259 in 1985 to 67 in 1993 (Harbridge et al. 1993).

New Zealand dissolved its existing private and public sector union confederations to form a single body, the New Zealand Council of Trade Unions (NZCTU), in the 1980s.[22] However, this display of cohesion was short-lived, since in May 1993, 14 unions with a total membership of 35,000 members formed another confederation, the New Zealand Trade Union Federation (NZTUF) (Roth 1993:267). The brief period between 1988 and 1993, when there was a single confederation in New Zealand, has proved the anomaly in confederation history.

The largest New Zealand confederation (NZCTU) had over 50 affiliates in early 1991, while the estimated number of unions was around 80. By the end of 1993 the number of unions fell to about 67, with around 33 being members of the NZCTU (Harbridge et al. 1993). These unions represented 78% of all union members, though the proportion of unionists in unions affiliated to the dominant confederation fell during the period. Differences in industrial strategy lie behind the failure of some unions to affiliate to the NZCTU and others to leave and establish a new confederation. However, the NZCTU remains the most significant confederation. The series of forced structural changes increased the prospects for organizational cohesion in the New Zealand trade union movement.

Although the New Zealand trade union movement created the New Zealand Labor party in 1916, the union movement's links with the Labor party were strained in the 1980s (although one-quarter of unions remain affiliated). The union movement now faces a number of left parties claiming union allegiance.[23] In sum then, the New Zealand union movement has experienced an increase in organizational concentration which could underpin increased unity and cohesion. However, the varied political and organizational responses to the major changes in labor relations in the 1980s, particularly the recent savage decentralization, have encouraged fragmentation rather than unity.

In New Zealand, wage bargaining was highly centralized and liable to government intervention through the postwar period (Deeks 1990). In 1984 the New Zealand Labor government began the shift to a more decentralized bargaining structure which, however, did not gain any impetus until the change to a national government and the highly controversial Employment Contracts Act of 1991.

While the wage bargaining system of the early 1980s in New Zealand raised the prospects for exercise of authority by the NZCTU, this was not realized. There was little evidence of control by the NZCTU over wage bargaining. This was in contrast to the tight ACTU control of centralized wage bargaining policies and outcomes in Australia. New Zealand now has a highly decentralized and fragmented wage bargaining system closer to the traditional North American system. Nor does the NZCTU have significant resources in terms of people or funds with which to wield authority over its affiliates. Although the New Zealand trade union movement has a dominant confederation, this confederation does not wield a high level of national authority.

The New Zealand trade union movement experienced a range of major organizational changes over the period. Most of these follow changes in legislation brought about by radical government agendas.[24] The unions had very little role in shaping these agendas and have had to grapple with their effects on union membership and traditional bargaining relationships. There has not been a coherent strategic response at the national level, largely because there is disagreement on the appropriate response. The first effect then has been an apparent increase in the level of fragmentation of the union movement as it concentrates on dealing with the effects at the workplace and industry level. It should be noted, however, that there is the structural organizational base for a revived unity and cohesion at the national level, although it is yet to be realized. There is, however, neither the history nor the prospect of the NZCTU wielding national authority over its affiliates or in relation to government or employers.

New Zealand Unions and Economic Restructuring: National Responses. There was little difference in the broad approach espoused by the Australian and New Zealand trade union movements in the late 1980s, but there was substantial difference in the actual policies adopted. In New Zealand, despite election of a Labor government in 1984, a wage-price freeze imposed under the previous national government remained in place through that year. This was the case, although parts of the New Zealand trade union movement had been hoping for an Accord-type agreement. New Zealand unions tried to negotiate a compact with the Labor party and failed (Brosnan et al. 1992; Bray and Walsh 1993). The Labor government then abolished the compulsory arbitration system and introduced legislative changes that had the effect of forcing unions into separate industry or enterprise negotiations with employers.

Despite a number of attempts, the New Zealand union movement was unable to achieve the compact it sought because of resistance from employers, elements of government, some reluctance in its own ranks, and finally the defeat of the Labor government in 1990 (Bray and Walsh 1993). The scope for further policy development articulating a broad national interventionist agenda for unions was restricted as the union movement concentrated on dealing with the major fall-out from economic restructuring measures introduced first by labor and then by the national party government. The effect of the changes wrought in industrial relations and the wider New Zealand political economy has been such that the new policies contemplated by the Labor party and weakly endorsed by the NZCTU (Foulkes 1993) do not envisage tripartism and a substantial role of unions in economic and social reform but return to considering industrial relations reform as separate from broader policy questions. The national policy articulated by the NZCTU relies on the market efficiencies of enterprise bargaining, with some legal underpinning of minimum codes as the way forward. This is a much reduced agenda from the ambitions of the 1980s.

The outcome of national economic restructuring was considerable wage restraint in which the weakly organized were unable to make gains and lost award coverage. As a result, wage inequality grew (Bray and Walsh 1993; Brosnan et al. 1992). While overall wage outcomes were not far from those of Australia, real wages fell more steeply over the period (Brosnan et al. 1992). The difference was that in Australia the unions "negotiated" a degree of wage restraint against union influence in other areas of policymaking, while in New Zealand the union movement was unable to gain influence over national economic and social policy. Unemployment grew substantially in New Zealand, and groups such as women and Maoris were represented disproportionately among the unemployed. The labor force shrank along with employment (Brosnan et al. 1992).

The picture that emerges at the national level in New Zealand then is of the initial similarities in the strategic focus of the Australian and New Zealand trade union movements in the 1980s. Both embraced a broad agenda premised on trade union involvement in the process of economic restructuring. The New Zealand union movement, through creation of a single confederation in 1988, also tried to provide the structural underpinning that did not exist in the early 1980s for implementation of such an agenda. This did not prove effective, and the New Zealand trade union movement's agenda was not realized. While New Zealand has undergone considerable economic restructuring, including major deregulation of the labor market, the union movement has not been able to craft an effective national response because its political influence and access to government was limited under Labor and then removed with the advent of a national government in 1990.

New Zealand Unions and Industry Bargaining. The role of unions at the industry level in New Zealand was shaped and constrained by the national political environment. This led to similar outcomes to those observed at the national level. Like their Australian counterparts, New Zealand unions recognized the need to deal with increased international competition through restructuring at the industry level. Unions in the manufacturing industry advocated the tripartite industry planning approach to change that was advanced through the accord in Australia. However, the New Zealand Labor government introduced tariff reforms at such a rate that the unions were unable to effectively intervene in the changes that occurred (Bray and Walsh 1993).

In the late 1980s, manufacturing unions and employers combined to try and introduce an industry planning approach to the continued restructuring. A report on international competitiveness was prepared but failed to gain support from government. Thus industry restructuring in New Zealand proceeded without explicit union involvement in its planning.

In this period, however, the unions moved to restructure bargaining relationships and agreements at the industry level. As in Australia, the major impetus for this came from manufacturing industry unions, particularly the engineering union.[25] The shift to industry bargaining was significant since the basis of unionism in New Zealand was occupational, and traditionally, wage relativities were bargained and set in this context. Through industry bargaining the New Zealand unions changed the basis of working arrangements by the restructuring of classification structures and enhanced focus on industry-determined skill development and training (Bray and Walsh 1993). However, while this union involvement in restructuring began in New Zealand through industry bargaining, its spread was undermined by the introduction of the Employment Contracts Act which forced a stronger focus on the enterprise.

Without a strong tradition of industry unionism, neither Australian nor New Zealand union movements were positioned for major intervention in industry restructuring. The aspirations of New Zealand unions were undermined by the unwillingness of the government or many employers to cooperate in a more managed approach to the major structural change that affected New Zealand industry in the 1980s. While some unions were able to shape the outcomes of industry restructuring in some sections of the manufacturing industry by following an industry bargaining agenda, this was not the norm. Moreover, the possibilities of this approach were undermined by the legislative changes introduced by the national government and their impact on the shape and direction of bargaining.

Enterprise Focus and Forces for a Declining Union Role. New Zealand, through its arbitration system, had little impetus for unions to be heavily involved with employers at the enterprise level. Critics of the system argued that it discouraged bargaining and flexibility at the work-place (Brosnan et al. 1990, 1992). When the national government intro-duced the Employment Contracts Act in New Zealand, it fundamentally changed bargaining laws and structures, introducing a system that is "decentralized, heavily voluntarist, and contractually based" (Boxall 1991: 285).

The Employment Contracts Act not only entrenches a decentralized bargaining system but does so by treating the individual contract of employment as the conceptual cornerstone of the system. In other words, it de-emphasizes or undermines the collective aspects of indus-trial relations. As Anderson and Foote (1994:78) argue:

> Responsibility for the negotiation of an employment contract now rests firmly on the parties themselves and the Act is writ-ten so that bargaining on a collective basis or through a repre-sentative is seen as a departure from the norm and one which involves considerable constraints and barriers.

Unions gain access to the bargaining table only through the direct autho-rization of employees nominating them as their bargaining agent. How-ever, authorization by employees as a bargaining agent carries no com-pulsion for the employer to recognize the union, since the act contains no obligation to bargain. The act also makes multi-employer bargaining very difficult, since strikes to compel multi-employer bargaining are ille-gal, thus reinforcing the overall intention of the act to focus bargaining at the enterprise level.

By 1993, 75% of employees were covered by contracts negotiated under this act (Whatman et al. 1994) and around 45% of employees are now covered by individual rather than collective contracts. Individual contracts are growing in number, and trade union representation of em-ployees has declined, although unions are the main representatives in collective contract negotiations. Where there are collective contracts, less than 20% are multi-employer (Whatman et al. 1994; Anderson and Foote 1994).

All this indicates that while bargaining in New Zealand has been forced to the enterprise level, union involvement has been severely cir-cumscribed by the legislative regime in which they work. The outcome has been a continuing role for unions where they previously had a strong bargaining position and their marginalization and elimination in many contexts where workers are both weak and weakly organized.

Surveys in 1992 and 1993 have reported a majority of employees disapproving of the Employment Contracts Act. Surveys have also reported that over 40% of respondents indicate an increase in work effort. However, there are major gulfs in the perceptions of employers and employees on areas of improvement at the workplace. For example, 60% of employers believed job security had improved, compared to only 14% of employees. Similarly, 42% of employers reported increased trust, compared to only 15% of employees (Whatman et al. 1994).

The experience of microeconomic reform in New Zealand has been accompanied by considerable redundancies and a general contraction in employment accompanying a series of other changes to enhance and intensify work effort.

Coming to Terms with Decentralized Bargaining. The New Zealand trade union movement has had to find itself in very new circumstances. While the movement's aspirations when the Labor party gained government in the early 1980s were very similar to the broadly centralized and interventionist role sought by the ACTU in Australia, neither structural nor historical circumstances favored this strategic approach. Instead, the New Zealand unions faced a wave of legislative change that swept away the industrial relations system and the legislative protections in which they had previously operated. In part, the unions were complicit in the early stages of this change. Unlike their Australian counterparts, they had been historically more skeptical of arbitration and more accepting of restrictions of its role in the 1980s. Nevertheless, they were not prepared for the dramatic changes that occurred in the last two decades and the radical restructuring of industrial relations this entailed.

The changes forced a leaner and potentially more cohesive trade union movement but also pushed the unions firmly back to their areas of industrial and organizational strength. In forging new industrial and organizational strategies[26] to meet the deregulated labor market, there has not yet been evidence of the structural changes in the trade union movement bringing a newly cohesive movement at the national level.

The legislative changes also forced union activity to the enterprise level; national and industrial strategies were unable to be implemented through political means[27] and could not be given effect industrially. At the enterprise level unions were forced to concentrate on establishing their credentials as bargaining agents and negotiating collective contracts that would not undermine previous conditions entrenched in awards. There was little room in this for engaging positively in shaping programs of workplace reform when fundamentals such as union recognition and basic employment conditions all had to be negotiated.

The New Zealand experience illustrates the difficulties of effective union intervention in economic restructuring at *any* level without a cohesive trade union movement with significant political and industrial influence at the national level. Clearly New Zealand unions had begun the 1980s espousing a national strategy for economic restructuring, but the structural and historical circumstances in which the movement found itself forced the unions back to a limited industrial agenda at the enterprise level. Optimistic observers of New Zealand suggest that a "battle-hardened" union movement will emerge with a stronger enterprise base on which to build new strategies. Even if this were the medium-term outcome of the changes wrought, it will be some time before New Zealand unionism is in a position to follow a united strategy on economic restructuring. For some time, if political circumstances remain essentially unchanged,[28] unions will be occupied with establishing the ground rules for union involvement at the enterprise level and unlikely to face the labor market circumstances that will allow much change to their current position.

The United States

The United States Union Movement: Confronting Change? Compared to Australia and New Zealand, the legislative framework within which U.S. industrial relations works has remained stable throughout the whole postwar period, including the 1980s and 1990s. This is not to suggest that U.S. industrial relations has remained unchanged over that period, however (Kochan and Wever 1991).

One particular change that aroused much attention was the decline in the level of union representation which sparked debate in the union movement about its strategies. In the U.S., union density was estimated at 22% in 1980 and fell to around 16% in 1989 (Chang and Sorentino 1991:50). While the U.S. historically has had low levels of union representation compared to Australasia and Europe, the decline was notable, particularly since Canada with a similar industrial relations system did not experience such a dramatic decline. Considerable research suggested that part of the explanation for this decline was structural changes in employment—something that the U.S. experienced along with many other countries, including Australia and New Zealand. However, this did not fully explain the decline, and some questioned the continuing interest in unionism by workers, U.S. union strategy, and the impact of the "New Deal" legislative framework (Farber 1985; Cornfield 1989; Goldfield 1987; Kochan and Wever 1991). By the mid-1990s, U.S. union density had apparently stabilized, albeit at a low level, but the debate begun in the 1980s about union movement directions had not been resolved. Apart from the level of union representation, however, the structure of union organization in the U.S. has remained constant over much of the postwar period. In 1995 there were some signs, however, that structural change was also on the horizon. Prospects of a merger between three of the largest and most progressive manufacturing unions (the Auto Workers, the Steelworkers, and the Machinists) to create one large mega union of over two million members suggests that the declines in unionization experienced over the postwar period had finally driven structural change.

Signs were also evident that the long-term stability of the AFL-CIO might be disturbed. The U.S. has had one central union confederation, the American Federation of Labor-Congress of Industrial Organizations (AFL-CIO), since the 1950s. The degree of organizational concentration, in terms of percentage of unions affiliated to the largest confederation, remains high. The AFL-CIO has about 90 affiliates, which include approximately 80% of all trade unionists (Windmuller 1981). The AFL-CIO has also had a very long-term stable leadership. Accompanying discussions of a merger is a struggle over a change of leadership of the AFL-CIO, reflecting a desire among influential national unions for a change in union strategy.

The national union structure, bolstered by legislation in the U.S., was erected around the principle of industrial unionism or at least eschewed craft or occupational unionism. In principle this should enhance the basis for organizational cohesion, but in contrast the relative size of national unions combined with the independence conferred by decentralized bargaining worked to undermine the authority of the AFL-CIO and the overall cohesion of the union movement.

The U.S. union movement, despite informal links with Democrats which have been relatively strong at the national level through the postwar period, has no formal party affiliation. Indeed, the U.S. political system at the federal level is such as to encourage a multiplicity of pressure groups, but to discourage the identification of one particular political party with a major organized pressure group such as trade unions, or at least to discourage strong party systems and the possibility for strong party-union alliances (Bruce 1989). This constrains the ability of the American union movement to engage in more than political lobbying and limits its effective political influence (Draper 1986). Links with the

Democrats are stronger in states with a substantial union presence. Moreover, some national unions have supported the Republicans at various times, as have union locals (Kochan and Wever 1991; Draper 1986). In part, the lack of effective political influence is the result of the nature of the U.S. political system which does not provide the opportunities available in parliamentary systems such as Australia and New Zealand. The potential political influence of the union movement is also restricted by the low level of union representation and the concentration of unionists in particular regions of the U.S. The limits to the relationship of the AFL-CIO to a political party also reflects the high level of independence of national unions and their locals in deciding their political strategy. In sum, the individually "rational" decisions of parts of the union movement collectively undermine effective national political influence.

The AFL-CIO has no authority over wage bargaining or industrial issues generally. This role is jealously guarded by the national unions.[29] Thus the U.S. had a decentralized wage bargaining system through the 1980s, as it had for many decades previously, over which the AFL-CIO exercised no control. Compared to its affiliates, the AFL-CIO does not have major resources, although because of the absolute size of the U.S. trade union movement, the AFL-CIO has resources in terms of funds and staff well in excess of its Australian and New Zealand counterparts.

Despite its limited formal and informal authority, the AFL-CIO instituted a review of union strategy in the 1980s in response to declining union organization and economic restructuring. The AFL-CIO Committee on the Evolution of Work comprised leaders of a number of major unions. It commissioned research and instigated discussion throughout the 1980s. One report on strategies for revitalizing the union movement was produced in 1985, and the process to produce two further reports led to only one further report being issued (Wever 1995). In general, the debate was unable to generate agreement by AFL-CIO affiliates on the way forward, although recent signs suggest that changed leadership may bring strategic review at the center.

The structures of the U.S. union movement, partially created and reinforced by the New Deal legislative framework, have proven stable and enduring. They reinforce highly independent national unions, jealous of their own authority and unwilling to cede it in the interests of a nationally cohesive movement. The nature of the U.S. political system and the low level of union representation limit the potential political influence able to be wielded by the union movement. With limited potential political influence there is little incentive for U.S. unions to embrace the changes necessary to mobilize effective political strategies. Like other movements, the U.S. union movement has had to confront the effects of economic restructuring, in part manifest in declining union representation and challenges to traditional work practices and employment relations. It responded, as did the Australian and New Zealand movements, by examining strategies and policies at the national level. However, while the Australian unions crafted and implemented new strategies, including major changes to their structures, and the New Zealand unions found major changes thrust upon them, the U.S. union movement responded to the challenges in a fragmented way that left existing structures and strategies for the movement as a whole largely untouched and unreformed through the 1980s and 1990s. Innovative responses to economic restructuring among U.S. unions occurred in individual national or local unions or in particular regions, rather than being orchestrated by the AFL-CIO. It is still to be seen whether pressure from innovative national unions can bring a change in overall U.S. union movement strategy.

U.S. Unions and National Economic Restructuring. The U.S. union movement, given the decentralized nature of the bargaining system and no history (outside wartime) of major national direction of economic policy based on tripartism, did not articulate demands for such a framework. In the U.S., wages policy in the 1980s was partially driven by difficult economic circumstances with a variety of wage settlements in key industries that broke existing industry patterns and provided multifarious tradeoffs (Katz 1985; Cappelli and McKersie 1985). Overall, real wages continued to decline as they had been in the 1970s. Unemployment grew but remained lower than in Australia or New Zealand, while employment growth was significant over the period.

The major national strategic focus of the U.S. union movement has been directed at legislative change. In the late 1970s and again in the 1990s (each time associated with the election of Democrat presidents) hopes about labor law reform rose. Apart from these unmet aspirations for legislative change which would improve the organizing environment for unions, other interventions directed at government have included initiatives such as the Job Training Partnership Act to deal with unemployment. In sum then, at the national level U.S. union response to economic restructuring has been limited to specific legislative reform targets. Given the political climate, the union movement has had to make do with small, piecemeal legislative changes, leaving the New Deal framework largely intact.

Thus there has been very limited coordinated national response by American unions to economic restructuring. The U.S. union movement has maintained its traditional approach of concentrating activities in the industrial arena and confining any national strategy to a program of political lobbying for legislative change.

U.S. Unions and Industry Bargaining. The decentralized nature of bargaining in the U.S. did not encourage an industry approach to bargaining. Moreover, unlike Australia and New Zealand (and many other European countries), employers were not organized into industry groups to facilitate development of industry relationships. Nevertheless, while bargaining was centered at the company and plant level, relatively stable cycles emerged in the postwar period that had the effect of creating identifiable industry patterns. These were particularly clear in industries such as auto, steel, and transport. Here strong national unions coordinated wage rounds across major companies in these industries.

The 1980s saw the collapse of many of these patterns as concession bargaining at the local level created both reductions and greater diversity of contract conditions and pay increases in each industry. This further impetus to decentralized industrial relations meant that opportunities for union responses to economic restructuring at the industry level were very limited.

Restructuring at the Workplace and U.S. Unions. The major focus of U.S. union strength and activity continued to be at the company and plant level. The highly fragmented nature of bargaining at this level increased over the 1980s. Prior to this period, there was a degree of stability and predictability about the general nature and shape of collective bargaining contracts (Kochan 1985; Wheeler 1987; Fairris 1991). This produced a clearly defined (if adversarial and reactive) role for unions (Walton et al. 1994; Kochan 1985). The 1980s brought an increased level of experimentation by unions as they responded to the pressures of economic restructuring.

There was an increased involvement by unions in various forms of industrial democracy experiments. These varied from employee shared ownership schemes, to quality-of-working-life (QWL) programs, and greater consultation over introduction of new technology or the formulation of investment plans. Much of this activity occurred in companies (and industries) that had a strong postwar tradition of unionism. For example, employee involvement programs centering around improved productivity but also major reskilling of the workforce were fostered by the UAW and General Motors and Boeing Corporation and the International Association of Machinists (Walton et al. 1994). The National Steel Corporation and the United Steelworkers signed a high profile agreement in 1986 involving substantial cooperation between union and management to secure revitalized economic prosperity. While there was great variety in the scope of QWL programs, it was estimated in 1982 that some 44% of firms with more than 500 employees had some form of QWL initiative (Fairris 1991).

Another aspect of changes in work organization in this period was the introduction of self-directed teams. The use of teams became comparatively widespread through the 1980s and 1990s (Osterman 1994; Fairris 1991). In many cases these changes involved modification in the way shopfloor industrial relations had been conducted, with less emphasis on the highly bureaucratic grievance system and consequent changes in the job classifications and reward systems.

Osterman (1991) estimates that around 36% of establishments had introduced some of the practices associated with flexible work organization. While these changes are responses to economic restructuring, only some are directly associated with union activity. Osterman (1991) found that management values about innovative work practices were the significant factor driving establishments to change.

Most managements did not willingly embrace a change to more cooperative and flexible forms of work organization. Unions faced severe challenges from managements in a range of industries and firms including the airlines, transport generally, parts of the auto industry, paper, and clothing (Turner 1991; Walton et al. 1994). While in some instances initial conflicts were resolved through greater involvement of unions in decision making and more flexible and cooperative work organization, in many other cases change was imposed without union input.

Unions did not remain passive in the face of managerial challenges to unionism, generally, and to previously hard-won contract conditions. The 1980s saw the development of corporate and comprehensive campaigns, to mobilize shareholder and community pressure to win concessions from management. Also in this time, "in-plant" strategies were developed that reduced traditional union reliance on the strike during contract negotiations and substituted broader forms of industrial action, including filing of mass grievances, work to rule, and the like (Shostak

1991). These were creative innovations to face managerial aggression in the 1980s and 1990s.

Despite the many examples of innovation in U.S. unions' responses to economic restructuring, the pattern that emerges is not one of a strong, unified, and proactive response. As Turner (1991:154) argues, "in the U.S. the range of outcomes is very wide, from innovative non-union to traditional . . . to innovative unionized." National unions and locals innovate, and there is some diffusion of these innovations, but there is no coherent or coordinated response evident at the company or workplace level to economic restructuring. Moreover, as Wever (1995) argues, in some cases local responses to economic restructuring create ambivalent reactions at the national union level. This contrasts with the Australian response to workplace restructuring in the 1980s[30] but is consistent with the New Zealand union experience.

In all then, the U.S. union movement has responded to economic restructuring, but its responses (despite local innovation) have occurred within the traditional pattern of company and plant-level autonomy and fragmentation. The union movement response has been the sum of a series of local responses conditioned by the particular relationships between the union and the companies with which it deals.

Conclusion

The degree of union inclusiveness has been argued to affect the goals and strategies of union movements. Broadly, inclusive or political unionism is associated with more moderate demands and greater flexibility in response to economic restructuring. Generally, while inclusive unionism may produce more modest gains for particular areas of the economy where unions are strongest, it is regarded as providing more lasting and widespread gains for all workers.

Comparing the union movements of Australia, New Zealand, and the U.S., only the Australian movement approached inclusiveness in this period, although the New Zealand labor movement was structured more like the Australian than the U.S. movement at the beginning of the period analyzed. The Australian movement was able to institute a series of changes that increased its inclusiveness and enhanced national cohesiveness over the period until the 1990s. The New Zealand movement faced circumstances that encouraged fragmentation, and the U.S. movement retained its fragmented approach. While the New Zealand union movement still exhibits some of the structural features of a relatively inclusive union movement, there are signs it is fragmenting and losing central authority rather than gaining it. In the U.S., the low level of union representation and weak central authority of the AFL-CIO have remained the critical factors throughout the period of the 1980s, making it a less inclusive movement than the other two. Of the three union movements, it is the U.S. union movement that exhibited the least change over the period.

The national political influence of these union movements has been in keeping with the structural base of their strength and national authority, although union structure does not determine political influence, as illustrated by the case of New Zealand. At various times all have devised policies and strategies that are dependent on broad political programs emphasizing structured economic and social intervention, including social contracts concerning employment and welfare spending, industry policies, and the like. These broad strategic goals have been the corner-stone of the Australian union movement response to economic restructuring in the period. Such goals were advanced but abandoned by the New Zealand movement in the face of hostile circumstances. That is, in New Zealand political contingencies intervened to influence both union structure and strategy. Broad strategic goals never achieved any dominance in the U.S. union movement's strategies.[31] Indeed, the changed strategies proposed for the U.S. union movement initially focused on new organizing strategies and then on ways of altering the labor relations framework to encourage greater labor participation in management. In other words, for the U.S., new strategies did not stray beyond the employment relations framework.

In part, the strategic approach of the three union movements reflected the degree of inclusiveness of the movement. More directly, it is clear that their access to political influence affected their commitment to broad strategic political programs and that this access was in part dependent on the degree of cohesiveness and strength of the movement but also reflected political contingencies. In essence, the Australian movement was able to rely on national political influence to broker a comprehensive reform package and to set in place an institutional framework that enhanced its influence, while the New Zealand and U.S. union movements were reliant on bargaining in the industrial arena for a more restricted set of goals. The innovations in the U.S. and New Zealand were confined to company or workplace level and were dependent in part on the bargaining strength of the unions involved. The mechanisms for diffusion of these innovations did not exist or, in the New Zealand case, had been removed.

Allowing for political contingencies, it can be argued that the structural features of the trade union movements were decisive in union movement choices by restricting the range of policy stances able to be implemented, rather than through shaping initially the type of goals sought. Of some importance was the ability of the confederations to represent effectively their affiliates. Thus the perceived degree of cohesion of the movement and authority of the confederation were significant, since without these factors there was no possibility of a negotiated compact between labor and government or political party. It is also clear from the evidence that the Australian movement was able to institute a rapid series of changes and responses to economic restructuring that touched the whole union movement. The New Zealand union movement was driven by circumstances and adapting to them, while the U.S. union movement has had difficulty gaining consensus on the direction for change.[32] In this sense it is clear that the structural features of national unionism have an effect on both strategies able to be implemented and the degree of flexibility evident in the face of rapid economic restructuring.

However, an important factor to emerge from this survey of the 1980s and 1990s is the fragility of the Australian union response. In the interests of flexibility, it may have undermined some of the structural factors that promoted cohesion and a degree of inclusiveness. The New Zealand story also indicates the major impact that forced changes in the employment relations framework can have on the possibilities for building a cohesive movement. Some New Zealand unions may emerge with a stronger industrial base, but it seems that the overall influence of the movement will be more difficult to rebuild. The U.S. experience speaks to the constraints that structural factors have on the range of possible strategies for union movements and the difficulties in its circumstances of building a more inclusive movement. Alone, a union movement cannot build the circumstances for inclusive and therefore flexible unionism. Where inclusive union movements are possible, they must look to the limits of flexibility.

Endnotes

[1] Much as Canada and the U.S. were very similar cases in industrial relations in the postwar period but began to diverge in the 1980s.

[2] Ofori-Dankwa (1993) modifies the Murray-Reshef model by arguing that union movements reflect different combinations of political and economic paradigms. For example, he suggests that Sweden is both high political and high economic, while China is low political and low economic; the U.S. is high economic and low political, and France the opposite. Therefore, unlike the Murray and Reshef typology that

would suggest some commonality between the Scandinavian and European trade union movements, this typology suggests significant differences between the Swedish and the French trade union movements, for example.

[3] Cella and Treu also make use of some of the variables central to Visser's framework, but they do not appear to have the same centrality to their framework as they do for Visser.

[4] Visser acknowledges that this last measure is ambivalent, since a small number of large but equivalent-sized affiliates might diminish vertical authority, while a large number of equivalent-sized small affiliates might enhance vertical authority. Windmuller (1981) also makes this point about the problems of high levels of union concentration for the authority of confederations.

[5] Visser's typology not only differentiates among the autonomous category in Martin's framework but is more consistent in its identification of similarity with the elaborated typologies of the "neocorporatist" literature.

[6] Generally, however, attitudes to this division vary among the authors cited. For example, both Visser and Murray and Reshef are clearly favorably disposed to a unionism that undertakes representation and issues broader than their immediate membership. Conversely, Martin treats this as corruption of union agendas. Moreover, tellingly he treats inclusive union movements such as Sweden as essentially similar to the U.S. in that they are pursuing an independent bargaining agenda for their members.

[7] Since 1983 the federal Labor government has won a series of elections and has now been in government for thirteen years.

[8] The more optimistic data from trade union membership surveys also report a decline from over 50% to 46% in 1993.

[9] This is a dramatic decrease from 1991 when there were 126 affiliates. This decrease in the number of affiliates is the result of a remarkably strong process of union amalgamations.

[10] Indeed, in Australia there is no significant national union not affiliated to the ACTU, although there remain some state-registered unions not affiliated.

[11] In Australia there were 140 federal unions in 1990 and 54 in 1994 (ABS 1994).

[12] Their outward manifestation is in clashes over the direction of wage policy between the NSW Trades and Labor Council and the ACTU. The NSW TLC is a provincial labor confederation, one of the oldest in Australia and the largest and best resourced.

[13] An agreement between the Australian Labor party and the ACTU ostensibly about economic and social policy but more directly the framework for a national income bargain in which economic and social policy were some of the bargaining chips.

[14] The Australian Labor party was formed in 1891 by the Australian trade union movement.

[15] There is some debate, however, whether this relationship with the government has been an unalloyed benefit for union members and trade unions in terms of outcomes. Some have argued declining real wages for trade union members and declining

union membership are the result of the union movement through the ACTU having to meet national economic objectives. The difficulty in resolving this debate is establishing the likely outcomes for the union movement in the absence of the ACTU approach. Those who support the ACTU strategy point to the outcomes in New Zealand as an indicator of what might have happened otherwise.

[16] This extended superannuation to all wage earners, where previously it had been available only to the highly paid, those in secure employment and predominantly nonmanual workers.

[17] The timing of the survey meant that only changes instituted as a result of the 1987 second-tier decision were able to be identified. The 1989 structural efficiency decision and subsequent changes as a result of enterprise bargaining will be able to be identified through the general survey and panel data when the second of these surveys is completed in 1995.

[18] Some of the legislative requirements for enterprise bargaining in Australia borrowed notions from North America, such as "bargaining in good faith."

[19] There was such concern about the potential of enterprise bargaining to disadvantaged groups, such as women and people from non-English speaking background, that the legislation provides special clauses for consultation with these groups and requires the minister for industrial relations to report to parliament on their pay outcomes annually.

[20] Although the public sector has been the subject of major change, including industrial relations changes, union density is rising, while the collapse in union membership has been in the private sector.

[21] It should be noted that these estimates of union density in New Zealand are based on membership as compared to their Quarterly Employment Survey. Density, when calculated against workforce data derived from the Household Labor Force Survey, suggests a much lower result, with density at 52% in May 1991 and 34% in December 1993 (Harbridge et al. 1994).

[22] The two confederations were the Federation of Labor (FOL) and the Combined State Unions (CSU).

[23] Recent changes in the New Zealand voting system from "first past the post" to proportional representation increases the possibility of minority political parties gaining parliamentary seats. It, thus, increases the viability of competing "left" parties.

[24] These radical agendas were not confined to one side of the political spectrum but were embraced in different form by both Labor and national governments.

[25] In Australia it was the metalworkers union which included the engineering workers that led much of the debate on industry policy and microeconomic reform.

[26] For a discussion of new approaches to organizing by New Zealand unions see Oxenbridge (1995).

[27] An interesting sidelight on union political pressure in New Zealand was communicated by Raymond Harbridge in an E-mail of April 7, 1995. He notes the problems of the Firefighters Union in attempting to negotiate with government. The union has now organized a Citizens Initiated Referendum (using newly introduced legislation to

allow this) with a petition to parliament to hold fire service staffing at current levels. We have yet to hear the outcome of this novel industrial/political tactic.

[28] The only unpredictable factor is the opportunities that might be offered by political change. The changes in the New Zealand electoral system open the possibility of election of a number of minor political parties in a system that was previously two-party dominated. Some of these minor parties may be to the left of the Labor party, some certainly will claim links with unions or workers. This may allow for legislative change which would alter favorably the environment in which New Zealand unions operate. However, it is not possible at present to predict with any confidence.

[29] While U.S. national unions style themselves as internationals due to links with Canada and the like, for ease of comparison they are referred to as national unions in this chapter.

[30] While enterprise bargaining encourages a more fragmented approach at the workplace level in Australia, unions are still attempting to direct overall outcomes through setting broad industry frameworks. The major question that remains is whether this will continue to be a viable approach.

[31] This does not mean that U.S. unions ignored issues such as welfare and health care in their lobbying activities, but merely that these issues did not form a central part of an overall strategic approach. Union concern over social wage issues continued in the traditional political lobbying approach.

[32] It is important to note here that the relative size of the Australian and U.S. union movements is of some significance. The large size of the U.S. union movement would make any strategic change slower than a smaller movement.

References

ABS (Australian Bureau of Statistics). 1990. *Trade Unions Members, Australia*. 6325.0. Canberra, Australia: AGPS.

_____. 1993. *Trade Unions Members, Australia* 6325.0. Canberra, Australia: AGPS.

ACTU/TDC. 1987. *Australia Reconstructed*. Canberra, Australia: AGPS.

Anderson, G., P. Brosnan, and P. Walsh. 1994. "Flexibility, Casualization and Externalisation in the New Zealand Workforce." *Journal of Industrial Relations*, Vol. 36, no. 4, pp. 491-598.

Anderson, G., and H. Foote. 1994. "The Employment Contracts Act and New Zealand Unions." In R. Callus and M. Schumacher, eds., *Current Research in Industrial Relations*. Sydney: AIRAANZ.

Boxall, P. 1991. "New Zealand's Employment Contracts Act 1991: An Analysis of Background, Provisions and Implications." *Australian Bulletin of Labour*, Vol. 17, no. 4, pp. 284-309.

Bray, M., and N. Haworth, eds. 1993. *Economic Restructuring and Industrial Relations in Australia and New Zealand: A Comparative Analysis*. ACIRRT Monograph No. 8. Sydney: University of Sydney.

Bray, M., and P. Walsh. 1993. "Unions and Economic Restructuring in Australia and New Zealand." In M. Bray and N. Haworth, eds., *Economic Restructuring and Industrial Relations in Australia and New Zealand: A Comparative Analysis*. ACIRRT Monograph No. 8. Sydney: University of Sydney.

_____. 1994. "Accord and Discord: The Differing Fates of Corporatism under Labour Governments in Australia and New Zealand." Paper presented to the 8th AIRAANZ Conference, February, University of Sydney.

Brosnan, P., D. Smith, and P. Walsh. 1990. _The Dynamics of New Zealand Industrial Relations_. Auckland: John Wiley and Sons.

Brosnan, P., J. Burgess, and D. Rea. 1992. "Two Ways to Skin a Cat: Government Policy and Labour Market Reform in Australia and New Zealand." _International Contributions to Labour Studies_, Vol. 2, pp. 17-44.

Bruce, P. 1989. "Political Parties and Labor Legislation in Canada and the U.S." _Industrial Relations_, Vol. 28, no. 2, pp. 115-41.

Callus, R., A. Morehead, M. Cully, and J. Buchanan. 1992. _Industrial Relations at Work: The Australian Workplace Industrial Relations Survey_. Canberra, Australia: AGPS.

Cappelli, P., and R. McKersie. 1985. "Labor and the Crisis in Collective Bargaining." In T. Kochan, ed., _Challenges and Choices Facing American Labor_. Cambridge: MIT Press.

Cella, G., and T. Treu. 1982. "National Trade Union Movements." In R. Blanpain, ed., _Comparative Labour Law and Industrial Relations_. Deventer: Kluwer.

Chang, C., and C. Sorentino. 1991. "Union Membership Statistics in Twelve Countries." _Monthly Labor Review_, Vol. 114, no. 12, December, pp. 46-53.

Cornfield, D. 1989. "Union Decline and the Political Demands of Organized Labor." _Work and Occupations_, Vol. 16, no. 3, pp. 292-322.

Davies, I. 1966. _African Trade Unions_. London: Penguin.

Deeks, J. 1990. "New Tracks, Old Maps: Continuity and Change in New Zealand Labour Relations." _New Zealand Journal of Industrial Relations_, Vol. 15, pp. 99-116.

Draper, A. 1986. "A Rope of Sand: The AFL-CIO Committee on Political Education." _Economic and Industrial Democracy_, Vol. 7, pp. 45-60.

Eaton, A. 1994. "The Survival of Employee Participation Programs in Unionized Settings." _Industrial and Labor Relations Review_, Vol. 47, no. 3, pp. 371-89.

Ewer, P., W. Higgins, and A. Stevens. 1987. _Unions and the Future of Australian Manufacturing_. Sydney: Allen and Unwin.

Ewer, P., I. Hampson, C. Lloyd, J. Rainford, S. Rix, and M. Smith. 1991. _Politics and the Accord_. Sydney: Pluto Press.

Farber, H. 1985. "The Extent of Unionization in the United States." In T. Kochan, ed., _Challenges and Choices Facing American Labor_. Cambridge: MIT Press.

Fairris, D. 1991. "The Crisis in U.S. Shopfloor Relations." _International Contributions to Labour Studies Series_, Vol. 1. London and San Diego: Academic Press, pp. 133-56.

Fishman, R., and C. Mershon. 1993. "Workplace Leaders and Labor Organization: Limits on the Mobilisation and Representation of Workers." _International Contributions to Labour Studies_, Vol. 3, pp. 67-90.

Foulkes, A. 1993. "The Culture of Tripartism: Can European Models Be Adapted for New Zealand Use?" _New Zealand Journal of Industrial Relations_, Vol. 18, pp. 185-93.

Frenkel, S., and O. Clarke, eds. 1990. "Economic Restructuring and Industrial Relations in Industrialised Countries." _Bulletin of Comparative Labour Relations_, Vol. 20, Deventer, The Netherlands: Kluwer.

Gallie, D. 1978. *In Search of the New Working Class*. Cambridge: Cambridge University Press.

Gardner, M. 1990. "Wage Policy." In C. Jennett and R. Stewart, eds., *Hawke and Australian Public Policy: Consensus and Restructuring*. Melbourne: Macmillan.

Golden, M., and J. Pontusson, eds. 1992. *Union Politics in Comparative Perspective: Economic Restructuring and Intra-Class Conflict*. Ithaca, NY: Cornell University Press.

Goldfield, M. 1987. *The Decline of Organized Labor in the United States*. Ithaca, NY: Cornell University Press.

Goodrich, C. 1928. "The Australian and American Labour Movements." *Economic Record*, Vol. 4, no. 7, pp. 193-208.

Gourevitch, P., A. Martin, G. Ross, C. Allen, S. Bornstein, and A. Markovits. 1984. *Unions and Economic Crisis: Britain, West Germany and Sweden*. London: Allen and Unwin.

Griffin, G. 1994. "The Authority of the ACTU." Working Paper No. 80, Department of Management and Industrial Relations, University of Melbourne.

Harbridge, R., and K. Hince. 1993. "Organising Workers: The Effects of the Act on Union Membership and Organisation." In R. Harbridge, ed., *Employment Contracts: New Zealand Experiences*. Wellington: Victoria University Press.

Hibbs, D. 1978. "On the Political Economy of Long-Run Trends in Strike Activity." *British Journal of Political Science*, Vol. 8, pp. 153-75.

Hoxie, R. 1919. *Trade Unionism in the United States*. New York: Appleton & Co.

Jacobs, D. 1990. "Comment on Murray and Reshef." *Academy of Management Review*, Vol. 15, no. 4, pp. 682-87.

Juris, H., M. Thompson, and W. Daniels, eds. 1985. *Industrial Relations in a Decade of Economic Change*. Madison, WI: Industrial Relations Research Association.

Kassalow, E. 1969. *Trade Unions and Industrial Relations: An International Comparison*. New York: Random House.

Katz, H. 1985. "Collective Bargaining in the 1982 Bargaining Round." In T. Kochan, ed., *Challenges and Choices Facing American Labor*. Cambridge: MIT Press.

Kendall, W. 1975. *The Labour Movement in Europe*. London: Allen Lane.

Kochan, T., and K. Wever. 1991. "United States of America." In J. Niland and O. Clarke, eds., *Agenda for Change: An International Analysis of Industrial Relations in Transition*. Sydney: Allen and Unwin.

Martin, R. 1966. "The Authority of Trade Union Centres: The Australian Council of Trade Unions and the British Trades Union Congress." In J. Isaac and W. Ford, eds., *Australian Labor Relations Readings*. Melbourne: Sun Books.

_____. 1980. *TUC: The Growth of a Pressure Group*. Oxford: Clarendon Press.

_____. 1989. *Trade Unionism: Purposes and Forms*. Oxford: Clarendon Press.

Millen, B. 1963. *The Political Role of Labor in Developing Countries*. Honolulu: East-West Center Press.

Mitchell, R., and M. Wilson. 1993. "Legislative Change in Industrial Relations: Australia and New Zealand in the 1980s." In M. Bray and N. Haworth, eds., *Economic Restructuring and Industrial Relations in Australia and New Zealand: A Comparative Analysis*. ACIRRT Monograph No. 8. Sydney: University of Sydney.

Murray, A., and Y. Reshef. 1988. "American Manufacturing Unions' Stasis: A Paradigmatic Perspective." *Academy of Management Review*, Vol. 13, no. 4, pp. 615-26.

_____. 1990. "Reply to Jacobs." *Academy of Management Review*, Vol. 15, no. 4, pp. 688-93.

Niland, J., and O. Clarke, eds. 1991. *Agenda for Change: An International Analysis of Industrial Relations in Transition*. Sydney: Allen and Unwin.

Ofori-Dankwa, J. 1993. "Murray and Reshef Revisited: Toward a Typology/Theory of Paradigms of National Trade Union Movements." *Academy of Management Review*, Vol. 18, no. 2, pp. 269-92.

Osterman, P. 1994. "How Common is Workplace Transformation and Who Adopts It?" *Industrial and Labor Relations Review*, Vol. 47, no. 2, pp. 173-88.

Oxenbridge, S. 1995. "Organising the Secondary Labour Force: The New Zealand Experience." Paper presented to the AIRAANZ 1995 Conference, Melbourne.

Rimmer, M., J. MacNeil, L. Watts, K. Langfield-Smith, and R. Chenall. Forthcoming. *Best Practice in Australia*. Melbourne: Longman Cheshire.

Roth, H. 1993. "Chronicle." *New Zealand Journal of Industrial Relations*, Vol. 18, no. 2, pp. 264-72.

Shostak, A. 1991. *Robust Unionism: Innovations in the Labor Movement*. Ithaca, NY: ILR Press.

Turner, L. 1991. *Democracy at Work: Changing World Markets and the Future of Labor Unions*, Ithaca, NY: Cornell University Press.

Visser, J. 1990. "In Search of Inclusive Unionism." *Bulletin of Comparative Labour Relations Series*, Vol. 18, Deventer, The Netherlands: Kluwer.

Walton, R., J. Cutcher-Gershenfeld, and R. McKersie. 1994. *Strategic Negotiations*. Boston: Harvard Business School Press.

Wever, K., and P. Berg. 1993. "Human Resource Development in the United States and Germany." *International Contributions to Labour Studies*, Vol. 3, pp. 31-49.

Wever, K. 1995. *Negotiating Competitiveness, Employment Relations and Organizational Innovation in Germany and the United States*. Boston: Harvard Business School Press.

Whatman, R., C. Armitage, and R. Dunbar. 1994. "Labour Market Adjustment under the Employment Contracts Act." *New Zealand Journal of Industrial Relations*, Vol. 19, no. 1, pp. 53-73.

Wheeler, H. 1987. "Management-Labor Relations in the U.S." In G. Bamber and R. Lansbury, eds., *International and Comparative Industrial Relations*. Sydney: Allen and Unwin.

Windmuller, J. 1981. "Concentration Trends in Union Structure: An International Comparison." *Industrial and Labor Relations Review*, Vol. 35, no. 1, pp. 43-57.

CHAPTER 3

International Trends in Work Organization in the Auto Industry: National-Level vs. Company-Level Perspectives

JOHN PAUL MACDUFFIE
University of Pennsylvania

Changes in shopfloor work organization are a central part of broader changes in industrial relations in many industries around the world. In the automotive industry (the focus of this chapter), international competition, new technological capabilities, and production system innovations have prompted many companies to move away from the dominant mass production model and to adopt new, flexible principles for organizing work that have demonstrable advantages in terms of economic performance. It is clear that these principles are often adopted selectively (and incompletely) and modified as they diffuse. What is less clear is how much variation in adoption occurs (and how extensive the modifications), whether the patterns of diffusion are driven more by national-level or company-level factors, and how closely work organization changes are related to the overall industrial relations system, which *does* vary considerably at the national level.

Past research on the transfer of principles of organizing work suggests that there is substantial national-level variation in how certain dominant principles are understood and applied and that such variation is historically persistent (Kogut and Zander 1992). For example, the overlapping principles of Taylorism and Fordist mass production that diffused broadly in the U.S. were also much studied by companies in Europe. However, the adoption of those principles in Europe was slow, partial, and affected by cultural influences at both national and company levels. In England, for example, Lewchuk (1988) argues that the persistence of craft traditions and the disdain of managers for involvement with shop-floor matters resulted in the adoption of Taylorist work organization with much less management control over work methods than in the U.S. At the same time, pressures from the institutional environment—from government and labor institutions and from company efforts to follow (what they believe to be) "best practice"—may lead to convergence in work practices within a given country (Kochan and Cappelli 1984; Baron, Dobbin, and Jennings 1986). Convergence within a given industry can be even more pronounced, to the extent that work rules standardized across the industry are prominent in collective bargaining contracts. Thus past perspectives on the transfer of work organization argue for persistent *differences across* countries and *convergence within* countries and companies.

But I will argue in this chapter that the emergence of a new set of dominant organizing principles in the auto industry has created the conditions for more *convergence across* countries and *divergence within* countries in work organization. These conditions affect the organization of work far more directly than they affect the broader industrial relations system, with the latter more likely to retain many country-specific characteristics despite the pressures for decentralization and responsiveness to local circumstances (Katz 1993; Locke 1992). But whereas national differences in industrial relations were likely in the past to dominate changes in work organization and create clear national patterns, I will argue that the forces for convergence across and divergence within countries are now more likely to overwhelm national differences.[1]

Jürgens et al. (1993) address this issue in the world auto industry for the period 1983-1986, attempting to differentiate "company" and "country" effects. The authors carried out extensive field work at a "core sample" of seventeen plants from three companies (labeled A, B, and C in the book but clearly identifiable as Ford, GM, and Volkswagen) in three countries (U.S., U.K., and Germany). They find evidence of company differences in strategies for change in work organization at Ford and GM (the two companies with plants in all three countries), although with much more convergence across the Ford plants than across the GM plants. Underlying these differences, they argue, was the crisis faced by Ford (but not GM) in the early 1980s; Ford's emphasis on changing work organization and human resource practices as the primary response to their crisis, compared with GM (and VW's) greater emphasis on technical solutions such as advanced assembly automation; and the greater centralization of Ford's implementation effort, compared with the more decentralized approach at GM.

However, they also find strong country effects, particularly with respect to industrial relations and the institutional context for training skilled workers. In the U.S., given a history of adversarial, "job control" labor-management relations, management at both Ford and GM emphasized work-rule changes to achieve more flexibility in labor deployment, coupled with efforts to boost employee participation and improve union-management cooperation. In the U.K., management struggles to pursue rationalization through greater shop floor control met with fierce union resistance and doomed most efforts at work organization changes. In Germany a surplus of skilled workers and union efforts to reduce working hours combined with management's technical orientation and concern about high absenteeism led to the use of advanced automation on the assembly line and the creation of "off-the-line" subassembly areas with longer work cycles.

For the tumultuous time period they document, Jürgens and his colleagues (1993) find it difficult to discern dominant trends, concluding that:

> We are faced with considerable difficulties in interpreting the direction and pace of change and getting to its essence. . . . A further problem lies in the fact that at the time of our research there was no established model for the new forms of work in the future, only many controversies about the direction to be taken. . . . The factor 'industrial relations' proved to be an extraordinarily important influence. But also within management there were many different ideas—about the necessity as well as the path of the reforms to be pursued. (p. 370)

On balance, however, they conclude that "the national affiliation of the factory site turned out to be a strong intervening factor which often came through more strongly than the influence of company affiliation" (p. 379). Thus the findings of Jürgens et al. suggest that while strategies for changing work organization differed significantly at the company level, national factors associated with the industrial relations system had a stronger influence on what work organization changes were actually implemented.

I will revisit these issues in this chapter to evaluate the many changes that have occurred in the auto industry since the time period of their study—in their words, "the end of an age in the auto industry," yet a time when "the contours of the new production regime are barely visible" (p. 397). In the last ten years there have been many new and intriguing developments in the auto industry to examine. U.S. and European companies have set up joint venture plants with Japanese competitors. Wholly owned "greenfield" plants, like GM's Saturn and Volvo's Uddevalla, have provided a "clean sheet of paper" for companies to experiment with new work practices. First Japanese companies and now German companies have set up new "transplant" facilities located away from their home base. Many existing plants have undertaken major changes in work organization when presented with both a carrot (the promise of new products or new investments in technology) and a stick (the threat of plant closure) by their company. Most significantly, with the rise in legitimacy and understanding of Japanese-influenced "lean production" principles, there has been more consensus across companies (although by no means unanimity) about the model for new forms of work that Jürgens et al. found to be manifestly lacking in the early 1980s and more acceptance of this model by unions as the starting point for negotiations.

Drawing on longitudinal data (1989 and 1993-94) from an international sample of 86 assembly plants, I will update and extend the Jürgens et al. analysis by statistically evaluating the relative weight of company and country effects for work organization change and addressing the question of which work organization trends have been convergent and which are divergent. While company effects appear to dominate country or regional effects for many variables—including certain human resource policies, automation levels, and plant performance—both kinds of effects remain strong with respect to changes in work organization. Furthermore, while the *direction* of change in work organization is convergent toward a "lean" or "flexible" production model, the *rate of change* differs dramatically across regional groups. Both the direction and rate of change in work organization can be linked in most regions to three prominent forces for convergence described in the next section. However, various country- and company-specific factors that lead to divergence in work practices—the focus of the chapter's third section—remain important for explaining variations from the dominant trends. The chapter will close by discussing the implications of this analysis for assessing national-level vs. company-level effects on the transfer of new ways of organizing work.

Conditions for Convergence across Countries

Three factors that promote convergence across countries will be discussed in this section: (1) the globalization of automotive markets; (2)

the move toward more flexible, programmable forms of automation; and (3) the diffusion of lean production ideas and innovations. While all of these trends can be traced back 20-30 years, they have had the most impact on companies worldwide in the past 10 years.

Globalization of Markets

It is relatively easy to document the common claim that the globalization of markets has had a massive impact on the competitive dynamics of the automotive industry and on the fortunes of auto companies worldwide. First, sales of vehicles made by non-domestic producers (either imports or produced at "transplant" facilities) have captured an increasingly large share of the market in many countries. The share of non-Big Three vehicle sales in the U.S. rose from less than 1% in 1955, the peak year for sales in the postwar period, to 18.4% twenty years later (1975), to a high of 28.5% in 1991, before falling back to 25.9% in 1994. The import share in European and Japanese markets is considerably less but climbing steeply, reaching 12% in Western Europe and nearly 5% in Japan by 1994 (Automotive News Market Data Book, various years).

Second, foreign-direct investment by companies in overseas production facilities and distribution networks is higher than ever, with the initial wave of investments (beginning in the 1920s and 1930s) by U.S. multinationals in Europe, Mexico, South America, Australia, and other developing economies now supplemented by a new wave (since the early 1980s) of Japanese investment in the U.S., Europe, Australia, and Asia and even more recently by European company investments in the U.S. in the 1990s.

Third, there has been an explosion of cross-national strategic alliances in the auto industry, as companies look for opportunities to learn from each other, to share the risks of technological development or expansion into a new market, to fill gaps in each other's product lines or distribution networks, and to build global economies of scale (Nohria and Garcia-Pont 1991).

To the extent that the globalization of markets brings more intensified competition for all automotive companies (whether or not they are global competitors), it creates pressures for convergence toward whatever approach to work organization is most associated with market success. At the same time, by driving some companies (or their plants) out of business, it helps select for those work organization practices associated with competitive survival.

Flexible Automation

While programmable machine tools have been readily available since the 1960s, it wasn't until the 1980s that automobile companies began making substantial investments in flexible automation. The diffusion of flexible automation was slow, due in part to being more expensive, particularly at first. But these new technological capabilities also did not fit well with the prevailing strategy of mass production companies—to achieve massive economies of scale through high-volume production of a single model, using fixed tooling designed only for that model. But as the price of flexible automation has fallen and companies have reassessed their competitive strategy and product portfolio plans, investments in flexible automation have risen dramatically.

Flexible automation allows for multiple products to be built in a single plant and/or for rapid model changes (both major and minor) over time. Investing in flexible automation facilitates strategies of more product variety and shorter product life cycles. It is thus a necessary complement to changes in product development processes that result in more products being generated from cross-project coordination and in faster time to market. Robotic weld and paint equipment can also be adjusted more easily to accommodate incremental process improvements or engineering changes.

Investments in flexible automation can potentially be a force for convergence in work organization in several ways. The link between flexible work organization and flexible automation is not technologically determined; robots do not require teams to operate effectively, nor multiskilled workers. But the decisions to invest in robotics and to invest in new forms of work organization are increasingly interconnected in company strategies. This is particularly true in light of the well-publicized failures of technology-only strategies in the mid-1980s (at General Motors in the U.S. and, to a lesser extent, at Fiat and VW in Europe) and the observation that many firms, under the influence of mass production traditions of high volume and minimal changeovers, do not always use the flexible capabilities of new automation (Jaikumar 1986).

There are many ways in which flexibly deployed workers capable of effective problem solving are critical to achieving the strategic goals associated with flexible automation. In plants building many different models, workers have heightened responsibility for accommodating greater product complexity without productivity or quality penalties, mastering a higher variety of tasks, making sure the right parts go on the right vehicle, working with team members to find the most efficient layout for parts and tools, and identifying the product-specific quality problems.

Flexible automation facilitates rapid changeovers from one model to another, but before such changeovers can be made, work methods must be revised and well tested in advance to avoid quality problems during product launch. Workers who are accustomed to job rotation within and across teams and to involvement in *kaizen* activities that refine work methods over time are critical resources in achieving an effective changeover. Programmable automation also lends itself more readily to worker involvement in making incremental process changes.[2]

Lean Production Ideas

A third strong influence promoting convergence across countries is "lean" or "flexible" production principles and innovations. This factor both complements and supplements the factors listed above, since lean production emphasizes flexibility in both production organization and technology, and several companies using lean production have achieved performance advantages that have helped them become extremely effective global competitors.

The key features of a lean production system are: just-in-time inventory systems and other buffer minimization policies; rapid machine setups to allow small lot production by reducing changeover times; the use of "on-line" work teams, job rotation, and extensive training to develop multiskilled workers who can be flexibly deployed; small, "off-line," problem-solving groups that involve workers in *kaizen* or continuous improvement activities. These innovations were mostly developed at Toyota by Taiichi Ono in the late 1950s and early 1960s and thus are often identified as the Toyota Production System (Schonberger 1982; Monden 1983; Ono 1988). They first diffused within Japan to Toyota's suppliers and eventually to its competitors (Cole 1989). Mazda, for example, nearly went bankrupt in the mid-1970s. Crucial to its recovery was a decision to implement Toyota-like lean production methods.

By the late 1970s the diffusion of lean production within Japan was well advanced and Japanese automakers had substantial performance advantages over their U.S. and European counterparts, particularly with respect to labor productivity and quality (Cusumano 1985). Then Japanese companies began to transfer lean production organizing principles to overseas plants in the U.S. and Europe—first Honda, Nissan, and Toyota, followed later by Mazda, Mitsubishi, Isuzu, Subaru, and Suzuki.

While not uniformly successful, virtually all of these transplants achieved performance advantages over many American and European plants, particularly in their ability to achieve both high productivity and high quality (Krafcik 1988). Furthermore, the transplants made relatively few modifications in their production system from the approach used in Japan (Florida and Kenney 1991). The modifications that were made (e.g., no seniority-based pay, no enterprise union, no rotation of workers across shifts, separate pay and promotion policies for "exempt" and "nonexempt" employees) did not affect work organization (Shimada and MacDuffie 1987; MacDuffie and Pil 1994).

The transplants had a strong "demonstration effect" in the U.S., particularly given prior expectations by American companies that Japanese competitive advantages were based on lower factor costs (e.g., wage rates) and on cultural attributes of their workforce (e.g., group orientation, strong work ethic), neither of which would be available to them in the U.S. Lean production came to be seen more and more as an alternative production paradigm that could be applied in a variety of cultural contexts.

Lean production acquired additional legitimacy through the business press, through company-initiated benchmarking of themselves against Japanese competitors, and through a variety of joint venture projects that gave U.S. and European companies close access to Japanese learning models. M.I.T.'s International Motor Vehicle Program (with which I am associated) no doubt contributed to this legitimization process as well, both through its formulation of the lean production model and its international benchmarking of manufacturing, supplier relations, and product development (Krafcik and MacDuffie 1989; Womack, Jones, and Roos 1990).

By the early 1990s, when industry recessions plunged such companies as General Motors, Mercedes-Benz, Volvo, and Fiat into crisis, the normative pressures to see lean production as the "best practice" route to recovery were very strong. Furthermore, with the discrediting of the "high tech" strategy for achieving competitive advantage at General Motors and (to a lesser degree) Volkswagen and Fiat, the idea took hold that new, flexible technologies needed to be coupled with the organizational flexibility provided by lean production to be used effectively (MacDuffie and Krafcik 1992). Finally, lean production plants seemed better able to handle high levels of product complexity without incurring cost or quality penalties (MacDuffie, Sethuraman, and Fisher, forthcoming)—a strategic advantage given the enthusiastic response of consumers to a proliferation of product offerings.

"Unfreezing" of the Mass Production Model

The confluence of the three forces listed above has created conditions ripe for convergence in work organization across countries. Globalization of markets has put serious competitive pressure on the old mass production model. The perceived performance advantages of lean production, together with evidence of its transferability, have given it powerful legitimacy as the new dominant model for auto manufacturing. Flexible automation offers considerable strategic advantages over fixed automation, particularly with respect to meeting the growing market demand for product variety, but is most strongly associated with improved economic performance when coupled with more flexible organizational practices.[3]

Thus this point in time can be characterized as the interruption of a long period of stasis for the dominant model (mass production), during which new technologies and organizing principles take hold and slowly displace the old model. As new organizing principles become dominant, all firms in the industry must adopt them to maintain competitiveness or face decline and possible death. Yet the change to the new principles can be extremely slow, since the new approach is likely to destroy old capabilities and require the development of new ones. Thus firms may resist adopting the new principles until they encounter a "competitiveness crisis." Such a crisis can "unfreeze" a company from its past strategies, structures, organizational routines, and labor-management relationships and create an opportunity for fundamental change. As each firm undergoes this transition, the net result (over time) should be movement toward the new organizing principles. Thus the combined force of the globalization of markets, new flexible technologies, and the increased influence of lean production ideas should be convergence in work organization across companies.[4]

Conditions for Divergence across Companies

Given the forces for convergence across countries described above and a tendency historically for industry-wide standardization of work practices *within* countries, why should work practices *diverge* across companies?[5] Answering this question requires examination of a number of company-level factors: differences in the timing of a "competitiveness crisis," perceptions from management and the union as to the source of a company's problems and the best path to recovery, management's strategy for changing work organization and the union's response or counterstrategy, management and union experience with earlier efforts to change work organization (or perception of the experience of competing firms), and company capabilities for learning and access to learning models. (See Table 1 for summary information about these factors for a subset of U.S. and European companies.)

The significance of a competitiveness crisis, as noted above, is its ability to "unfreeze" a company from its past strategies, structures, organizational routines, and labor-management relationships to allow the opportunity for some fundamental rethinking. This "punctuates" the equilibrium situation to allow a new set of organizing principles to exert influence on a company. Yet the impact of such a crisis can vary depending on its timing. The first company to experience a severe crisis may benefit, paradoxically, by having an earlier incentive to change to more effective strategies, structures, and organizational practices. A company's response to such a crisis will also vary depending on what diagnosis they reach about the source of the crisis (e.g., internal vs. external) and how they frame the solution (e.g., technical vs. organizational).

Furthermore, some management strategies for implementing work organizational changes are more effective than others and are heavily affected by whether unions support or oppose management's plan (and whether unions have an alternate strategy of their own). The history of past company experiences with work innovations (or the perceived experience of competitors) will affect the expectations and receptivity of workers, managers, and union officials to any new change efforts. Finally, some companies are better able to learn from the experience of other companies (often through explicit "benchmarking" comparisons), and some have greater access to such "learning models."

The U.S. Big Three

In the U.S., each of the Big Three faced a "competitiveness crisis" at different times. Chrysler was first, nearly going bankrupt in the late 1970s. At that point, knowledge about Japanese production methods at the Big Three was limited and financially strapped Chrysler had the fewest resources to investigate a different manufacturing approach. The perceived remedy for Chrysler's problems in manufacturing was defined mostly in terms of cost cutting. Wage and benefit concessions and some loosening of work rules negotiated with the UAW became crucial to the company's recovery. But Chrysler's overall approach to work organization and the production system changed little in the early 1980s.

TABLE 1
Factors Leading to Divergence across Companies

Company	Timing of Crisis	Perceived Path to Competitiveness	Mgmt. Strategy for Work Org. Change	Union Response to Work Org. Change	Past Experience with Work Innovations	Capabilities for External Learning
GM—U.S.	Early 1990s	"High tech" ('80s), cost-cutting ('90s)	QWL and teams, synchronous mfg. and quality network	Supportive in early '80s, mixed to negative in late '80s	Scattered efforts discredited in eyes of mgmt., union ('90s)	Low—unable to learn much from NUMMI or Saturn
Ford—U.S.	Early 1980s	Quality, employee involvement ('80s), "world car" ('90s)	Integrating quality resp. into line jobs, off-line EI groups	Mostly supportive	Cautious about teams due to GM experience	Moderate to high—work effectively with Mazda and Nissan
Chrysler	Early 1980s, early 1990s	Cost-cutting ('80s), new products ('90s)	MOA (teams, new pay systems) at some, POA (reduced job classes) at others	Mixed for MOA, not involved in POA	None	Moderate—learned some from Mitsubishi more from Honda; less in mft. than product development
GM—Europe	Early 1980s	Cost-cutting ('80s), lean production ('90s)	Off-line subassembly ('80s), teams ('90s)	Supportive but feel scope of change is too broad	Influenced by Volvo, VW problems	High—able to learn from NUMMI, CAMI
Ford—Europe	Early 1980s	Cost-cutting, quality ('80s); "world car" ('90s)	Integrating quality resp. into line jobs	Supportive, except in UK	Follows Cautious lead of Ford U.S.	Moderate—able to learn from Ford U.S., Mazda
Volkswagen	Mid-1970s, early 1990s	"High tech" ('80s), "lean production" ('90s)	Off-line sub-assembly, skilled workers run high-tech areas ('80s), cost-cutting ('90s)	Supportive	Off-line efforts influenced by Volvo experiments	Low—few alliances, see themselves as innovators; little need for external learning seen pre-'90s
Volvo	Mid-1970s early 1990s	"Socio-tech" plants ('80s), "lean production" ('90s)	Autonomous teams, off-line sub-assembly, Uddevalla w/no line	Supportive	Each experiment seen as partial, next one goes further	Low—few alliances, see themselves as innovators; no need to learn seen pre-'90s
Renault	Mid-1980s	Lean production	Teams	Adversary pre-crisis, then supportive	None	High—able to learn about lean production
Fiat	Mid-1970s early 1990s	"High tech" ('80s) lean production ('90s)	Teams	Adversary pre-crisis, then supportive	None	Mod. to high—able to learn about lean production

Chrysler's first experimentation with new forms of work organization came in the mid-1980s, a time of relative prosperity for the company, in the form of the Modern Operating Agreements (MOA) that were implemented at two assembly plants and four component plants (Department of Labor 1991; MacDuffie, Hunter, and Doucet 1995). The impetus for the MOA was threefold. First, the head of the Chrysler department of the UAW wanted to sponsor an "industrial democracy" initiative. Second, Chrysler hired a new vice-president of labor relations from the steel industry and gave him a charter to develop joint labor-management initiatives similar to those that had been successful at Ford. Third, Chrysler was finally in a position to make long-overdue investments in capital equipment and new products and decided that investments should be contingent on changes in work organization at various plants.

The MOA initiative was bold in its reliance on collective bargaining as the means for full-scale changeovers of existing "brownfield" plants, involving the use of work teams, "pay for knowledge," and the decentralization of quality responsibilities. However, implementation was extremely slow. MOA was seen primarily as a labor relations initiative and not as being central to manufacturing strategy. As such, it was often disrupted by labor-management disputes on other matters. At plants where the local union was unwilling to implement MOA, Chrysler often introduced a Progressive Operating Agreement (POA) that was management-initiated and focused on increasing the flexibility of labor deployment through the elimination of job classifications and work rules. Chrysler showed little ability for cross-company learning during this time. While Chrysler had access to a "lean production" plant through their joint venture involvement with Mitsubishi in Illinois, this had little influence on the thinking about MOA.

MOA implementation was also affected by Chrysler's return to crisis conditions in 1989-91. This time Chrysler's response focused on reforming product development. They sought out a variety of learning models among the Japanese companies (particularly Honda) and were able to move quickly to implement a "platform team" approach that enabled them to develop successful new products in three years—matching or exceeding Japanese product development benchmarks. With the return of high market demand, particularly for the product segments where Chrysler is strong (e.g., minivans), the company made a very successful comeback in 1993-94.

However, there has been little effort to build beyond the MOA experience to achieve broad changes in work organization at Chrysler's assembly plants. Persistent quality problems in Chrysler plants reveal that much scope for improvement still remains. At least so far, Chrysler's competitive ups and downs have had relatively little to do with changes in their approach to work organization in manufacturing. In both competitive crises during the past 15 years, work organization has not been perceived as either a major problem or an important remedy for the company. This example reveals the limits to which competitive crises alone can explain changes in the approach to work organization.

Ford faced a financial crisis soon after Chrysler in the early 1980s, although it was less visible because profits from Ford of Europe concealed the extent of problems in North America. Ford had acquired 25% of Mazda in the late 1970s and so had been exposed to Mazda's process of learning about the Toyota Production System. Ford's top managers also defined the company's problems partly in terms of the company's rigid structure, its emphasis on narrow functional specialization, and its adversarial labor-management relations. Employee involvement and quality were endorsed as twin initiatives that could help the company overcome these past organizational problems.

While Ford engaged in less plant-level innovation than General Motors, it was more successful at changing labor relations at top levels. The effort to break down barriers between functional groups helped pave the way for more cross-departmental communication at the plant level and for more cross-training for workers. Finally, Ford's decision to focus heavily on quality improvement with its "Quality is Job 1" campaign helped promote more decentralization of quality responsibilities from inspectors to shopfloor workers.

As Ford's fortunes began to improve in the mid-1980s, it became cautious about more far-reaching changes in work organization such as teams. In part, Ford wanted to preserve good relations with the UAW's Ford department, whose public position was one of opposition to teams. Ford also knew from experience that the UAW was willing to allow considerable flexibility at the plant level, as long as potentially controversial changes in work organization, such as the adoption of work teams, were avoided. Thus for Ford, changes in work organization were quite modest on the surface, yet more fundamentally linked to the quality-oriented strategy for competitive recovery than the more visible MOA changes at Chrysler.

Ford's caution about teams also derived from its observations of rival General Motors. GM had embarked on an ambitious "Quality of Work Life" program jointly with the UAW in 1979, emphasizing "off-line"

QWL groups that addressed non-production-related issues in an attempt to boost worker satisfaction. At the same time, GM tried to open some nonunion "team concept" plants in the South (the so-called "Southern Strategy") as well as at some "greenfield" plants around Detroit. The Southern Strategy failed almost immediately, as the UAW successfully organized the new plants in Oklahoma City and Shreveport, Louisiana. But teams became associated in the UAW's mind with an antiunion strategy. Team efforts in Michigan and elsewhere soon ground to a halt. The most advanced team plant at GM during this time, the Fiero plant in Pontiac, Michigan, marked the first time that teams had been centrally involved in dealing with production-related issues. The closing of the Fiero plant due to poor product sales prompted further skepticism about the value of teams from the union and workers alike.

GM had another opportunity to learn about lean production from its involvement at NUMMI, its joint venture with Toyota. While the NUMMI story is well known (Krafcik 1986; Brown and Reich 1989; Adler 1992; Adler and Cole 1993), it will suffice to say that GM did a terrible job of learning from NUMMI. GM top management and engineers expected that Toyota's advantages derived from technology and that hiring back the workers and union officials from the former GM Fremont plant would be a liability for Toyota. So GM completely overlooked the different approach to organizing production work and the greater emphasis on worker skill and motivation as the source of NUMMI's impressive performance. Although they exposed hundreds and possibly thousands of GM employees to NUMMI for short, one-day visits, complete with plant tour, these visits did not reveal the different "logic" at NUMMI and, if anything, bred skepticism about NUMMI's value as a learning model.

The crisis at GM came much later than at Chrysler and Ford, in part because of the company's size and wealth. By the time it hit GM in the early 1990s, the company had lost so much market share and closed so many plants that it was in an extremely difficult position from which to implement new work practices. With staggering losses, big cost savings were needed quickly. Workers were cynical about management intentions and trust was low. As a result, GM has taken a more "top-down" approach to lean production in the last few years, primarily through its Synchronous Manufacturing program, which carries out process reengineering efforts (driven by industrial engineering staff) at the plants.

So depending on the timing and nature of their "competitiveness crisis," each of the Big Three companies experienced the "unfreezing" effect that can facilitate the adoption of new work practices to a different extent. The companies also differed in their perception of whether "lean production" was the right path to follow strategically, with Ford the first to move in this direction, followed by Chrysler and only belatedly by GM. Ford appears to have made the best use of its learning relationship with a Japanese company, with both Chrysler and GM having more difficulty absorbing the lessons from their joint-venture experiences. GM's unhappy experiences with QWL and "team concept" served to scare off Ford and slow Chrysler's willingness to pursue this approach, as well as making it more difficult for GM to bring about work organization changes when it was finally faced with a major competitiveness crisis.

Europe

In Europe the movement toward lean production has been more recent and, to a greater extent than the U.S., reflects the trends toward convergence. Furthermore, for European companies that have all their plants within a single country, it is difficult to untangle company and country effects. But the factors identified above—the timing of a competitiveness crisis, perceptions of the best path to recovery, management strategies and union responses, and capabilities for learning—do help identify important differences across companies in Europe, particularly during the 1980s.

By the mid-1980s, for example, Renault was facing a major competitiveness crisis and chose to embrace lean production as a way out of their difficulties and as an alternative (given severe financial constraints) to making heavy investments in technology. This required the company to reach agreement with its unions in both France and Belgium on a new contract allowing significant changes in work organization at its existing plants. Peugeot, in contrast, faced no such crisis. With its CEO leading the campaign within the EC to keep Japanese companies from building plants in Europe or boosting their exports, Peugeot had little interest in adopting a Japan-influenced model and did not pursue the same kind of work restructuring through collective bargaining as Renault.

Also in the mid-'80s, Fiat was just reopening its Cassino plant, heralded as the most automated assembly plant in the world and a reflection of Fiat's intent (following a financial crisis in the late 1970s and a bitter strike which was won decisively by management) to reduce its dependence on workers (Locke 1992; Camuffo and Volpato 1994). During this time, Volvo was preparing to open its Uddevalla plant, the most ambitious in a series of plants with sociotechnical designs—in this case with no moving assembly line—intended to help it attract Swedish workers into manufacturing jobs and reduce high levels of absenteeism and turnover. Volvo was also continuing its efforts to implement "off-line assembly" and other sociotechnical design concepts at its other plants in Sweden, Belgium, and Holland (Berggren 1992).

Volvo's example was in turn influencing both Volkswagen and Mercedes in their planning of "off-line" assembly areas for new plants at Emden and Rastatt in Germany. But Volkswagen at this time was also committed, like Fiat, to a "high tech" strategy for reducing direct labor in assembly, though motivated more by a desire to utilize its highly skilled technical workers and improve ergonomic working conditions than by a move away from reliance on workers (Jürgens et al. 1993; Turner 1991).

When a competitiveness crisis hit these four companies—Fiat, Volvo, Volkswagen, and Mercedes—in the early 1990s, each responded in different ways. Fiat abandoned its "high tech" strategy and negotiated plans with its unions for a new plant (Melfi) that would utilize team structures (UTE, or Elementary Technical Units), performance-based pay, and other new forms of work organization (Camuffo and Micelli 1995). Volvo closed its two innovative sociotechnical plants (Kalmar and Uddevalla) in response, according to some observers (Hancke 1993; Berggren 1993), to pressure from Renault (briefly their partner-in-alliance), which was convinced of the greater virtues of Japanese-style team structures. Volkswagen negotiated new arrangements with IG Metall and its works councils for work-hour reductions and pay freezes to minimize layoffs during a period of reorganizing of production and increased its utilization of "group work,"[6] building on pilot projects from the mid-to-late 1980s (Jürgens 1995a; Roth 1995). Mercedes-Benz accelerated its move away from craft methods and boosted investments in automation, while backing away from the Volvo-influenced production system at Rastatt and hiring a Japanese consulting firm to implement "lean production" at its new U.S. factory.

For the American-owned companies in Europe, company differences were also pronounced. As in the U.S., Ford of Europe got a fast start in the early '80s (with its "After Japan" program) on implementing employee involvement activities directed at quality and improving labor-management relations. However, unlike Ford in the U.S., these were boom years for Ford Europe and the early experiments with work reorganization were short-lived. However, Ford had laid the foundation for more cooperative relations with its unions and works councils, enabling them to revive some quality-oriented initiatives later in the '80s (in connection with learning exchanges with Mazda plants), while proceeding cautiously (as in the U.S.) with teams and other new work structures. GM of Europe, on the other hand, did face a severe financial crisis in the early 1980s that set the company on a path of learning about lean production, unlike GM in the U.S. This strategic redirection resulted not only from the competitiveness crisis but from the appointment of new top managers (first Jack Smith and then Lou Hughes) who had helped to set up the NUMMI joint venture and had become convinced of the value of lean production principles. While there is still more variation in Europe across GM's plants than for Ford, GM has gone further than Ford in establishing more far-reaching reforms in work organization at some of its plants (Turner 1991).

For example, the most advanced lean production plant in Europe that is not Japanese-owned is the new GM Europe plant in Eisenach in eastern Germany, which is run primarily by young American and Canadian managers and advisors who previously worked either at NUMMI or at GM's joint venture plant with Suzuki in Canada (CAMI). Eisenach's achievement owes much to GM Europe's strategy of trying to replicate lean production principles developed elsewhere, without major efforts to reinvent or modify them, and to the extensive transfer of managers with extensive "hands-on" experience with lean production to oversee the launch effort. Eisenach has also benefited from its greenfield status and its workforce—skilled workers from the former East Germany who have no previous experience in a traditional mass production plant and who have shown considerable receptivity to "group work" (MacDuffie 1995b; Jürgens 1995b).

So most European companies that faced competitive crises early in the 1980s pursued different strategies for improvement, depending on whether they were primarily oriented toward technology (Fiat, VW) or "people" (Volvo, Ford) solutions (Jürgens et al. 1993), whether they had adversarial (Fiat, Renault) or cooperative (Volvo, VW) relationships with unions and works councils, their past experience with work organization reforms (especially at Volvo and VW) and the influence of "learning models" (e.g., Volvo's sociotechnical experiments for VW and Mercedes, Mazda for Ford Europe, NUMMI for GM Europe). GM Europe and Renault were the only European companies during the 1980s to make serious moves companywide toward lean production, due to the timing of competitive crises, the orientation of their leadership, and their capacities for learning. Thus it is only after the competitive crises of the early 1990s that the responses of the European companies begin to look more convergent, as will be discussed below.

Japan

Even in Japan there is substantial divergence across companies, although largely within the bounds of the lean production model. The diffusion of Toyota's production methods in the 1970s mentioned above did mean that most companies were adhering to the most visible aspects of lean production, particularly the just-in-time inventory system and the use of formal work teams and quality circles. However, sizable differences remain in how well companies understand Toyota's innovations and how successfully they have been able to maintain lean production practices in the face of various challenges—e.g., industry downturns, increasing product variety, major automation initiatives within the assembly area. Nissan, for many years, resembled U.S. companies in its emphasis on automation and economies of scale and its relatively traditional work organization (Cusumano 1985). Even after adopting much of the structure of Toyota's work organization, Nissan was much less successful at getting workers involved in *kaizen* activities. During a visit to a Nissan plant in 1992, I received an extensive presentation about a newly initiated campaign for "workshop management" consisting of *kaizen*-type activities that had been carried out at Toyota plants for at least 15 years.

These differences are also apparent when examining the "transplant" operations of various Japanese companies in the U.S. Nissan yielded substantial authority to the first American manager of its Tennessee plant over such issues as plant design and ended up with the most space-inefficient plant in North America. In addition, many of Nissan's HR policies in Tennessee bear a closer resemblance to the U.S. nonunion model than to employment practices in Japan (Shimada and MacDuffie 1987). Unlike Toyota, which built a very effective working relationship with the union at NUMMI, Mazda made several mistakes in its handling of the union and the workforce at its plant in Michigan— with management first building overly rosy expectations during an endless hiring and training process, then reversing its position on several key issues such as training and temporary workers during the pressures of the first year of production (Fucini and Fucini 1990). The smaller Japanese companies—Mitsubishi, Suzuki, and the Subaru-Isuzu joint venture—have all had some difficulties simultaneously managing lean production and an American/Canadian workforce at their transplant facilities (e.g., Huxley, Rinehart, and Robertson 1995).

A thorough examination of the source of differences among the Japanese companies is beyond the scope of this chapter. But it can be said that, like U.S. and European companies, each of the Japanese companies has experienced competitive crises at different times and has a different history of experiments with work reforms and a different relationship with its enterprise union. While the Japanese companies may share a greater consensus about pursuing the Toyota Production System model for work reorganization than in other countries, there still appear to be strong differences in the learning capabilities of the different companies, particularly with respect to transferring these work practices to countries outside of Japan.

Summary

In all three regions, company-level factors lead to significant divergence in the adoption of new forms of work organization despite the strong forces for convergence outlined above. Some of this divergence represents differences in the timing and severity of a competitive crisis that "unfreezes" the company and increases its readiness for fundamental changes, some of it is based on differences in company capabilities for implementing such change, and some of it reflects more durable differences in company strategies. While considerable company-level divergence is apparent during the past 10-15 years, a time of major transition in organizing principles, it is less clear whether these differences will persist or whether they represent different starting points and different rates of change toward what may be a more convergent "steady state" in another 10-15 years.

Comparing Regional Changes in Work Organization over Time

The previous sections describe the convergent and divergent forces for change in work organization. In this section we examine the regional trends in the adoption of "flexible" or "lean" work practices as well as trends for flexible automation and product variety, which are hypothesized to be promoting the diffusion of new work practices. These trends provide an initial basis for evaluating the main hypothesis of greater convergence in work practices across countries and regions.

Evidence concerning changes in work practices (and other factors affecting the adoption of work practices) across countries and regions is presented in Table 2a and 2b. I draw upon 1989 and 1993-94 data from the International Assembly Plant Study (see also MacDuffie and Pil

TABLE 2a

Regional Averages for Work Organization Variables—Round 1 (1989) vs. Round 2 (1993/94)
Matched and Unmatched Samples

Variable	Jpn/Jpn		Jpn/N.A.		U.S./N.A.		US&E/Eur.		NIC		Aust.	
	1989	93/94	1989	93/94	1989	93/94	1989	93/94	1989	93/94	1989	93/94
Matched Sample (n=38)												
% Workforce in Teams	78	70	71	76	10	6	0.4	75	2	30	0	34
% Workforce in EI Groups	93	90	12	14	17	20	5	54	42	68	24	62
Job Rotation (0=none; 4=lots)	3.8	4.2	2.7	3.7	0.9	2.1	1.8	3.9	2.2	3.7	1.7	3.7
Suggestions per Employee	56	48	1.1	1.9	0.3	0.2	0.3	1.0	2.3	N/A	0.1	0.2
% Suggestions Implemented	91	90	68	79	22	34	15	49	39	59	8	6
Work Systems Index	82.1	80.8	49.1	50.7	22.5	24.0	16.0	52.6	36.8	55.4	19.7	36.4
Unmatched Samples (n=62 and n=81)												
% Workforce in Teams	84	70	78	72	12	18	0.5	62	3	37	13	49
% Workforce in EI Groups	100	81	13	25	21	26	11	49	31	73	16	51
Job Rotation (0=none; 4=lots)	3.1	3.9	2.7	3.9	0.9	2.0	1.7	3.6	2.0	3.2	1.7	4.0
Suggestions per Employee	61	51	1.0	3.6	0.3	0.3	0.4	0.9	1.4	N/A	0.1	0.2
% Suggestions Implemented	88	84	61	65	22	41	23	41	32	48	20	23
Work Systems Index	77.9	78.9	47.3	50.4	22.6	28.1	24.1	46.7	27.9	57.3	19.4	43.5

TABLE 2b

Regional Averages for Production Organization Indices, Technology, and Product Variety Variables
Round 1 (1989) vs. Round 2 (1993/94)—Matched and Unmatched Samples

Variable	Jpn/Jpn 1989	Jpn/Jpn 93/94	Jpn/N.A. 1989	Jpn/N.A. 93/94	U.S./N.A. 1989	U.S./N.A. 93/94	US&E/Eur. 1989	US&E/Eur. 93/94	NIC 1989	NIC 93/94	Aust. 1989	Aust. 93/94
Matched Sample (n=38)												
% Total Automation	38	36	35	38	34	35	26	32	13	17	9	8
Robotic Index	3.9	7.4	4.2	5.7	2.4	2.5	2.4	3.9	1.0	2.3	0.6	0.6
Model Mix Complexity	52.0	44.9	14.0	15.9	19.3	18.2	37.0	27.9	48.0	35.3	18.2	42.2
Parts Complexity	71.5	39.7	33.0	8.2	42.3	18.7	74.9	22.6	50.7	20.8	22.6	11.0
Use of Buffers Index	96.0	83.7	77.4	76.2	65.3	66.6	51.0	68.8	71.1	70.6	66.4	44.4
HRM Policies Index	63.2	55.5	65.1	68.5	31.5	35.6	38.1	58.9	47.7	51.7	14.6	62.3
Work Systems Index	82.1	80.8	49.1	50.7	22.5	24.0	16.0	52.6	36.8	55.4	19.7	36.4
Unmatched Samples (n=62 and n=81)												
% Total Automation	38	35	36	38	30	34	26	31	8	21	10	9
Robotic Index	4.4	6.3	4.6	6.5	2.2	3.3	2.2	3.4	0.6	3.2	0.5	0.7
Number of Models Produced*	5.1	5.4	1.9	2.3	2.7	2.2	2.6	2.5	2.8	3.0	4.0	4.0
Number of Countries for Export*	6.9	16.7	23.6	26.6	2.9	5.6	23.7	26.6	38.9	51.4	1.5	2.3
Wire Harnesses*	430	580	35	37	15	12	83	84	39	61	8	8
Exterior Colors*	24	33	12	14	10	11	15	16	12	14	10	10
Engine/Trans. Combinations*	180	167	52	63	30	29	83	86	77	N/A	11	15
(*data are from 1990 and 1993-94)												
Use of Buffers Index	93.1	79.3	79.6	70.8	59.0	66.6	54.1	67.9	61.9	49.6	68.3	25.3
HRM Policies Index	56.0	52.4	67.3	75.3	30.6	41.9	31.1	57.6	35.9	48.3	18.2	62.6
Work Systems Index	77.9	78.9	47.3	50.4	22.6	28.1	24.1	46.7	27.9	57.3	19.4	43.5

1995). I will compare regional averages across six groupings of plants—Japanese-owned plants in Japan (Jpn/Jpn), Japanese-owned plants in North America (Jpn/NA), U.S.-owned plants in North America (US/NA), all U.S. and European-owned plants in Europe (Eur/Eur), plants in Newly Industrialized Countries (NIC), and plants in Australia (Aust).

Table 2a first considers regional changes from 1989 to 1993 for specific work practices—the percentage of the workforce in teams and employee involvement groups, the extent of job rotation, the number of suggestions per employee, and the percentage of suggestions that are implemented—and then shows the Work Systems Index score which is based on aggregating these practices.[7]

The top half of the table contains data from the matched sample of 38 plants participating in both Rounds 1 and 2 of the assembly plant survey, while the bottom half of the table contains data from the entire Round 1 (n=62) and Round 2 (n=81) samples. The matched sample offers the most precise look at change in the same set of plants over time but with a small sample size. Conversely, the larger unmatched samples offer a more representative view of dominant practices in each region at the two points in time, albeit with compositional differences in the plants included in each sample. The fact that both views of the data reveal roughly similar patterns suggests that the results discussed below are not substantially affected by sample bias problems.

Work Organization

The most striking trend in Table 2a is the huge increase in European, New Entrant, and Australian plants in the use of small group activities—both "on-line" work teams and "off-line" employee involvement groups—as well as increased job rotation and reliance on suggestion systems. In contrast, small group activities at the U.S.-owned plants in North America affect fewer employees than in any other region and problem-solving activities (i.e., suggestions received per employee and the percentage of suggestions implemented by management) also remain low for the Big Three plants even as they increase for European, NIC, and Australian plants (as well as the Japanese transplants).[8] Job rotation is the only practice to have significantly increased in all regions. Increased concern about ergonomic problems and repetitive strain injuries may provide a common motivation for job rotation across companies, irrespective of the company's commitment to job rotation as a means of learning multiple skills.

Plants in Japan remain the most consistent followers of "lean" work practices. They do show some diminution in their adherence to certain practices, which seems to be most likely due to recessionary conditions in the Japanese auto industry that carried through 1993 and 1994. In contrast, the Japanese transplants in North America appear to be on a steady trajectory converging upon the practices of their counterparts in Japan, although their percentage of workers in employee involvement groups and suggestions received and implemented remains considerably lower than in Japan.

On the strength of this evidence, it seems reasonable to claim that the *direction* of work organization changes is converging toward lean or flexible production work practices.[9] The changes in Europe, NIC, and Australian plants can perhaps also be accurately described as convergent in *degree* or extent of change as well. Here I would argue that the appropriate comparison is to the Japanese transplants rather than Japanese plants in Japan. The implementation of lean production in Japan has been going on for over 30 years, while implementation in the transplants as well as in any other plants that are moving toward lean production has occurred in the last 5-10 years. For most of these variables, the difference in means in 1993-94 when comparing the Japanese transplants with European, NIC, and Australian plants is not statistically significant. However, while Big Three plants in the U.S. and Canada may be converging in direction, their *degree* of implementation of flexible work organization clearly *diverges* substantially from other regions.

Automation

Table 2b provides data on two measures of technology: total automation, which measures the total number of physical production steps that are carried out by automated equipment rather than people (e.g., the number of welds, the square inches of paint applied, the assembly operations); and the robotic index, which measures the number of robots (defined as programmable automation with three or more axes of motion) in the weld, paint, and assembly areas adjusted for the plant's production volume.

Considering total automation first, which does not distinguish between fixed and flexible automation, we can see a small increase in automation in most regions. While the direction is consistent with the historical trend, the relatively small size of the increase may be due to the fact that automation levels have remained relatively flat in the weld shop (where many modern plants in the U.S., Europe, and Japan are approaching

90-95% automated welds) and in assembly operations (where automation remains costly, unreliable, and surprisingly difficult to shift across models, causing companies in all three regions to back away from ambitious investment plans in this area). Thus major boosts in automation level at modern plants are mostly occurring in the paint shop. In contrast, results for the robotic index reveal a strong shift toward flexible automation. With levels of total automation relatively unchanged, this means that flexible automation is being substituted for earlier generations of fixed or hard automation at a rate that is facilitated by steady improvements in the price/performance ratio for this equipment.

Japanese-owned plants, both in Japan and the U.S., have the highest level of flexible automation in both 1989 and 1993 and a higher rate of growth in the use of robotics over this time period than U.S. and European plants, which are similar in their level and rate of growth in robotics. The high percentage change in the level of robotics for the NIC plants, particularly in the unmatched sample, is primarily the result of a number of newly built Korean plants that were designed to be "high-tech." There is virtually no change in flexible automation among the Australian plants because they typically have neither the production scale (most make under 50,000 vehicles a year) nor the manufacturing capabilities (having operated for years in a protected market) to attract much capital investment.

Thus these data provide mixed support for the hypothesis that investments in flexible automation create an incentive to move toward more flexible forms of work organization. The extremely high level of flexible capabilities, both technological and organizational, at the Japanese plants in Japan and North America supports the idea that "fit" between these capabilities is important, even if it does not conclusively indicate the direction of the causality.[10] Similarly, the relatively large jump in the robotic index for European and NIC plants matches the jump in their scores for various work practices. U.S. Big Three plants are again an exception to this trend.[11]

Product Variety/Complexity

The product variety/complexity data in Table 2b are drawn completely from the Round 2 survey in which respondents were asked to answer a more specific and detailed list of questions about changes in product variety for 1990 and 1993.[12]

Plants that build lots of models are likely to benefit from heavier reliance on flexible automation and flexible work organization. Trends for the number of models are mixed but do not show dramatic change over this three-year period.[13] Japanese plants in Japan make the most models in each plant, consistent with their high-variety product strategies. Low-volume NIC and Australian plants also produce relatively high variety since there is insufficient market demand to justify dedicating a single plant to one product. The Japanese transplants, which started with extremely low product variety to facilitate the learning process, continue to add more different models to their plants over time. While the number of models holds steady in Europe, it actually drops in the U.S., where the Big Three have been more inclined to see product variety as being detrimental to achieving high productivity and quality in manufacturing and have made determined efforts to cut it back.[14] Thus one source of incentive to develop more flexible forms of work organization—increasing product variety—is lacking for the Big Three plants (MacDuffie, Sethuraman, and Fisher 1996).

Another indicator of increasing product variety driven by the globalization of markets is the trend of plants exporting vehicles to more and more countries, which is consistent across all the regions, although with high variation in the amount of export activity. Although Big Three plants showed the highest percentage increase (93%) from 1990 to 1993, their level of export activity is still comparatively low and may not yet exert much influence on decisions about work organization. In contrast, export activity is quite high for European plants in 1993-94, which fits with their greatly increased utilization of flexible work practices. However, the causality is uncertain since the level of European exports was not much lower in 1990, while work practices that year were still mostly traditional. This would support an argument that the European move to flexible work organization has been overdue, given their past levels of flexible automation, product variety, and export activity.[15]

The other three measures—the number of wire harnesses, the number of exterior colors, and the number of engine/transmission combinations built at each plant—represent more intermediate levels of product variety that are not so apparent to the consumer but pose massive difficulties in terms of greater manufacturing complexity.[16] For these variety indicators, there are again large regional differences, with the highest levels in regions that export heavily.[17] The overall trend is for modest increases in all three kinds of product variety, except, once again, for Big Three plants in the U.S. that have been attempting to reduce manufacturing complexity. Both the differences in levels across regions and the trends over time fit the patterns of utilization of flexible work organization most notably in Japan (high variety = high flexibility) and the U.S. (low variety = low flexibility).

Other Production Organization Policies

Table 2b also includes data for two indices of production organization that in past work I have found to be highly intercorrelated with (and complementary to) changes in work organization: the use of buffers and HRM policies index (MacDuffie 1995a). The former refers to manufacturing policies affecting inventory levels for both incoming parts and work-in-process and thereby captures the extent to which a plant is following a just-in-time inventory policy. A higher score means a *reduction* in buffers, i.e., a move to "leaner" buffers. The latter refers to such HRM policies as the use of contingent compensation, the presence of status differentiators, and the level of training for new and experienced employees. A higher score indicates "high commitment" HRM policies.

Examining primarily the unmatched samples, we find substantial convergence in level across regions for the use of buffers index, with Japanese-owned plants (both in Japan and the U.S.) increasing their inventory levels (very likely because of the impact of the recession on the JIT system in Japan and the increased amount of domestic sourcing of parts for the transplants) and U.S., European, and NIC plants decreasing their buffers. (Australia's huge increase in buffers is an unresolved puzzle.) This suggests that the lean production view of buffers as *muda* (waste) to be eliminated has been quite influential on inventory practices worldwide. But given the lack of variation in buffer policies and high variation in work practices, it is clear that a move toward JIT inventory practices is not always linked to the adoption of flexible work practices.

In contrast, patterns of change for the HRM index are better predictors of work organization changes. European and Australian plants are the most enthusiastic adopters of new HRM policies in recent years, as they are for small group activities. Japanese plants, both in Japan and the U.S., have remained relatively constant in their HRM policies, while Big Three and NIC plants have shown a modest increase in their HRM index scores, primarily due to an increase in training activities.

The massive change in the HRM index score for Australia requires some explanation. It is the direct result of a country-specific initiative related to industrial relations—a new agreement reached between the industry association and the metalworkers union in response to the deregulation of the Australian industry (Automotive Industry Authority 1989). This agreement introduces a new "pay-for-skill" compensation plan and a training qualification program intended to boost both basic and technical skill levels throughout the automotive workforce (Lansbury and Bamber 1995). Since both new pay plans and increased training are part of the HRM index, these changes have a substantial impact on the scores of the Australian plants.[18]

Also worthy of further discussion is the dramatic increase in the implementation of formal work teams and problem-solving groups in European plants and the absence of such changes in the U.S. In Europe the rapid move to "group work" reflects the confluence of a number of conditions. Many European companies were already experimenting in the 1980s with work teams in subassembly areas of some plants (Turner 1991; Jürgens et al. 1993). At the same time, European unions, particularly in Germany and Sweden, were studying different approaches to "group work" internationally, contrasting in particular the Japanese model found at NUMMI and other U.S.-based transplants with the sociotechnical model used by Volvo at its car and truck plants (Berggren 1992; Roth 1995). For much of the 1980s, these unions were more likely to advocate the adoption of "group work" than management, which was not convinced that this change in work organization would lead to performance gains. As Turner reports in his case study of GM Europe's Bochum plant:

> As early as 1982. . , the union and works council demanded better protection for displaced or downgraded workers and called for alternative forms of organization, including group work. According to works councillors, management bargainers laughed at proposals for group work (a union pipe dream) until 1987-88, when management developed its own interest in teams (p. 128-29).

In the late 1980s and early 1990s, the combination of a competitive crisis for many European companies and the legitimation of "lean production" as a model appears to have convinced managers of the need to implement "group work" as part of an overall shift in production system strategy. Unions have supported this move, it appears, because they see the opportunity to advance their own agenda and the interests of workers by supporting this initiative. There is certainly some ambivalence about this change among managers, union officials, and workers. It is too early to tell whether "group work" will be viewed as instrumental in boosting performance. Also, it is unclear whether "group work" will win widespread acceptance and become a permanent feature of work organization in European plants.

The rapid move toward "on-line" and "off-line" group activities in these regions is a strong contrast with the U.S. and Canada, where movement toward lean production work practices has been quite limited, although many associated manufacturing policies (e.g., buffer reduction) have been implemented. There are many company-specific factors that help explain this limited diffusion, as noted above, and some common factors associated with industrial relations: first, the political controversy around the idea of a "team concept" within the United Automobile Workers (UAW) union, where opposition to teams was a central feature of the New Directions faction in the 1980s (the Canadian Auto Workers [CAW] have also opposed work teams); and second, management caution after the failure of several early experiments with teams in the late '70s and early '80s. As a result, less convergence toward flexible work practices can be seen in the U.S. in 1993 than would have been evident five to ten years ago. This pattern may also be changing again, with evidence that the U.S. companies (most notably Ford) are increasingly likely to convert plants to team-based work organization whenever a major retrofit of a plant for a new product allows time for extensive training and other preparation. If the most recent (and pending) implementations of new work practices at Big Three plants turn out to be more durable than the wave of experimentation in the early 1980s, the U.S. trend may come to resemble trends in the rest of the world within the next 5-10 years. However, U.S. plants may also continue to be anomalous cases. If so, it will be important to determine whether U.S. companies are also resistant to other global trends (e.g., toward high product variety) or whether it is only the area of work organization that shows distinctly different patterns from other regions.

Company-level vs. Country-level Explanations for Change

Given that there is evidence of both convergent and divergent trends in work organization, the next question is how to assess the relative importance of national/regional vs. company influences, both for work organization and other aspects of the production system. This requires a comparison of plants from the same company that are located in multiple regions and of plants in the same region that are owned by multiple companies.

In this section I will examine a subsample of 31 plants from the 1993 survey that meet these conditions, with at least three plants from a given company in two regional groups (i.e., a minimum of six plants per company). Three companies are represented—labeled A, B, and C for confidentiality reasons—and all plants are located in North America, Europe, or Japan. These three companies do have plants outside of these three regions, but we do not have data from a sufficient number to warrant including them in the comparison. Of the 31 plants, 18 are in North America, 9 are in Europe, and 4 are in Japan. To preserve confidentiality agreements with the companies, I cannot reveal any additional details about companies A, B, or C, and I will present only limited data. Also, while analyses of this kind typically emphasize country effects rather than regional effects, the data do not allow for country-level analyses. For example, the nine plants in Europe are divided among four countries, too few per country for any meaningful statistical analysis. While there are certainly differences among plants in Europe, they are relatively small for these nine plants in relation to the more significant differences across regions.

I will focus on the three categories of variables analyzed above: automation; product variety; and production organization (e.g., use of buffers, work systems, and HRM policies). In addition, I will examine differences in plant productivity and quality.

To illustrate the logic of this analysis, consider the automation variable. If the level of automation across all the plants in this subsample is similar (i.e., no statistically significant difference in group means), it may indicate an industry effect rather than company or regional effects. A certain level of automation may be necessary for competitive survival across the industry, at least in the advanced industrial nations in this subsample, with relatively little benefit in acquiring automation beyond the level necessary to meet the competitiveness threshold. If automation levels reveal significant differences by company but not by region, it would imply differences in company automation strategies that prevail across different locations. If, on the other hand, automation levels differ by region but not by company, it would imply that company investment choices are differentially affected by regional factors, such as the availability of technical support or skilled workers or wage rates.

The same logic would apply to other variables, such as the use of work teams. Similar levels across all companies and regions would imply competitive necessity. Significant company (but not regional) differences would suggest that company strategies are the dominant influence on diffusion patterns. Significant regional (but not company) differences would suggest that country/regional factors such as worker characteristics, labor-management relations, the union position on teams are more influential than company-specific strategic plans.

Table 3 (p. 102) presents means across the various company/regional groupings of plants, and Table 4 (p. 103) shows the results of t-tests for statistically significant differences. For the performance variables, confidentiality agreements prohibit revealing company-specific averages (even with the companies disguised) in Table 3, but the significance level of t-tests for differences in productivity and quality means across the six groupings in this subsample are included in Table 4.

Plant Performance

T-test results here indicate that the "company effect" for both performance measures appears to be dominant. The only significant regional difference among the three productivity comparisons and one quality comparison is for productivity between company A's U.S. and European plants. In contrast, there are pronounced differences in both productivity and quality across companies in three out of four of the productivity comparisons and two out of three of the quality comparisons.

Automation

The two automation measures show strikingly different patterns. Levels of total automation are relatively similar across these plants, but more pronounced company differences are evident for the robotic index. For both automation measures, there are both company differences and a "home country" effect; the company A and company B plants in the U.S. have more automation than their European counterparts, as do the company C plants in Japan compared to their U.S. transplants. It seems likely that the higher production volume that companies normally produce in their home country might provide the economies of scale to justify more extensive automation investments.

T-tests in Table 4 reveal different results for the two automation variables. For total automation, there are no significant differences across any of the groupings, suggesting that overall automation levels are indeed determined more by industry competitive requirements, at least for these advanced industrial economies, than by regional or company differences. For the robotic index, company differences are more pronounced, although there is a significant difference between company B's U.S. and European plants on this variable.

Production Organization Indices

Recall that the use of buffers index captures such manufacturing policies as levels of incoming and work-in-process inventory and the approach to vehicle repair, with higher scores reflecting smaller or "leaner" buffers. A priori, these policies would seem to be primarily influenced by company-level choices and capabilities. (Although there are likely to be regional differences in the capabilities of suppliers to support a just-in-time system.) Here company-level influences do appear to be predominant, with company C plants being the "leanest," followed by company A and then company B.

The HRM policies index includes training, contingent compensation, hiring philosophy, and degree of status differentiation. With the possible exception of training, these are primarily established at the corporate level. The training variable measures in-plant training activity, both on-the-job and off-the-job, and thus would not pick up the apprenticeship-based training that is prominent in some European countries (and not in the U.S.). Here the most striking pattern is the similarity of the means for company A and company B in both the U.S. and Europe. Furthermore, although plants of European-owned companies are excluded from this subsample, their mean score for the HRM policies index (not shown) is higher than the mean for U.S.-owned company A and company B plants in Europe. This pattern suggests that corporate guidelines for these HRM policies at companies A and B are sufficiently strong to produce relatively uniform outcomes across different regions.

For the work systems index, the summary measure of work organization practices, there are intriguing signs of both regional and company effects. Clear differences in company strategy are apparent. Company C plants tend to have the highest scores on this index, followed by company A and then company B. Factors discussed in the "company-level divergence" section above—such as the timing of competitive crises, management and union perceptions of past experiences with work organization changes, and organizational capacities for learning—help explain these differences.[19] Nevertheless, consistent with the overall trend for Europe, the work systems mean is higher for the European plants of company A and company B than for their U.S. plants. As discussed above, this regional difference is rooted partly in the different stance of European and American unions toward "team concept" or "group work."

For both the use of buffers and HRM policies, the t-tests in Table 4 are only significant across companies, not across regions. But for the work systems index, the t-tests reveal significant differences in means for both regional and company comparisons. The implications of this finding will be discussed further below.

TABLE 3

Company and Regional Comparisons of Means for Key Variables (1993-94 Data)

Variable	Firm A-U.S.	Firm A-Europe	Firm B-U.S.	Firm B-Europe	Firm C-U.S.	Firm C-Japan
%Total Automation	37	32	31	29	35	38
Robotic Index	3.6	3.7	1.9	2.8	4.5	6.8
Use of Buffers	68	77	43	62	87	93
HRM Policies	35	48	34	43	79	NA
Work Systems	35	60	15	33	56	86

NA = Insufficient data

TABLE 4

T-tests for Company and Regional Means for Key Variables—1993/94 Data

Variable	Comparison of Means within-Company, across Region			Comparison of Means across Company, within Region			
	Firm A-U.S. vs. Firm A-Europe	Firm B-U.S. vs. Firm B-Europe	Firm C-U.S. vs. Firm C-Japan	Firm B-U.S. vs. Firm A-U.S.	Firm B-U.S. vs. Firm C-U.S.	Firm A-U.S. vs. Firm C-U.S.	Firm A-Europe vs. Firm B-Europe
Productivity	°°°	—	—	°°°	—	°°°	°°
Quality	NA	NA	—	—	°	°°	NA
Total Automation	—	—	—	—	—	—	—
Robotic Index	—	°°	—	°	°°	—	—
Use of Buffers	—	—	—	°°	°°	°°	°°
HRM Policies	—	—	—	—	°°°	°°°	—
Work Systems	°°°	°	°°	°°	°°°	°°	°°

°°°   t-test is significant at p < .01
°°   t-test is significant at p < .05
°   t-test is significant at p < .10
—   t-test is not statistically significant
NA = Insufficient data to do t-test

Link between Flexible Technology and Flexible Work Organization

This analysis reveals an intriguing relationship between the pattern of findings for the robotic index and work systems. The use of "flexible" work systems—characterized by teams, problem-solving groups, job rotation, and active suggestion systems—tracks the use of flexible automation very closely.

The highest mean score for both technology and work organization variables is found at company C plants in Japan, with substantially lower mean scores at company C's U.S. plants. The lowest mean score for both variables is found at company B plants in the U.S. Company B's European plants have mean scores for both variables that are higher than company B's U.S. plants and statistically significant. The only variation from this pattern is found at company A's U.S. plants, which have the same (relatively high) level of robotics as company A's European plants but a lower usage of flexible work systems, to a statistically significant extent. This suggests that in company A's U.S. plants there is insufficient investment in flexible work systems relative to the investment in flexible automation—unlike company B, where the low scores for both variables are well matched.

Conclusions and Implications

The chapter updates and extends the inquiry of Jürgens et al. (1993) into convergent and divergent forces for change in work organization in the world auto industry, with a hypothesis suggesting more convergence across countries and divergence across companies than in the past. A regional examination of Round 1 and Round 2 data from the International Assembly Plant Study reveals a mix of convergent and divergent trends with respect to the adoption of flexible work practices. The *direction* of change in work organization is convergent toward a "lean" or "flexible" production model, while the *rate of change* differs dramatically across regional groups. Both the direction and rate of change in work organization can be linked, in most regions, to the general forces for convergence highlighted above—the globalization of markets (reflected in more models being produced, more export activity, and hence more manufacturing complexity); the move toward flexible automation; and the influence of lean production ideas and policies (particularly complementary policies on the use of buffers and HRM policies). Where these links are not seen, the various country- and company-specific factors that account for divergence must be examined.

European plants show the most fundamental shift in their approach to work organization from 1989 to 1993-94, with NIC and Australian plants close behind. This can be partially explained by technology and product variety trends in these regions but also requires a more institutional analysis of the influence of lean production ideas and, for Europe and Australia, the impact of a strong union role in shaping (and implementing) new policies affecting work organization. Japanese plants both in Japan and the U.S. provide the best evidence of the "fit" between flexible work organization, flexible technology, and a high variety product strategy. Finally, Big Three plants in the U.S. and Canada show the least amount of movement toward flexible work practices and present the most anomalous results. This is particularly true given that most of the global trends highlighted above can be seen in the U.S. and Canada as well as in the other regions. However, it must be noted that the U.S. companies seem to have made less investment in flexible automation than companies in other regions and are also intent on reducing their levels of product variety—both strategic decisions that reduce their incentive to make changes in work organization.

For Europe in particular, the extent and rapidity of the shift toward more flexible work practices owes a great deal to the long-time interest of European unions in experimenting with "group work." Compared to the U.S. situation, the relatively well-developed policy stance of European unions toward "group work," the higher level of political consensus within these unions about the potential benefits of these new work structures for workers, and the tradition (and past experience) of working with management to find mutual gains at a time of competitive crisis are all factors that facilitated this change.

In cross-sectional comparisons across companies and regions for the subsample of 31 plants, the results of t-tests shown in Table 4 reveal far more statistically significant differences in means on the right-hand side of the table—across companies, within regions. This suggests the primacy of a "company" effect over a "regional" effect for many of these variables (e.g., performance, automation, human resource policies) although, as noted above, for new work practices both company and regional effects appear to be strong. These results must be interpreted with caution. It is possible that some of the regional differences in means revealed here are not statistically significant because the sample size is too small. Nevertheless, the greater strength of company-level factors relative to regional-level factors seems clear despite constraints on statistical power.

In both analyses, company differences in automation and product variety strategies appear to play an important role in influencing adoption of flexible work organization. The "pull" toward flexible work organization created by these strategic variables may be the most important reason for the dominance of company-level effects. Indeed, differences in the competitive strategy of companies may be driving divergent approaches to work organization within the more global trend of convergence toward lean production principles described above.

For example, with the caveat that not all company strategies reflect the linkage between flexible work systems and flexible automation hypothesized here, we can make certain predictions for the companies examined above. We would expect company C to continue to move, at its U.S. plants, toward the level of flexible work systems found at its plants in Japan. In contrast, company B could be expected to retain low levels of both flexible automation and flexible work systems until (or unless) it shifts strategy in the direction of higher product variety and significantly shorter product life cycles. Company A should be willing to invest more in flexible work systems in its U.S. plants to complement its already-high investment in flexible automation. However, all of these changes may be affected by regional or national-level factors affecting work organization.

In conclusion, the purpose of this chapter is not to argue that national-level differences in work organization have disappeared completely or will someday. In fact, national-level differences are certain to remain, at the very least because of differences in the legal, regulatory, and industrial relations institutional environment that *will* persist at the national level. However, I am arguing that the value of using the "country" lens to understand changes in work organization is less and less, particularly during a time when various forces are promoting the diffusion of a new set of organizing principles. It may make sense to first examine company-level factors affecting the adoption and diffusion of new approaches to work organization and then to turn to national-level explanations to explain residual variation. Conversely, the "country" lens will continue to be the best starting place for understanding those aspects of industrial relations not directly linked to product market strategies, e.g., mechanisms of worker representation, collective bargaining processes and outcomes, and union structure.

This brings us back to the issue of how changes in work organization will relate to national-level differences in industrial relations which are likely to persist. European companies and unions with an institutional structure that ensures more union involvement in strategic decision making have shown a greater ability to make connections between the technical and the "people" aspects of work organization, both in their strategizing and in their day-to-day operations. The speed with which many European plants have moved toward "group work" and other new work practices may be evidence of capability for learning and flexible responsiveness to changing environmental conditions in the union-management relationship that has been less achievable in the U.S. Or there may simply have been a more clearly legitimized "model" for change in the early 1990s, when the most "unfreezing" took place for European companies and unions, than in the 1980s, a more turbulent period of transition that left both the Big Three and the UAW more ambivalent about work organization changes. In any case, the ongoing experiences of companies and unions in Europe, the NIC countries, and Australia—the regions that have moved substantially in the direction of flexible work practices—will surely influence the relative mix of convergent and divergent trends in work organization by the year 2000.

Acknowledgments

Many thanks to Ulrich Jürgens and the co-editors of this IRRA volume for helpful comments. I am also grateful to the International Motor Vehicle Program at M.I.T. and the Sloan Foundation which sponsored the research upon which this chapter was based.

Endnotes

[1] One note about the assessment of convergence or divergence is in order here. Both convergence and divergence are dynamic processes of change that must be assessed within some frame of reference that captures both time frame and assumptions about the feasible rate of change. If one assumes that change in the direction of some well-understood "best practice" should occur quickly, then anything less than full convergence upon such practice in a reasonable period of time could be taken as evidence of partial or unsuccessful diffusion. Yet most available literature (e.g., Kochan and Useem 1992) would suggest that change within organizations is inherently slow and that the key traits that underlie some example of "best practice" are rarely well understood before they are transferred into other organizational settings (e.g., Kogut and Parkinson, 1991). From this perspective, even modest movement toward a new production model across a range of companies and countries and within a relatively short period of time could be taken as impressive evidence of convergence.

[2] For example, workers can easily do minor reprogramming of weld robots (where allowed to do so) by physically "teaching" the robot where the new weld spot should go by moving the weld tip to the exact spot. This removes the technical barriers to incremental changes in weld placement—unlike fixed automation, where any changes require engineering involvement and substantial cost.

[3] The causality is not clear in the link between flexible technology and flexible work organization. Although the acquisition of flexible technology may in some cases be "pulled" by earlier changes in work organization, they may also "push" changes in work organization in order to gain maximal value from the capital investment.

[4] Ironically, this is a time when a prolonged recession in the Japanese industry, the apparent end to years of uninterrupted growth, and various problems (e.g., traffic congestion from just-in-time deliveries, difficulty attracting young Japanese to factory work, going overboard on product variety) are giving rise to new questioning of lean production in Japan (Cusumano 1993). While this has sounded a cautionary note for U.S. and European companies, it does not appear to have weakened their perception that they can benefit from moving toward lean production.

[5] There are also a number of factors that promote divergence in work practices *within* companies, including "greenfield" vs. "brownfield" facilities, the strength of market demand for the products made in a particular plant, and plant-specific arrangements with competing companies for collaborative "benchmarking" or joint venture production. Companies typically use new "greenfield" sites for the most comprehensive changes in work practices. In older plants, the management philosophy at many companies is to attempt major changes in work practices only when there will be a "significant emotional event" (GM's term)—generally a corporate decision about investment and product placement—that will shake up employees and ready them for change. Such management pressure is unlikely to be applied at a plant that is building a best-selling product and running at or above full capacity, given the risk of disrupting both economies of scale and profitability with an unwelcome initiative to change work practices. For example, Chrysler plants making the minivan have regularly been able to resist pressure from both top management and the Chrysler department of the UAW to adopt a Modern Operating Agreement (MOA) contract. Finally, it appears that plants engaged in benchmarking comparisons inside and outside their company—an increasingly common phenomenon—are often more willing to share information with a competitor's plant than with a plant within their own company due to internal company rivalries over resources (including investment, promotion opportunities, the chance to hire new employees). This situation may contribute to both convergence across companies and divergence within companies in work practices.

[6] In the German context, many of those involved in the debates over new forms of work organization differentiate between "group work" and "team work." The former term is associated with high autonomy from both managerial oversight (i.e., "self-managing" with no supervisor) and technical constraints (i.e., eliminating a machine-paced assembly line), in the tradition of sociotechnical theory and many Scandinavian experiments, while the latter term is associated with Japanese-style lean production and is characterized as low in autonomy and dominated by management. These distinctions in terminology are less often observed in practice, in part because many companies choose to create their own unique term for their group/team-based activities (e.g., "elementary technical units" at Fiat, "work modules" at Saturn).

[7] See MacDuffie 1995a for more information on the construction of the work systems index and other production organization indices.

[8] For the U.S. plants, it is worth noting that the unmatched sample shows a more substantial increase in the percentage of employees affected by small group activities (from 12% to 19% for work teams and from 21% to 29% for employee involvement or problem-solving groups) than the matched sample (a drop from 10% to 6% for work teams and a smaller increase, from 17% to 20%, for employee involvement groups). This is because some traditional plants in the 1989 sample have closed and the new plants in the Round 2 sample make more use of such small group activities.

[9] The reduction in the level of some of these practices in Japan is not substantial enough at this point to be judged as a move away from the "lean production" principles of work organization, particularly since these modifications may represent an adjustment to recession. However, future trends in Japan bear watching closely for evidence of further shifts, either toward traditional mass production practices or in some new direction.

[10] Japanese plants have had flexible work organization much longer than they have had programmable automation, suggesting that the former helped make investments in the latter more feasible and/or cost effective.

[11] For the U.S. plants, comparing the matched and unmatched samples provides one important insight. For the matched sample, the increase in the robotic index for the U.S. plants is negligible, as is the change in their use of flexible work practices. Yet for the unmatched sample, a larger change for both automation and flexible work practices is reported. This suggests that Big Three plants in the matched sample are more traditionally "mass production" in orientation than the unmatched sample for 1993-94, which includes some new plants that are more oriented toward flexibility in both areas. Still, even for the unmatched U.S. sample, the increase in flexible work practices is much less, compared to Europe, in relation to a similar increase in flexible automation across the two regions.

[12] Given that these questions about product variety concern physical characteristics of the products made in each plant, the 1990 data are unlikely to be affected by any retrospective bias.

[13] Data on the number of platforms at each plant—the most fundamental indicator of product variety (since multiple models can be built from the same platform)—are not included here because of definitional problems that make the data difficult to interpret.

[14] It should be noted that after 1993, Japanese companies also made concerted efforts to reduce the number of models and other aspects of product variety which were perceived as getting out of hand with negative consequences for company cost structures. This caveat applies to all the complexity measures discussed here.

[15] I have made a similar argument about the discrepancy during much of the 1980s between the high levels of training and education for the workforce in many European plants and their traditional work organization practices (MacDuffie and Kochan 1995).

[16] For example, wire harnesses provide the infrastructure for electrical options, so as products offer more sophisticated audio systems, more power accessories (windows, locks, seats), and fancier electronic engine regulation and environmental controls, the

number of harnesses proliferates. Different export markets often regulate electrical equipment differently, so more export markets typically means more different wire harnesses. The increase in exterior colors to please consumers doesn't pose many problems for the paint shop but does have a cascading effect on the number of color-dependent trim parts (e.g., bumpers, mirrors, interior upholstery and other decoration) that must be unpacked, delivered, and organized for easy and reliable installation. The more different engine and transmissions are offered to consumers, the more possible combinations must be scheduled and planned logistically.

[17] The amazingly high numbers of wire harnesses and engine/transmission combinations for plants in Japan are due in part to different design principles for wire harnesses and a different definition of engine variants as well as the very high number of different export markets.

[18] These scores must also be interpreted with some caution. Australian colleagues have told us that these answers reflect the *plans* for compensation and training that are required in the new agreement, not necessarily what has yet been implemented.

[19] Due to confidentiality agreements, I cannot elaborate on these company differences here.

References

Adler, Paul S. 1992. "The 'Learning Bureaucracy': New United Motor Manufacturing, Inc." In Barry M. Staw and Larry L. Cummings, eds., *Research in Organizational Behavior*. Greenwich, CT: JAI Press.

Adler, Paul S., and Robert E. Cole. 1993. "Designed to Learn: A Tale of Two Auto Plants." *Sloan Management Review* (Spring), pp. 33-45.

Automotive Industry Authority. 1989. "Award Restructuring." Report of a Tripartite Study Mission to Japan, the United States, Germany, and Sweden. Melbourne, Australia.

Automotive News Market Data Book. Various years.

Baron, James N., Frank Dobbin, and P. Devereaux Jennings. 1986. "War and Peace: The Evolution of Modern Personnel Administration in U.S. Industry." *American Journal of Sociology*, Vol. 92, pp. 350-83.

Berggren, Christian. 1993. "Volvo Uddevalla—A Dead Horse or a Car Dealer's Dream?" Working paper, Royal Institute of Technology, Stockholm.

_____. 1992. *Alternatives to Lean Production: Work Organization in the Swedish Auto Industry*. Ithaca, NY: ILR Press.

Brown, Clair, and Michael Reich. 1989. "When Does Union-Management Cooperation Work? A Look at NUMMI and GM-Van Nuys." *California Management Review*, Vol. 31, no. 4 (Summer), pp. 26-44.

Camuffo, Arnaldo, and Giuseppe Volpato. 1994. "Labor Relations Heritage and Lean Manufacturing at Fiat." Paper presented at International Developments in Workplace Innovation Conference, Toronto.

Camuffo, Arnaldo, and Stefano Micelli. 1995. "Mediterranean Lean Production? Supervisors, Teamwork, and New Forms of Work Organization in Three European Car Makers." Paper for International Industrial Relations Association 10th World Congress, Washington, DC.

Cole, Robert. 1989. *Strategies for Learning: Small Group Activities in Japanese, American, and Swedish Industry*. Berkeley, CA: University of California Press.

Cusumano, Michael. 1985. *The Japanese Auto Industry: Technology and Management at Toyota and Nissan*. Cambridge, MA: Harvard University Press.

_____. 1994. "The Limits of 'Lean'." *Sloan Management Review* (Summer), pp. 27-32.

Department of Labor. 1991. *Chrysler's Modern Operating Agreements*. Report prepared by Malcolm Lovell and Susan Goldberg, George Washington University, and Robert McKersie, Thomas A. Kochan, John Paul MacDuffie, Larry Hunter, and Andrew Martin.

Florida, Richard, and Martin Kenney. 1991. "Transplanted Organizations: The Transfer of Japanese Industrial Organization to the U.S." *American Sociological Review*, Vol. 56 (June), pp. 381-98.

Fucini, J., and J. Fucini. 1990. *Working for the Japanese: Inside Mazda's American Auto Plant*. New York: Free Press.

Graham, Laurie. 1993. "Inside a Japanese Transplant: A Critical Perspective," *Work and Occupations*, Vol. 20, no. 2, pp. 147-73.

Hancke, Robert. 1993. "Technological Change and its Institutional Constraints: The Politics of Production at Volvo Uddevalla." Working paper #93-05, Science, Technology, and Public Policy Program, Kennedy School of Government, Harvard University.

Huxley, Christopher, James Rinehart, and David Robertson. 1995. "Challenging Lean Production: Workers and Their Union at a GM-Suzuki Transplant." Paper for International Industrial Relations Association 10th World Congress, Washington, DC.

Internal Labor Markets. Cambridge, MA: MIT Press.

Jaikumar, Ramchandran. 1986. "Post-Industrial Manufacturing." *Harvard Business Review*, Vol. 64 (Nov.-Dec.), pp. 69-76.

Jürgens, Ulrich. 1995a. "Volkswagen at the Turning Point: Success and Crisis of a German Production Concept." Working paper, Actes du GERPISA #10.

_____. 1995b. "From Socialist Work Organization to Lean Production: Continuity and Discontinuity in the Transformation." *Annual Report of the Economic Society*. Tohuku University.

Jürgens, Ulrich, Thomas Malsch, and Knuth Dohse. 1993. *Breaking from Taylorism: Changing Forms of Work in the Automobile Industry*. Cambridge University Press.

Katz, Harry C. 1993. "The Decentralization of Collective Bargaining: A Literature Review and Comparative Analysis." *Industrial and Labor Relations Review*, Vol. 47, no. 1, pp. 3-22.

Kochan, Thomas A., and Peter Cappelli. 1984. "The Transformation of the Industrial Relations/Human Resources Function." In Paul Osterman, ed.

Kogut, Bruce, and Udo Zander. 1992. "Knowledge of the Firm, Combinative Capabilities, and the Replication of Technology." *Organization Science*, Vol. 3, no. 3 (August), pp. 383-97.

Krafcik, John F. 1986. "Learning from NUMMI." International Motor Vehicle Program, MIT. Working paper.

_____ 1988. "Comparative Analysis of Performance Indicators at World Auto Assembly Plants." Unpublished masters' thesis, Sloan School of Management, MIT.

Krafcik, John F., and John Paul MacDuffie. 1989. "Explaining High Performance Manufacturing: The International Automotive Assembly Plant Study." Working paper, International Motor Vehicle Program, MIT.

Lansbury, Russell D., and Greg J. Bamber. 1995. "Making Cars in Australia: New Models of Work and Production." Paper for International Industrial Relations Association 10th World Congress, Washington, DC.

Lewchuk, Wayne. 1988. *American Technology and the British Car Industry.* Cambridge: Cambridge University Press.

Locke, Richard. 1992. "The Demise of the National Union in Italy: Lessons for Comparative Industrial Relations Theory." *Industrial and Labor Relations Review,* Vol. 45, no. 2, pp. 229-49.

MacDuffie, John Paul. 1991. "Beyond Mass Production: Flexible Production Systems and Manufacturing Performance in the World Auto Industry." Unpublished doctoral dissertation, Sloan School of Management, MIT.

_____. 1995a. "Human Resource Bundles and Manufacturing Performance: Organizational Logic and Flexible Production in the World Auto Industry." *Industrial and Labor Relations Review,* Vol. 48, no. 2 (January), pp. 192-221.

_____. 1995b. "The Transfer of Organizing Principles in the World Auto Industry: Cross-Cultural Influences on Replication Efforts." Working paper, Wharton School, University of Pennsylvania.

MacDuffie, John Paul, Larry W. Hunter, and Lorna Doucet. 1995. "What Does Transformation Mean to Workers? The Effects of the 'New Industrial Relations' on Union Employees' Attitudes." Presented at Academy of Management meetings, Vancouver.

MacDuffie, John Paul, and Thomas A. Kochan. 1995. "Do U.S. Firms Underinvest in Human Resources? Determinants of Training in the World Auto Industry." *Industrial Relations,* Vol. 34, no. 2, pp. 147-68.

MacDuffie, John Paul, Kannan Sethuraman, and Marshall L. Fisher. Forthcoming. "Product Variety and Manufacturing Performance: Evidence from the International Automotive Assembly Plant Study." *Management Science.*

MacDuffie, John Paul, and John F. Krafcik. 1992. "Integrating Technology and Human Resources for High Performance Manufacturing." In Thomas A. Kochan and Michael Useem, eds., *Transforming Organizations.* New York: Oxford University Press, pp. 209-25.

MacDuffie, John Paul, and Frits K. Pil. 1994. "Transferring Japanese Human Resource Practices: Japanese Auto Plants in Japan and the U.S." Presented at Academy of Management meetings, Dallas, Texas.

_____. 1995. "'High Involvement' Work Systems and Manufacturing Performance: The Diffusion of Lean Production in the World Auto Industry." Working paper, Wharton School, University of Pennsylvania.

Monden, Yasuhiro. 1983. *Toyota Production System.* Norcross, GA: Industrial Engineering and Management Press, Institute of Industrial Engineers.

Nohria, Nitin, and Carlos Garcia-Pont. 1991. "Global Strategic Linkages and Industry Structure." *Strategic Management Journal,* Vol. 12, pp. 105-24.

Ono, Taiichi. 1988. *Workplace Management.* Cambridge, MA: Productivity Press.

Roth, Siegfried. 1995. "Rediscovering Its Own Strength? Lean Production in the German Automobile Industry." Paper for International Industrial Relations Association 10th World Congress, Washington, DC.

Schonberger, Richard. 1982. *Japanese Manufacturing Techniques*. New York: Free Press.

Shimada, Haruo, and John Paul MacDuffie. 1987. "Industrial Relations and 'Human-ware': Japanese Investments in Automobile Manufacturing in the United States." Working Paper, Sloan School of Management, MIT.

Turner, Lowell. 1991. *Democracy at Work: Changing World Markets and the Future of Labor Unions*. Ithaca, NY: Cornell University Press.

Westney, Eleanor. 1987. *Imitation and Innovation*. Cambridge, MA: Harvard University Press.

Womack, James, Daniel Jones, and Daniel Roos. 1990. *The Machine That Changed the World*. New York: Rawson-MacMillan.

CHAPTER 4

Economic Development Strategies, Industrial Relations Policies and Workplace IR/HR Practices in Southeast Asia

SAROSH C. KURUVILLA
Cornell University

The rapid economic development of several East (e.g., Japan, Korea, and Taiwan) and Southeast Asian (e.g., Singapore, Malaysia, Philippines, and Thailand) countries during the last decade has attracted considerable research attention. While the role of labor policy in East Asian development has been the subject of research interest (e.g., Deyo 1989), relatively little attention has focused on industrial relations in the now faster growing Southeast Asian region.

Focusing on two Southeast Asian countries, Malaysia and the Philippines, this chapter traces the linkages between industrialization strategies, national industrial relations policies, and workplace industrial relations practices. Although many authors (Kerr et al. 1964; Sharma 1985; Deyo 1989) have emphasized the role of industrialization in explaining industrial relations development, the argument here is that economic development strategies and industrial relations policies are closely intertwined and mutually reinforcing. It is therefore not the levels of industrialization per se, but the shift from one industrialization strategy to another that is important in understanding IR system transformation.

In this chapter, my focus is limited to the examination of the linkages between industrialization strategies and industrial relations policy at the national level and industrial relations and human resource practices at the level of the workplace. I use evidence from Malaysia and Philippines, along with some examples from the experience of Singapore to illustrate and support the argument. The next section details the argument.

The Argument

Southeast Asian countries have typically followed three types of industrialization strategies for economic development. The first strategy was import substitution industrialization (ISI), where the focus was to stimulate local industry to produce consumer and industrial goods that would substitute for imported alternatives and thereby conserve valuable foreign exchange (Kuruvilla 1995a). The second strategy has been export-oriented industrialization (EOI), where the basic thrust was the manufacture and export of simple manufactured goods, based on the competitive advantage of cheap labor and financed by foreign direct investment. I call this "first-stage export orientation." Some countries have embarked on a more advanced form of export orientation (second stage), where the focus is on the manufacture of higher technology and higher value-added manufactured products (again dominated by foreign investment), utilizing more highly skilled labor. Singapore and Malaysia both follow second-stage EOI, while the Philippines currently follows the first-stage EOI strategy.

My argument is that industrialization strategies and industrial relations policies are closely intertwined and mutually reinforcing. Earlier writers have suggested a linkage between these two factors. The most notable work here has been that of Kerr, Dunlop, Harbison, and Myers (1964), who argued that as all nations industrialized, their IR systems would be increasingly similar, although their hypothesis has not been supported by historical evidence since then.

Other authors have tried to differentiate IR systems by arguing that it is the levels or stages of industrialization that best explain cross-country differences in industrial relations. For example, Bjorkman, Lauridsen, and Marcussen (1988) noted that different levels of industrialization will imply different forms of capital accumulation, resulting in different ways that labor is utilized, an argument that has been supported by Sharma (1985). According to this argument, similarities in IR systems will be more pronounced if the countries are at the same level of industrialization. The reality of course is different, i.e., several countries who are arguably at the same level of industrialization, for example, U.S. and Germany or Hong Kong and Singapore (both service dominated economies), have vastly differing industrial relations policies, institutions and practices.

My argument builds on some of the existing work to provide an explanation for why certain kinds of industrial relations policies are adopted and what factors cause IR policies and institutions to change over time.

The first part of the argument suggests that the adoption of a certain type of industrialization strategy for economic development implies specific industrial relations and human resource policy goals at the national level. For example, the adoption of an export-oriented industrialization strategy—characterized by exports of low-cost assembled products, financed largely by foreign investment, and with low labor costs as the primary source of comparative advantage—has fundamental implications for industrial relations policy. Under such an industrialization regime, it is necessary for the state to ensure that the source of comparative advantage (i.e., labor costs) is maintained for the longest possible time. Besides, maintenance of low labor costs also ensures the continued attraction of foreign investment. Typically, low labor costs are maintained through industrial relations policy instruments, such as some degree of centralization of wage bargaining to maintain competitiveness or some degree of restraint on the ability of trade unions to push wages up through bargaining. Unfortunately, in much of Southeast Asia, control of trade unions during this industrialization phase has been more repressive, including bans on unionization or restrictions on the subject of bargaining or through restrictions on the ability of unions to strike. Korea, and Taiwan, as well as the two countries in studies in this chapter have taken this repressive strategy.

Another strategy has been to ensure that competitiveness is maintained through cooptation of trade unions as has been practiced in Singapore. To ensure stable industrial relations, the state sponsored the establishment of a tripartite industrial relations system with union input into all aspects of national decision making (see Kuruvilla 1995a for more details on the mechanisms by which this was accomplished). A tripartite National Wages Council ensured that wage increases did not hinder competitiveness. At the same time, in order to provide foreign investors with some degree of workplace control, the state introduced significant restrictions on the ability of unions to bargain and to strike (Kuruvilla 1995a).

Other industrialization strategies have different implications for IR policy. A strategy of inward-looking import-substitution industrialization (ISI), like that adopted by India until 1991, is largely based on heavily protected industries catering to a large domestic market. Given the absence of international competition and the highly regulated nature of domestic competition, the need to keep labor costs low is less central and thus permitted the Indian government to adopt a pluralistic IR system. The fact that the Philippines had a pluralistic IR system under ISI but a repressive IR system under first-stage EOI suggests support for this point.

Similarly, second-stage EOI is an industrialization strategy where the comparative advantage is not low costs but higher value-added products. Given that the comparative advantage of low costs is a transitory phenomenon (other less developed countries often offer lower costs), each developing state will gradually move up the cost ladder to higher value-added production. Higher value-added production implies highly trained workers who are also highly paid, since production systems to produce higher value-added items are more complex, perhaps more automated, and require greater skills to operate. Consequently, the focus of industrial relations and human resource policy must change, emphasizing greater productivity and skills development. This kind of transition can be seen in Singapore's industrial relations system. Under first-stage EOI, Singapore ensured that wage bargaining was centralized through the National Wage Council (NWC). However, under second-stage EOI, the NWC has decentralized wage bargaining to a considerable extent, stating that wages must be based on the differential requirements of each industry and firm. Moreover, under second-stage EOI, the state reformed the education system and started a skills development fund that forced employers to invest in training and skills upgradation (Kuruvilla 1995a). Clearly, therefore, different types of industrialization strategies adopted for economic development have different implications for industrial relations policy at the national level.

Given that different industrialization strategies imply different IR policy goals, it is relatively easy to postulate the second part of my argument (i.e., industrial relations systems will change according to changes in the industrialization strategy). A shift from import-substitution industrialization to export-oriented industrialization implied a fundamental change in industrial relations policy goals. As described in this chapter, both Malaysia and the Philippines commenced ISI policies consequent to independence and thereafter shifted to a first-stage EOI regime based on low costs. Malaysia, however, is currently shifting to a second-stage EOI regime characterized by high skills and higher costs. Both cases demonstrate transitions in industrial relations policy and industrialization strategy. The argument therefore is that the shift from one industrialization strategy to another constitutes an important turning point for industrial relations policy.

It is important to note that although each industrialization strategy has definite implications for specific IR policy goals, the institutions that countries adopt to meet those goals will vary. For example, Singapore has a tripartite system, while the Philippines under Marcos had a highly

repressive system. What causes these variations? I argue that these variations reflect both the institutional history and specific political considerations in each state. In most Southeast Asian economies the state has been
the dominant actor in both economic development and industrial relations spheres. However, relatively democratic Singapore adopted a con-
sensus-based tripartite strategy, while the lack of significant political
opposition to the Marcos dictatorship permitted the adoption of a highly
repressive labor policy. However, this aspect (i.e., the specific causes for
variation in industrial relations *institutions*) is not addressed in this chapter given space constraints. In addition, given the dominance of the state
and the existence of repressive policies, labor unions in Southeast Asia
have either been co-opted as "junior partners" in the rapid economic development (e.g., Singapore) or completely marginalized (e.g., Philippines). Given their relatively weak position, I do not focus on trade union
strategies and the variation in those strategies in this chapter.

Although I view the industrialization strategy as deterministic of industrial relations policy, in some countries industrial relations policy
changes are due to other factors. For example, in both Taiwan and
South Korea, the major transformations in industrial relations policy in
the late 1980s can be linked to political liberalization and the transition
to democracy, although previous shifts in IR policies can be linked to
industrialization strategies. However, as Freeman (1994) argues, the
transition to democracy in both Taiwan and South Korea have some
roots in their successful economic development experience and the
growth of a middle class. Therefore, political and economic forces are
also intertwined in some respects. I focus more on industrialization
strategies effects on IR policy.

The third part of my argument concerns workplace industrial relations. I argue that both the industrialization strategy and national IR policies impact the pattern of workplace IR/HR practices. IR policies outline
the rules by which the actors, labor, and management can operate. The
industrialization strategy ensures the creation of distinct economic sectors, which attract only certain types of firms, and the economic circumstances of these firms promote a specific pattern of workplace practices
subject to the rules articulated by IR policies. For example, under a first-
stage EOI strategy that emphasizes the export of cheap manufactures
such as electronics, IR policies will focus on cost containment and workplace IR/HR practices will also evidence a cost containment focus that is
consistent with the strategies of firms that will invest in this country. And
similarly, a country that adopts second-stage EOI will have national

IR/HR policies that aim at increasing skills development with workplace IR/HR practices reflecting more "progressive" human resource practices, focusing on skill attainment and flexibility, consistent with the strategies of firms choosing to invest in the country.

FIGURE 1

Economic Development Strategies, Industrial Relations Policies and
Workplace IR/HR Practices

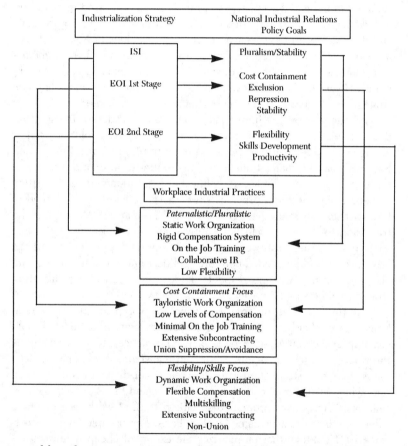

Although my argument is causal, i.e., industrialization strategy determines IR policy and workplace IR/HR practices, it is important to highlight the mutually reinforcing roles played by both industrialization strategy and IR policy in promoting economic development. Industrial relations policy instruments can be used effectively to make the transition from one industrialization strategy to another. A good example of this can be seen in Singapore's experience. When the comparative advantage of low labor costs faded, Singapore needed to rapidly shift to a second-stage high-value-added EOI strategy. The National Wage Council recommended double digit wage increases for three years in succession in the early 1980s, successfully driving out low-cost producers, and instituted new sets of investment incentives to attract more high-cost, high-value-added producers (Katz, Kuruvilla, and Turner 1993).

Although the linkages between industrialization strategy, national IR policy, and workplace practices (depicted in Figure 1) have been developed through detailed case studies of the Singapore experience (see Kuruvilla 1995a), in this chapter, I use Malaysia and the Philippines to illustrate the argument. These two countries are chosen because they both started out with ISI policies, then shifted to first-stage EOI, and now Malaysia is shifting to second-stage EOI. For my argument to be supported I must be able to show that there have been changes in the focus of national IR policies with every change in the industrialization strategy (i.e., shifts in policies over time). In addition, given that the two countries are currently following different industrialization strategies (Philippines at stage one EOI, while Malaysia at stage two EOI), there must be differences in IR policy when viewed cross-sectionally. The chapter will also use examples from the Singapore experience to further illustrate these linkages.

Industrialization Strategies

The rapid development of Singapore and Malaysia can be linked to their adoption of export-oriented industrialization in 1965 and 1977, respectively. Both countries had adopted import-substitution industrialization strategies (ISI) following independence from Britain in the 1950s but shifted to EOI for different reasons[1] (see Kuruvilla [1993] and Huff [1987] for a more detailed socioeconomic analysis for why these shifts occurred in Malaysia and Singapore, respectively). The Philippines adopted an ISI strategy following a balance of payments crisis in 1949-1950 arising from the imports of U.S. consumer goods under a free trade regime. Although the Philippines had shifted to export-oriented industrialization in the 1960s, it was only in the 1980s that it fully implemented the strategy. And, in contrast to the experience of Malaysia and Singapore whose economic performance (discussed below) increased steadily after adoption of EOI, the economic performance of the Philippines after EOI has been less impressive and more cyclical (see Macaraya and Ofreneo [1992] for a more detailed analysis).

Although the motivations and timing for the shift into EOI have been different in each country, the process and outcomes have been more similar. In terms of process, common elements in the attraction of foreign investment for EOI included infrastructural development (the development of transport, communication, free trade areas, export processing zones), financial incentives (land subsidies, electricity and power subsidies, building subsidies, exemption from corporate taxes, and export duty subsidies), labor incentives (bans on unionization and strikes, exemption from prevailing labor standards regulations), and various other regulatory exemptions.[2]

The results of the adoption of the EOI strategy are detailed in Table 1 which shows the average economic growth rates in each economy. During the 1970-1980 period, average growth rates in all three economies were higher than 5.7%, higher than the world average, and similar to growth rates in Korea and Taiwan. Since then, Singapore and Malaysia have continued growing at an annual average of 6% to 7%, although the Philippines has seen negative growth rates in 1981-1985.

TABLE 1

Average Annual Growth of Gross Domestic Product in 5 Year Intervals

Interval	Malaysia	Philippines	Singapore
1971-75	7.2	5.7	9.4
1976-80	8.6	6.0	8.5
1981-85	5.2	-1.2	6.2
1986-90	6.1	5.1	7.9

Source: World Bank World Tables, 1992.

Second, all three countries have experienced an increase in the relative share of manufacturing to both GDP and employment. Table 2 indicates that in all countries during the early EOI phase, the size of the manufacturing sector increased rapidly, and its current contribution to GDP ranges from 30% in Singapore and 27% in Malaysia to 25% in the Philippines, a substantial change from the figures in 1960. The growth in manufacturing appears to have leveled off in the Philippines and has actually seen some decreases since 1992 (Kuruvilla 1995a).

Third, the export performance of all economies has been dramatic. Given that Malaysia and Philippines have sizeable agricultural and other primary sector exports, to examine export growth I use the contribution

TABLE 2

Percent of Gross Domestic Product by Activity, 1960-1990

	1990	1985	1980	1975	1970	1965	1960
Malaysia							
Agriculture	18.7	20.8	22.9	27.7	28.8	26.6	33.8
Manufacturing	26.9	19.7	19.6	16.4	14.7	9.0	7.2
Trade / Services	22.7	23.1	22.4	23.5	22.7	21.0	20.4
Philippines							
Agriculture	22.1	24.6	25.1	28.8	27.8	27.0	27.1
Manufacturing	25.5	25.2	25.7	24.9	22.6	15.2	16.0
Trade / Services	30.7	29.7	26.2	28.3	32.6	26.9	29.2
Singapore							
Agriculture	0.3	0.7	1.2	1.9	2.3	4.4	5.7
Manufacturing	29.1	23.6	29.1	24.1	20.4	12.7	8.5
Trade / Services	53.8	48.2	44.7	46.3	48.0	65.1	71.2

Source: World Bank World Tables, 1992.

of manufacturing to total export earnings, a key indicator for evaluating the success of a manufacturing-based export strategy. As Table 3 indicates, in all three economies, manufacturing-export earnings as a percentage of total exports have risen sharply over the 30 year period. Currently, 72.9% of Singapore's exports consist of manufactured goods, while the figures for Malaysia and the Philippines in 1990 are 43.9% and 61.8%. In the 1970s, these figures were substantially lower—30.5% in Singapore, 7.4% in Malaysia, and 7.6% in the Philippines.

TABLE 3

Contribution of Manufacturing to Total Export Earnings, 1970-1990
(Percent)

Country	1970	1974	1977	1980	1984	1987	1990
Malaysia	7.4	13.6	15.4	19.0	26.7	39.5	43.9
Philippines	7.6	12.9	24.9	36.8	55.1	61.8	61.8
Singapore	30.5	41.3	44.0	53.9	57.3	71.6	72.8

Source: World Bank World Tables, 1992.

Fourth, it is also clear that the EOI strategy has been successful in attracting foreign investment. Although I do not have comparable figures for foreign direct investment, given that the definition of "investment" differs from country to country, the percentage of foreign firms share in manufacturing in each of these economies exceeds 30% when measured in terms of sales and assets and exceeds 60% when measured in terms of their contribution to exports. Foreign investment, as Table 4 shows, has been central in the dramatic export performance.

TABLE 4
Foreign Firms Share in Manufacturing, 1988 (%)

Country	Employment	Fixed Assets	Sales	Exports
Singapore	60	—	72	86
Malaysia	49	32	45	60
Philippines	—	32	41	66

Fifth, although the initial concentration of foreign investment was in textiles, footwear, and low-end electronics such as TVs and radios, the focus has shifted to higher-end electronics products such as semiconductors and other consumer and industrial electronics in Malaysia and the Philippines, while the investment in Singapore is more diverse, including many firms operating in the commercial services sector. In the case of Malaysia, its export-oriented electronics industry accounts for 60% of manufacturing exports, while textiles accounts for 8%. The growth in the electronics industry's share of manufacturing output in Malaysia increased from 13.9% of GDP in 1970 to 27% in 1990 decades later (Lai 1991), while foreign corporations own 91% of electronics firms (Dhanraj et al. 1992). In the Philippines, the electronics sector currently accounts for 33% of Philippine manufacturing exports (Philippine Department of Labor 1993).

Perhaps the most critical piece of evidence regarding the success of the EOI strategy can be seen in the increases in real wages over the last two decades. Table 5 shows the rates of growth in real wages and reductions in the incidence of poverty (percentage of families below the poverty line). Real wages have increased steadily while poverty levels have declined since the 1970s in both Malaysia and Singapore. The Philippines has seen declines in real wages in the early periods of its EOI strategy and continues to see declines in the 1980s. Philippine poverty levels have declined further since 1983.

Clearly the EOI strategy adopted by these economies has paid dividends. The relative failure of the Philippines has been attributed to the inability of the government to fully articulate its EOI strategy, given "crony capitalism" under the Marcos dictatorship and the economic

TABLE 5
Growth in Real Wages in Manufacturing and Incidence of Poverty

Country	Year	Growth in Real Wages	Year	Incidence of Poverty
Philippines	1960-74	-4.0	1971	50.7
	1974-79	-1.4	1980	40.8
	1981-87	2.4	1983	39.0
	1973-87	-0.5		
Malaysia	1963-73	-1.2	1970	49.3
	1971-80	2.0	1976	35.1
	1980-88	3.5	1979	29.2
	1971-88	2.7	1984	18.4
	1988-93	4.6	1988	15.0
Singapore	1960-72	1.7	1972	7.0
	1972-80	2.8	1978	1.5
	1981-85	5.4	1983	0.3
	1973-89	6.1		

ILO Yearbook of Labor Statistics, calculated by author.

mismanagement of the Marcos regime that resulted in dramatic increases in the Philippine debt situation in the 1980s.[3]

The general pattern of shifts in industrialization strategies from ISI to first-stage EOI and then to second-stage EOI (e.g., Malaysia) noted in these countries is consistent with the general pattern of industrialization and economic development prevalent in other Asian countries (e.g., Taiwan, South Korea, and Hong Kong), according to Kuruvilla and Pagnucco (1994). In the next section, I present more detailed analysis of the Malaysian and Philippine experiences.

Linkages between Industrialization and IR Policy

Malaysia

The first phase of ISI (1957-1963) focused on infrastructural and rural development, while industrialization was left to the private sector. The second phase of ISI (1963-1970) shows the state as a leading actor in investment motivated by the new economic policy (NEP) that promised the economic advancement of Malays via regulation as well as direct investment of the state on behalf of Malays.[4]

Industrial relations during this period reflected the system inherited from the British and was subject to substantial control by the state and the specific rules reflected the state's efforts to contain conflict in the interests of economic development (Kuruvilla 1993). The prohibition of political strikes and the restrictions on the ability of labor federations to carry out trade union functions (they were registered as societies) also ensured government control over the labor movement. At the national level, the government has always followed a multiple federation approach (currently there are three different federations). At the level of the workplace, even during the ISI stage, there have been restrictions on the subjects of bargaining, such as in Singapore with transfers, promotions, layoffs, retrenchments and job assignments being outside the subject of bargaining. In addition, as in Singapore, there are restrictions on the ability of unions to strike while a dispute is pending before third-party conciliation or arbitration, and several administrative requirements circumscribe the unions' right to strike. However, there was significant growth in labor unions during this period, with union density increasing to 12% of the nonagricultural workforce. I characterize this period as a "controlled pluralism," since the government did not always use the considerable powers at its command.

The resource crunch resulting from NEP policies, the state's failed heavy industries program, and Malaysia's increasing foreign debt (which was 30% of GNP by the mid-1980s) forced Malaysia to embark on an intensive export promotion drive.[5] The EOI drive was largely successful in that by the end of 1989, the manufacturing sector accounted for 42% of GDP and 40% of export earnings, and the low-cost export sector, dominated by foreign investment, accounted for 33% of export earnings, while the contribution of transnational corporations to exports increased from 28% of total exports in 1971 to 58% in 1988. The electronics industry, the centerpiece of the dramatic export performance, employed 16.7% of the manufacturing workforce in 1988 (Onn 1989), and exports of semiconductors exceeded M $4 billion comprising 24.8% total manufacturing exports in 1989 (Grace 1990). Although the EOI drive has resulted in impressive growth rates, the EOI strategy has made Malaysia dependent on foreign-dominated (foreign corporations accounted for 60% of exports), low-cost, labor-intensive manufacturing for industrial growth. This dependence on cheap labor forced the country to adopt various industrial relations policies geared toward attraction and retention of foreign capital (Grace 1990) outlined below.

The first direction of change in government labor policy reflected the need to contain costs in the export sector. Policy changes included extending tax and labor exemptions for foreign corporations (companies were exempted from several labor protection laws), the refusal to enact minimum wage legislation for the export industry, alteration of the definition of wages for the calculation of overtime to reduce costs in the export sector (which used overtime given the labor shortage), a reduction in the rate of overtime pay for working on holidays and rest days, and the government's continued refusal to enact equal pay for equal work in the export sector, where 78.6% of those employed were female.

The second direction of change focused on union control. In general terms, as part of the "look East" policy of the Prime Minister, in 1980 the government encouraged the formation of Japanese-style enterprise unions, and currently about 30% of unions are enterprise based (Arudsothy and Littler 1992). In addition, in the export sector unions were banned. Although the ban on electronics unions was lifted in 1988 due to international pressures (see Kuruvilla 1993), electronics workers were not permitted to affiliate themselves to national or industry-level federations (unlike their counterparts in the electrical industries). A combination of state suppression and employer opposition (see Kuruvilla 1993 for specifics) ensured that the electronics sector was and still is largely union free (out of 140 electronics firms operating in Malaysia currently, only two are unionized with in-house unions). The decision to allow only in-house unions in electronics is largely attributed to pressure from foreign investors (Grace 1990), although it is also consistent with the government's own acceptance of the low-cost export-oriented strategy.

The third direction of change in industrial relations policy could be seen in a more activist stance of the government, arguably linked more to its role as an investor and employer as a consequence of the heavy industries program. Kuruvilla (1993) documents the different ways in which the new activism is manifested, including extensive powers given to the labor minister to declare industries as "essential," to suspend trade unions acting against the "national interest," a greater involvement in union recognition cases (with increased rejection of registrations in manufacturing), and in dispute settlement where an increased number of cases were referred to compulsory arbitration. The greater involvement of the government in industrial relations reflected efforts at containing industrial conflict in the interests of fast-paced development.

The impetus for change from this low-cost, manufacturing export strategy came from within the electronics industry. The export strategy was successful in attracting foreign investment but resulted in a shortage of both skilled and unskilled labor. (Currently out of a workforce of about 13 million, roughly 2.5 million are guest workers, according to government statistics, while unofficial estimates place the figure at 4 million). The shortage of labor resulted in increases in wages and manufacturing costs (wage increases exceeded 6% annually during the latter half of the 1980s). The rising wage costs, combined with worldwide recessions in 1985 in electronics, forced the industry to restructure itself toward increased automation and adopt new forms of flexible work organization requiring workers of higher skill (see Rajah [1993] for a detailed description of this change in Malaysia). The competition from other low-cost producers and the need for forward and backward linkages with the electronics industry motivated the state to formally announce a shift in its EOI strategy emphasizing higher technology investment and industrial deepening via linkages with the export-oriented electronics industry.

Under this strategy (articulated more clearly in the state's Vision 20/20 plan which envisages Malaysia being an advanced industrial country by 2020), apart from financial incentives to attract higher technology and research and development firms, the government started its small scale industries policy with the objective of stimulating linkages, primarily as subcontractors, to the electronics industry (PSDC 1993). In addition, immigration policies were changed to allow the import of both skilled and unskilled workers given the labor shortage. Further, the education sector was reformed and deregulated, leading to a mushrooming of private colleges with exchange arrangements with universities in Australia and Canada. Between 1985 and 1992 enrollment in polytechnic has increased by 113%, while enrollment in colleges had increased by 45%. Education expenses accounted for 4% of GDP in 1993. Consistent with the reforms in education, the central elements of IR policy have shifted away from cost containment and union control to training and skills development designed to provide a better quality workforce necessary to attract higher technology investment. More specifically, the government enacted the Human Resources Development Act in 1992 and established the Skills Development Fund, whereby manufacturing companies employing more than 50 employees pay 1% of their monthly payroll costs—an amount that is matched by the government. The fund offers subsidies to companies who require training for workers. Employers can apply for blanket grants of their entire training plans for the year or on a case-by-case basis. Each contributing employer can rake back as much as 60% of their contribution. Also, at the local and regional level, skills development centers have been set up by the government to work in collaboration with business. These efforts are complemented by initiatives in the private sector, such as the new agreement between the Federation of Malaysian Manufacturers and the University of Science and Technology for skill training programs and the initiatives by foreign firms in Penang, where foreign multinationals who are fierce competitors in the international semiconductor market, cooperate locally in the development of skills at the Penang Skills Development Center. The export-manufacturing sector in Malaysia is now characterized by rising wages (see Table 5) and an increasingly nonunion environment.

In sum, in Malaysia industrial relations at the workplace level exhibits the goal of workplace IR flexibility, while at the national level, the government has followed a suppressive strategy. Unlike the Singaporean case, the Malaysian government has resisted the efforts of labor federations to unite into a single federation, and the government's recent "behind the scenes" support of a rival labor federation is indicative of its intention to keep the labor movement fragmented (Arudsothy and Littler 1992). Union density has steadily declined in Malaysia, and the trend is toward an increasingly nonunion model, especially in electronics sector. However, real wages have continued to increase steadily, as Table 5 indicates, and during the period 1988-1990 average wage increases in manufacturing exceeded 6%.

What the Malaysian case suggests is a correspondence between low-cost export-oriented industrialization and an industrial relations system geared toward repression and cost containment. Second, like the Singaporean case, the transition to an EOI stage characterized by higher technology is associated with a change in industrial relations policies focusing on skill development. Third, it is clear that EOI based on higher skills is bringing about the integration of IR policies with other human resource policies at the local level (see the workplace-level discussion) and with several other macro-level policies such as education, immigration, and economic development. Finally, the case also suggests the possibility that changes in the workplace practices and economic environment in the electronics industry have exerted upward pressure for changes in the industrialization strategy at the national level.

Philippines

During the ISI phase, the Philippine economy registered impressive growth rates in manufacturing, exceeding 14% in the 1949-53 period and 11% in the 1953-59 period. By 1960 it was clear that this boom in manufacturing resulted in a dependence on imports of technology beyond the ability of the Philippines to pay. To alleviate the negative balance of payments situation that arose, stabilization loans were sought from the World Bank which were granted on the condition that the Philippines open its economy, deregulate, and adopt an export-oriented strategy. The focus of labor relations was pluralistic, with little effort to tinker with the inherited IR institutions which were primarily American (the Industrial Peace Act of 1953 was based on the Wagner Act) and characterized by free collective bargaining, voluntary arbitration, unfair labor practice legislation, and business unionism. Union density and strikes showed a steady increase during this period (Villegas 1988).

During the period 1960-1972, the state made efforts to pursue an export-oriented strategy with mixed results, given the influence of different sets of elites on the government. The traditional agricultural elites supported a free trade strategy, while the domestic manufacturing elite who had prospered during the ISI years successfully obtained protection for their industries (Bello and Verzola 1993). The different elites maintained their hold over the government even during the Marcos years when some decontrols were accomplished. The social unrest resulting from the devaluation of the peso set the conditions for the declaration of martial law in 1972 (Bello and Verzola 1993).

The declaration of martial law in 1972 allowed the technocrats and the World Bank advisers to implement the recommendations contained in the Ranis Mission report (a World Bank-funded mission) and the World Bank Country Report of 1975, both of which argued for a full-scale export-oriented agro and industrial strategy based on the comparative advantage of cheap labor. The government accelerated decontrols and increased foreign borrowing to finance reforms in education, industry, and financial systems. Tariffs and customs codes were simplified, and investment incentives for multinationals were rationalized. Free trade zones (export processing) were established in Bataan and Mariveles.[6]

Since the strategy of export-oriented industrialization was predicated on the provision of cheap labor to foreign investors, labor policy was amended drastically to boost exports (Villegas 1988; Kuruvilla 1994). The first change was to guarantee industrial peace. A ban on strikes was instituted, but later modified to apply to "vital" industries "including those engaged in the production and processing of commodities for export" (Villegas 1988:61). The Secretary of Labor was empowered to obtain injunctions against strikes. Second, compulsory arbitration was introduced through the National Labor Relations Commission. Third, unions were not allowed to build up strike funds. Fourth, unfair labor practices by employers were "decriminalized." Finally, by decree no. 1458, striking workers were allowed to be permanently replaced (Villegas 1988).

The second direction of change in labor policy focused on a co-optation strategy adopted by President Marcos. The labor movement was restructured on a "one union in each industry" principle to be affiliated with one recognized labor center—the Marcos-controlled Trade Union Congress of the Philippines. The purpose of the reform in union structure was to promote tripartism, with the government, the TUCP, and the newly formed Employers Confederation of the Philippines (ECOP). This form of state corporatism with state control over the labor movements via its control over the TUCP was never fully institutionalized given the opposition from other labor groups.

The third direction of change in labor policy focused on the provision of cheap labor to the growing numbers of foreign investors in the export sector. The National Manpower Youth Council ensured a constant supply of trained workers and the apprenticeship program, which allowed children aged 14 and higher to be employed in export industries at a fraction of the prevailing minimum wage (Villegas 1988). Although minimum wages were revised numerous times, they fell far short of the rise in living costs as Marcos did not want to place the export program in jeopardy by a rapid rise in wage levels (Villegas 1988). The final direction of change was a downward revision of existing labor protection standards, based on the argument that existing labor protection standards did not reflect Philippine realities (Villegas 1988).

The martial law period did not fully accomplish the realization of full-scale EOI, although foreign investment did increase during this period. Repeated financial crises stemming from the failure of domestic industries under an export regime and the inability of exports to offset the debt payment requirements in the 1980s (debt had reached 93% of GNP in 1986) resulted in further dependence on World Bank financing (Bello and Verzola 1993). The result was a series of structural adjustment loans in 1983 and 1986. The strategic thrust of structural adjustment was a more determined implementation of EOI, deregulation and liberalization of the economy, coupled with a systematic easing out of inefficient Filipino firms (Ofreneo 1994; Villegas 1988). The World Bank report emphasized "priority should be given to the continued expansion of labor-intensive manufacturing taking advantage of the competitive aspect of labor costs" (Villegas 1988:70). The structural adjustment phase since 1983 has finally moved the Philippine economy to the high level of low-cost export orientation that the World Bank had targeted since 1970.

Foreign investment increased by 1,156% post-structural adjustment. The nontraditional manufactures (electronics and garments) attracted 80% of the investments, and by end 1983, the electronics sector accounted for 32% of total Filipino exports. However, the removal of protection for domestic industries and the export-oriented policies had a devastating impact on domestic industry. The number of domestic firms closing had increased from 831 in 1981 to 2,284 in 1984. In terms of industrial relations, to contain the strikes against martial law, the government enacted BP 130 and BP 227. The former prohibited strikes against the national interest, while the latter allowed the use of law enforcement agencies to control strikers. In addition, procedures for termination of workers were simplified. In terms of the IR impact of structural adjustment, between 1981 and 1982, 65,000 workers were laid off, and between 1983-85, 82,000 workers were laid off annually. At least 60% of workers in the growing export sector were still receiving less than the minimum wage (Villegas 1988), and this period witnessed a decline in union membership from 12.2% to 9.3%. These developments intensified the schism between the pro-government TUCP and other illegal labor centers, such as the KMU and FFW, that opposed structural adjustment policies—the beginnings of a deep schism in the Filipino labor movement that continues to this day.

Structural adjustment continued under the Aquino and Ramos governments. The labor relations legislation of the Marcos era has been largely withdrawn, and the Philippines is back to the pluralistic IR system that it commenced with in the 1950s.

Currently, at the national level there are 155 national labor federations and over 5,600 independent unions. The labor movement is fragmented and weak, and bargaining is largely based on the increases in minimum wages announced by the government from time to time (Ofreneo 1993). Bans on strikes in essential industries continue, replacement of striking workers is still allowed, and the intense interunion rivalry often results in lower union wins in representation elections. Real wages have fallen in the 1990s, while union density has declined with the closures of many ISI firms. Although the unions together claim a membership of three million workers, the actual number of workers covered by collective bargaining contracts is under 600,000 (Philippine Department of Labor and Employment 1993). The weakness of the labor movement provides the employer with control over workplace flexibility.

The Philippine case also suggests a correspondence between low-cost export-oriented development and a cost containment-oriented and repressive industrial relations policy. However, in this case, it took almost thirty years between the announcement of the EOI policy and its full implementation. As noted earlier, the slower development of EOI in the Philippines is attributable to the vacillation of the early Marcos years

(1965-1971) when Marcos was caught between the positions of two different sets of elites—those who favored export orientation and those who preferred import substitution. Post dictatorship, the continued failure of the Marcos regime to fully implement EOI has been linked to economic mismanagement, "crony" capitalism, and corruption. It was thus only in 1983 that the EOI program was fully implemented. The Philippines is still in its low-cost export-oriented stage, and although the extremely repressive policies of the Marcos regime have been withdrawn, the declines in real wages, job security, and the downward revision in labor standards, suggest the weakness of the labor movement which sustains the strategy. Unlike the other two countries, the Philippine state has been unable to orchestrate the development process with as much success. Finally, the Philippines also suggests the importance of the pressures of external actors on its industrialization strategy and, thereby, its industrial relations system.

In sum, the shift from an ISI strategy to an EOI strategy based on cheap labor resulted in changes in the IR policies toward cost containment, repression, and workplace flexibility, while the shift from first-stage EOI to second-stage EOI (in Malaysia) has again changed IR policies emphasizing skill development, productivity, and the enhancement of workplace IR flexibility. These examples clearly demonstrate the linkage between the industrialization strategy and industrial relations policies as argued in this chapter. The next section examines industrial relations practices in Malaysia and the Philippines, and here I attempt to show that both the development strategy as well as national IR policies impact patterns of workplace IR practices.

Workplace Industrial Relations and Human Resource Practices

The argument suggested that workplace IR/HR practices were influenced by both the industrialization strategy as well as the industrial relations policy in each country. Given my focus on identifying the links between industrialization strategy, IR policies, and workplace practices, I do not emphasize other factors relevant to the development of workplace practices, notably the business strategy of firms, in the discussion that follows.

In this section, I focus on workplace practices in the electronics industry in both Malaysia and the Philippines. Two reasons govern my choice of the electronics industry. First, it has been the largest industry in the export-oriented sector of both Malaysia and the Philippines and is the trendsetter in terms of workplace IR/HR practices. Second, the electronics industry allows a cross-sectional comparison between the two countries in ways that will help me isolate the separate impact of the industrialization strategies, given that Malaysia and the Philippines are currently at different stages of export-oriented industrialization. In this section, I intend to show that workplace IR/HR practices in Malaysia are consistent with its second-stage EOI strategy and IR policy, while workplace practices in the Philippines are consistent with its first-stage EOI strategy and IR policy. My information is drawn from both case studies recently completed in Malaysia and the Philippines as well as results from previous research.

The Electronics Industry in Malaysia

As noted earlier, the electronics industry in Malaysia accounts for over 60% of its export earnings and is completely dominated by multinationals (Lai 1991). Salih, Young, and Rajah (1987) suggest two clear phases in the development of the electronics industry in Malaysia. The first phase, during Malaysia's low-cost EOI stage was in the 1970s when National Semiconductor Corp (USA) located the first electronic assembly plant in Penang, Malaysia. By 1984, 23 of the world's largest semiconductor plants had set up operations in Malaysia, employing in excess of 85,000 workers. During the first phase the type of investment focused on the low end of electronic assembly and testing using the comparative advantage of cheap labor, with the higher technology processes of wafer fabrication, circuit design, and mask fabrication being located in the parent country.

The second phase in the development of the electronics industry started in the late 1980s, following the worldwide recession in semiconductors in 1985 and 1986 and denotes the beginning of the shift into a high tech EOI strategy. The second phase saw a broadening of foreign investment in semiconductors and consumer electronics and an increase in employment to 175,000 by 1993. The type of production in semiconductor manufacturing also changed, including higher end processes such as wafer fabrication and mask fabrication and, in some cases, even some process research units have been started. Circuit design still is done elsewhere, although the government has increased its efforts to attract R&D operations of multinationals by announcing a series of special incentives for R&D investment.

The shift into higher tech EOI in Malaysia was in part due to changes in the technology used in electronics production. The 1980s witnessed several technological breakthroughs in electronics production. In the area of assembly and testing itself, there has been increased automation especially in the dicing, die-attaching, bonding and molding operations (Salih, Young, and Rajah 1987). As chips become more complicated, automated production systems become increasingly necessary, as the bonding of a hundred wires on a very small VLSI chip cannot be done by hand. The expansion of the semiconductor market and the entry of several manufacturers have further pressed the need for reduced costs, reduced process times, and new production organization. These changes require increasingly higher skilled labor with the ability to provide input into production processes. The restructuring of the industry toward more automation and higher skill production, coupled with the labor shortages in Malaysia, was the basis for the government's initiative to upskill the Malaysian economy. Below, I compare workplace policies across the two phases in Malaysian industrialization the low-cost EOI phase and the high tech EOI phase.

Work Organization

During the low-cost EOI phase, semiconductor industry focused on simple assembly operations carried out by mostly female operatives. Grace (1990) notes that the production system was largely authoritarian, with operatives allowed little flexibility in deciding start and stop times and even being required permission to use the toilet. The system can be best described as Fordist, with assembly line workers engaged in repetitive tasks requiring minimal skill and training.

However, during the second phase, given that the industry is being rapidly automated, new manufacturing systems based on flexible production have been introduced (Rajah 1988). A few manufacturers such as Intel, Motorola, Hitachi, Phillips, and Thompson have moved away from assembly operations to more high technology-based production. Their production systems are now based on flexible work practices and include techniques such as TQC, JIT, and MRP. The team concept of production has been introduced in many of these plants, giving workers more and more input into decisions on the shopfloor. Texas Instruments, for example, has reported exemplary success with the introduction of self-managed teams for production and quality control (Arensman 1991). With the new form of production in INTEL, turnover rates dropped to 3% while 85% of employees have been in their jobs for more than five years, a surprisingly high figure given that labor turnover in the electronics sector has been about 35% in the mid-1980s (Yang 1988).

Compensation

Under the low-cost phase, compensation policies in the electronics industry were geared toward keeping costs low. Wages were kept to minimum levels, and the government's persistent refusal to enact equal-pay-for-equal-work legislation allowed the industry to employ young women at wages less than 60% of average male wages (Grace 1990). Workers were paid by a variety of piece rates and production incentives above the daily base rate (Rajah 1988; Grace 1990). The compensation policies of firms was buttressed by national IR policies that focused on cost containment (Kuruvilla 1993).

In the second phase, pay systems increasingly look like pay systems in more advanced economies. New forms of work organization have brought with them new methods of training and wage payment systems. Increasingly, wages are tied to learning new skills, and Rajah (1988) notes that in many semiconductor companies, a production worker needs to know at least three processes to become a super operator with salaries reaching almost 750 M$ a month ($301 US). The average wage in the electronics industry is about 350 M$ ($167 US) per month.

Employment and Staffing

During the low-cost EOI phase, job security was not well entrenched in Malaysia. The dominant strategy was to downsize the core labor force during economic downturns using a number of different flexibility enhancing techniques, such as extensive use of overtime, use of temporary workers, temporary shutdowns, use of casual workers, and recontracting (Salih and Young 1988). Standing (1991) provides evidence that many of them rehired the retrenched workers often at lower salaries. Standing also suggests that the practice of extending probationary periods of workers for unlimited periods without the promise of permanent employment had become an effective method of obtaining external flexibility.

Given the labor shortage in Malaysia, during the second phase the emphasis shifted to increased job security. The use of temporary and casual workers has been reduced considerably, given the labor shortages of the 1990s. In addition, the labor shortages have given rise to increased subcontracting. The increase in subcontracting largely stems from the labor shortages but has been considerably enhanced by the government's own program to promote local linkages to the electronics industry by providing small-scale entrepreneurs with development assistance which has spawned a number of small firms servicing the industry.

Therefore subcontracting meets the government's goal of establishing backward linkages to smaller firms and meets the employers' goal of increased flexibility. The workers employed by subcontractors are paid lower wages, but in their case also, wages have increased steadily due to the shortage, and often, given that they are immigrant labor, they are not allowed to form unions. At least 45% of the firms use subcontracting regularly. The tendency toward vertical integration of processes (Lai 1991) further ensures the possibility of more stable employment.

Training

During the first phase the focus of training was largely on-the-job training. However, case studies of three major semiconductor firms suggest that training now emphasizes job rotation and multiskilling as well as training for effective teamwork. Given that the newer technologies and production processes require rapid expansions to worker skill, the electronics companies have had to invest in skills training. In a surprising cooperative effort, the electronics companies in Penang (who are fierce competitors in the global market) have begun collaborative efforts for skills development. They have formed the Skills Development Center, where each company contributes equipment and training professionals to train skilled workers for the entire industry (PSDC 1993). These corporate efforts have been buttressed by policies of the government, whose focus on skills development has been a key part of its IR strategy in the second phase of advanced EOI. The skills development fund requires employers to pay a certain percentage of the payroll costs into the fund which is matched by government contributions, and each firm can get its training expenses paid for by the fund up to a maximum of 80% of its contribution. In addition, the government has opened a number of vocational training and polytechnic centers and has expanded the university system to produce more skilled workers and engineers needed by the electronics industry. Therefore the efforts of both government and firms show an increased focus on skills development.

Collective Bargaining

During the low-cost EOI phase, the restrictions placed on unions in the electronics sector under national IR policy was complemented by the antiunion stance of employers. Employers used both union suppression and union substitution strategies in dealing with workers. Motorola, for example, increased pay and benefits one month after the government's announcement regarding unionization in the industry (Grace

1990). Grace notes that several companies threatened their workers that they would move operations to Thailand and China if a union was formed. Workers who exhibited pro-union sentiment have been routinely transferred to other plants and otherwise intimidated. In June 1990, Hitachi's Malaysian subsidiary fired 1,003 striking workers after they walked out protesting the government's refusal to allow representation of their in-house union by a national electrical workers union. Although most of the workers were hired back after apologies, workers considered activists were not reinstated. Although Hitachi was clearly within the law, in this case their unwillingness to reinstate activists suggests an unwillingness to deal with the union—a view shared by many American and Japanese employers. Notably, national IR policy permitted employers to adopt antiunion strategies.

The shift to more advanced EOI has not changed the union status of the electronics industry in Malaysia. Despite the government announcing that unions could be formed in the electronics industry, currently only two out of forty multinational semiconductor workplaces are unionized. The electronics industry remains union free. Grace (1990) suggests three reasons for this phenomenon. One is that the workers view enterprise unions with skepticism (given the restrictions on bargaining subjects and inability to affiliate with national unions), the second is that they fear employer reprisals if they join, and finally, it has become clear to workers that examples of unionization drives in other companies will result in increases in wages and benefits in their own (i.e., a union substitution effect). The labor shortages have also ensured steady increases in wages which are expected to grow by 12% during 1994-1995 (PSDC 1993). The average hourly wage of skilled workers in electronics is about $1.25 per hour compared to $.84 an hour in 1985, a significant increase by Malaysian standards.

In summary, workplace IR/HR practices have changed along with the changes in the industrialization strategy in Malaysia. Under first-stage EOI, where IR policy was based on cost containment and repression, workplace practices mirrored the policy objective. Employers followed union suppression strategies that were consistent with the state's own regulations regarding unionization; work organization was based on Fordist assembly line principles; consistent with low-cost, low-value-added production; compensation systems emphasized piecework; control systems emphasized authoritarianism; and training was largely based on the job training for narrowly classified jobs. With the shift into second-stage EOI, the policy shift from cost containment to skills development and flexibility has been accompanied by workplace IR/HR practices that are consistent with the change in development strategy. Compensation systems emphasize greater flexibility and are linked to skill acquisition, training is broader, worker participation in decision making has increased, and work organization is increasingly based on the team concept with greater autonomy provided to workers. While this change was clearly brought about due to changes in the technology of the industry as well as the business strategies of firms, the restructuring of foreign investment incentives to attract higher technology-based investment and the policy initiatives of the Malaysian state to alter its education policies and enhance training through the skills development funds and centers have been important in bringing about transformation in workplace practices. Both the development strategy, therefore, as well as IR policies have had an impact.

Workplace Practices in the Philippines

As noted earlier, the Philippines is still in the stage of export orientation based on the comparative advantage of cheap labor. Consistent with the figures in Table 6, the Philippines offers the cheapest labor in the three countries, and with its large unemployed labor force, there is little evidence of the move to higher technology-based production systems in electronics that has been the case in Malaysia. The electronics industry in the Philippines is much smaller in size than that of Malaysia although it accounts for the largest share of Philippine exports. Workplace practices also mirror the cheap labor focus of its development policy as shown below.

TABLE 6

Comparison of Compensation (Hourly wages and Fringes)
U.S. Dollars

Country	1969	1974	1980	1985	1987
U.S.			8.00	8.37	
Singapore	0.29	0.57	2.00	2.58	3.00
Malaysia		0.37	0.60	0.84	.90
Philippines		0.20	0.50	0.63	.60

Work Organization

Much of the electronics industry in the Philippines is characterized by labor-intensive assembly of chips using simple assembly line operations organized into a Fordist work organization model. The predominant pattern as suggested by our case studies of major electronics firms is one of rigid work rules and strict job classifications. Workers are typically assigned quotas of chip cuttings or installations (Kowaleski 1986:392). These quotas can be so large that workers' use of break time to meet them is not uncommon. Team production is rare for such jobs. Though computer-aided and automated technologies exist for some of these tasks, little evidence suggests that they have been widely used in the Philippines. There are exceptions, however. Motorola is particularly famous for its fully autonomous team-based production systems in the Philippines, but it appears to be a unique Motorola characteristic rather than the norm in the industry. Matsushita's work organization also mirrors successful Japanese practices in both Japan and in Malaysia, although their Malaysian operations are characterized by higher technology and a greater degree of employee participation than in their Philippines operation.

Kowalewski (1986) discusses health hazards prevalent in Philippine electronics production. They include lung disease from toxic fumes, acid burns, skin rashes, and allergic reactions. The most common occupational injury is eye problems brought about by lengthy work with microscopes. Only 6 out of 106 electronics workers in the Bataan Export Processing Zone surveyed by the Philippines Ministry of Labor and Employment reported using safety equipment of any kind (Ministry of Labor and Employment 1993). Poor enforcement of labor protection standards by the government provides a clear opportunity for firms to depress work conditions. Clearly the low-wage, export-oriented strategy emphasized by the government is being played out in these electronics firms.

Compensation

The dominant strategy of employers is to take advantage of the low wages. Our case studies indicate that most employers pay just above the minimum wage with pay systems composed of rigid components with no incentive component. Although the average minimum wage in the national capital region is 145 pesos per day, the average wage in the electronics sector is 163 pesos per day, only 12% higher. In one major electronics company, 40% of the skilled workers were paid below the minimum wage. Among the employers we talked to the unique exception was Motorola which had highly flexible pay systems linked to skill acquisition and whose workers were paid 50% more than the industry average (including benefits).

Electronics firms are largely free to determine their own wage levels, as neither labor unions nor the government has much control over the process. The regime's only significant role in setting wages is its occasional revision of the minimum wage, a process in which unions seek to participate through rallies, strikes, and political pressure. Though this does not directly affect firms since many pay less than the minimum wage, it does provide a signal for a general increase in labor costs (Ramos 1990; Jimenez 1984). Ofreneo's (1993) investigation of subcontracting and casualization suggests an increasing importance for employers to contain wage costs. Note that among the three countries, labor costs in the Philippines are the lowest (See Table 6).

Employment and Staffing

Surplus labor in the Philippines allows firms to rely on external flexibility-enhancing techniques. About 27.3% of electronics firms report having surplus labor (Windell and Standing 1992). More than half of electronics firms (52.3%) report using temporary labor regularly during the last three years. Three-quarters of electronics establishments mandate that employees go through a probationary period of up to two years before attaining full-time status. Probationary employees invariably earn lower pay (85% in electronics, according to Windell and Standing 1991) and benefits than full-time workers (Torres 1993). Torres suggests that roughly 8% of electronics employees are contract workers employed only for a fixed period and usually for a specified task. They earn almost 85% of regular employees' pay for similar jobs. Though contract workers account for a small proportion of the workforce, half or more of electronics firms used them at some point during the period of 1988-90 (Torres 1993). Windell and Standing survey results indicate that the primary reason for the employment of temporary and casual workers is due to market uncertainty.

Subcontracting was another buffer device used by 18% of electronics firms during 1988-1990 (Torres 1993; Windell and Standing 1992). Export-oriented firms exporting more than 75% of their production were twice as likely to contract out (Windell and Standing 1992). Virtually all firms who subcontracted did so for component production (Torres 1993). Since 1985 the government has set up the National Subcontracting Exchange which links small and medium subcontractors with manufacturers and exporters. It appears that in the case of multinational firms, Philippine subsidiaries and subcontractors are used to perform labor-intensive elements of the production process. Domestic workforces are buffered by frequent use of casual and probationary workers. When layoffs occur, the majority of firms (57%) provide notice, usually of four weeks or less. Retrenchment benefits are extremely rare. In general, employment in electronics is regarded as insecure—a perception buttressed by the fact that 16% of firms laid off more than 10% of their workforce in recent years. Ofreneo (1993) suggests that the movement toward casualization and subcontracting of both manufacturing and services is much higher in other sectors, such as garments. The divided labor movement has little power to counteract these changes in employment practices, and Windell and Standing (1992) assert that Philippine labor regulations have little or no effect on personnel decisions.

Training

We have relatively little information regarding training in the electronics industry. Our case studies indicate significant differences based on the type of production organization in each plant. In UNIDEN, one of the major employers, we found training to be based on OJT only. In Matsushita, training systems were considerably more advanced, including OJT but also involving some teamwork training. In Motorola, training systems were highly advanced with a clear skills development policy and an emphasis on multiskilling. Given the low-tech nature of electronic jobs in the Philippines, Matsushita, and Motorola are exceptions to the general rule. The industry has requested the government to finance more semiconductor training centers, perhaps attached to universities, in order to increase the supply of skilled technicians and maintenance personnel (Philippine ESP 2000). If this happens, then expansion into higher technology operations would be more feasible—a process the government would like to see.

Collective Bargaining

Although the repressive laws of the Marcos regime have been withdrawn, a ban on strikes in essential industries is still in force. The principal strategy of employers in electronics is one of union avoidance, although one-quarter of the electronics firms are unionized (Ramos 1990:135). Our interviews with union organizers in the industry suggest that, in some cases, organizing efforts have gone on for three years (e.g., in INTEL) without success due to employer opposition. In cases where they are unionized, they are invariably "yellow" unions, since Philippine labor law allows employers to set up their own in-company unions to ward off authentic ones (Pineda-Ofreneo 1985). Even when collective bargaining exists, wage bargaining is not widespread, as the practice now is that revisions in the minimum wages by the government are the basis of general wage increases (Ramos 1990). Although there has been an increase in the number of individual and collective disputes, government labor-management dispute resolution systems are so notoriously slow and inefficient that even government officials freely admit it (Ofreneo 1994). In short, management in the electronics industry has a virtually free hand in controlling its operations.

My interviews with several electronics firms (Kuruvilla 1995b) in the Philippines suggest that problems related to transport and communications were significant barriers to increasing investment. Consequently, firms are attracted to the Philippines primarily for low-cost but well-educated labor which is consistent with the low-cost EOI strategy espoused by the state. It appears that firms having a business strategy based on price are more likely to invest in the Philippines as opposed to Malaysia. UNIDEN is a good example. UNIDEN is a Japanese electronics manufacturer notable for its low-cost electronic products, such as answering machines. Given increasing costs in its factories in Taiwan and Korea, they have since relocated their plants to Philippines and China, both areas noted for their low-cost operations. While UNIDEN is more representative, exceptions to the rule can be found in both Matsushita and Motorola which have adopted a higher wage/higher skills strategy in the Philippines.

Clearly the workplace IR/HR practices in the Philippines mirror the low-cost orientation of the Philippines development strategy. The Philippines has done relatively little to induce foreign firms to locate higher end processes here, unlike in Malaysia. Therefore, although workplace IR/HR practices should be based on the business strategies of firms, clearly the development strategy adopted by nations influences the kinds of firms that will invest, and through that, their IR/HR practices. In addition, the workplace practices in both Malaysia and the Philippines have been influenced by IR policies as well. In Malaysia, the focus on skills development at the national level is also apparent at the local level, and clearly human resource policies of companies have changed to a high wage/high skills focus in conjunction with national strategy. In the Philippines, the low-cost focus of national strategies is apparent in workplace human resource practices.

The relative labor cost differentials (see Table 6) across the three countries indicate that all three nations have attractions for electronics firms. High tech investors invest in Singapore, where chip design is concentrated, given the high quality of its labor (see Table 7). Lower tech investors chose Malaysia, where wafer fabrication is now popular; and low end operations, such as assembly and testing, are typically done in the Philippines. This suggests that their location at different stages of the Asian development model will continue to provide a competitive advantage for all three nations, until this tableau is upset by the entry of lower cost producers such as Vietnam and Laos which have recently begun to attract foreign investment in manufacturing, based on the competitive advantage of cheap labor and less regulations.

TABLE 7

The Relative Competitiveness of Asian Labor

	Production Labor			Managerial Labor			TOTAL	Rank
	Q	A	C	Q	A	C		
Philippines	3	1	2	3	1	1	10	1
China	5	1	1	10	10	1	28	4
Hongkong	1	10	8	1	10	10	40	9
Indonesia	5	1	1	10	10	2	29	5
Japan	10	10	10	1	1	10	33	7
Malaysia	3	3	3	5	5	5	24	3
Singapore	1	10	8	1	10	8	38	8
S. Korea	1	8	7	5	10	9	40	9
Taiwan	1	9	8	1	8	9	38	8
Thailand	4	2	1	10	10	4	31	6
Vietnam	3	1	1	10	5	1	21	2

Note: Q=Quality, A=Availability, C=Cost

Source: Political and Economic Risk Consultancy LTD., 1991.

Conclusions and Implications

These two cases, along with Singaporean examples, support the argument that the focus of industrial relations policy changes when there is a change in the industrialization strategy. In the case of Malaysia, the shift into EOI was accompanied by industrial relations policies geared toward cost containment, including the ban on unions in the export-oriented sector. Again, with a shift into second-stage EOI, IR policies were altered to provide foreign investors with highly skilled labor to sustain the second-stage EOI strategy. In the Philippines, the shift from ISI to EOI under the Marcos dictatorship was accompanied by a highly repressive IR policies aimed at preserving the low-cost advantage.

Second, it is also clear that workplace industrial relations and human resource practices are linked to both industrial relations policies as well as economic development strategies. In the case of Malaysia, workplace IR/HR policies under first-stage EOI exhibit the focus on cost containment, while workplace IR/HR practices under second-stage EOI are consistent with the second-stage EOI and IR policies of skills development and workplace flexibility. Similarly, workplace IR/HR practices in the Philippines exhibit the low-cost focus that is consistent with its current first-stage industrialization strategy.

The interdependent nature of industrialization strategies and IR policies and institutions can be seen in several instances, notably in the use of the National Wage Council to facilitate the shift into second-stage EOI in Singapore. In addition, both Malaysia and Singapore would not have been able to successfully transform into second-stage EOI successfully if they had not focused on improving education and provision of incentives for skill acquisition to provide higher tech foreign investors with skilled labor.

Clearly, the above points demonstrate that economic development strategies and industrial relations policies are linked in a variety of ways and form a mutually sustaining system. From the perspective of comparative industrial relations research, the inclusion of national development strategies in frameworks for comparative analysis appears warranted. The implications for IR research is that we must view industrial relations from a broader developmental perspective, rather than analyzing IR as a semiautonomous subsystem as has been the practice previously.

This chapter also raises a question regarding convergence in industrial relations. The traditional argument regarding convergence offered by Kerr et al. (1964) was that as economies industrialized, their IR systems would be more alike. Clearly, in these cases, convergence can be seen in both economic development strategies and the goals of IR policy, although this convergence is arrived at through divergent methods. Convergence is also seen in terms of some industrial relations outcomes, such as the declines in union density and in the move toward nonunion export-oriented sectors in all three economies. An important question here relates to what we mean by convergence? Do we mean similarity of institutions or similarity in IR policy goals?

This comparative analysis also yields some important policy lessons. In second-stage EOI, the Malaysian and Singaporean experiences show that there was a greater integration of IR policies with other macro policies to further the success of the economic development strategy. In both cases, education, immigration, wage policies, and industrial relations policies appear to support and reinforce each other, resulting in the success of the national development strategy. Arguably, the central role played by the state facilitates such policy interaction. In the context of the current debates in the United States regarding the need for development toward a high wage/high skill economy, the experience of these countries suggest that a stronger state role will facilitate cross-policy linkages necessary for success in this area.

Apart from integration across different macro-level policies, the experience of these countries also highlight the importance of IR policies at macro and workplace levels to be internally congruent. These cases show that although national-level policies have been diverse and have had different outcomes (often negative ones from the point of view of labor unions in Malaysia and the Philippines) they complement the workplace-level strategies. In Singapore, the tripartite approach provides stability and worker voice at the national level that results in labor acceptance of the workplace-level strategies or compensates for the lack of voice workers have over workplace policies. Yet workplace flexibility has been a key factor in the success of Singapore's development strategy. This example emphasizes the need for policymakers to conceive of IR reform keeping in mind that IR policies at national and workplace levels should be internally congruent and mutually reinforcing.

The policy implications for the future of Southeast Asian trade unions are less clear, however. Clearly, trade unions do not appear to have the institutional or political means to increase their voice at the national level (with the exception of Singapore). Dramatic changes in legislation are less likely, given the relative political stability of the countries in the region, and worldwide trends toward decentralization will only further weaken the already weak trade unions at the enterprise level. The only silver lining for unions is that as the countries develop and adopt higher cost and higher skill-based production organizations, the increased skills of the workforce and the new production technologies may bring with them increased worker participation and involvement in shopfloor decision making, resulting in more democratic and independent representation for the workforce. This scenario is more likely than a change in the legislation that allows labor significant voice at the national level.

The central message in this chapter is the need for comparative industrial relations researchers to broaden their framework to study industrial relations. The specific case highlighted here is the need to view industrial relations from the perspective of economic development. In the context of an increasingly integrated world economy—characterized by global production networks, an increased international division of labor, and the rise of regional trading blocks—we need broader analytical frameworks in industrial relations that take into account the effect of actors and institutions both inside and outside the traditional nation-state boundary. The traditional view of the IR system as an autonomous subsystem characterized by three national actors is less relevant in today's global economy.

Endnotes

[1] More detailed descriptions of the reasons underlying the shift from ISI to EOI can be found in Huff (1987) for Singapore, Kuruvilla (1993) for Malaysia, and Ofreneo (1994) for Philippines. In the Singapore case, the central reason was the inability to sustain an ISI policy due to the small size of its internal market and the dependence on foreign technology for ISI. Its subsequent shift into more higher skill EOI can be traced to rising wages, labor shortages and competition from other low-cost producers in Asia. In the Malaysian case, the primary motivation for shift into low-cost EOI can be traced to the state's financial involvement in affirmative action policies to empower Malays, and the resulting financial crunch in terms of foreign exchange required to pay external debts. The EOI strategy was the only way to increase foreign exchange earnings and for accelerated development. Later, changing conditions in the global market for electronics and rising wages and labor shortages forced its shift into more capital intensive exports. In the Philippine case, the primary impetus for EOI came from the World Bank, who provided stabilization loans in the 1960s on the condition the Philippines open its economy. Since then, the World Bank has imposed two structural adjustment policies geared to make the Philippines into an export-oriented economy.

[2] For a more detailed description of the specific policies associated with these strategies see Spinanger (1986) for Malaysia, Begin (1992) for Singapore, and Villegas (1988) for the Philippines.

[3] Both Bello and Verzola (1993) and Macaraya and Ofreneo (1993) discuss these in greater detail.

[4] For more detail on Malaysia's industrialization choices, see Kuruvilla (1993), Bowie (1991) and Spinanger (1986).

[5] For the reasons behind this drive and the specific measures, see Spinanger (1986) and Kuruvilla (1993).

[6] For more details on these transformations, see Kuruvilla (1994), Villegas (1988), and Macaraya and Ofreneo (1992).

References

Amjad, Rashid, and Mritiunjoy Mohanty. 1991. "Industrial Restructuring and Implications for Human Resource Development in ASEAN." The Asian HRD Planning Network, ILO-UNDP project. Working Papers.

Angebrandt, Ann Marie. 1990. "Labor Top Concern for Chip Executives." *Electronic Business Asia* (November).

Arudsothy, Ponniah, and Craig Littler. 1992. "State Regulation and Fragmentation in Malaysia." In Steven Frenkel, ed., *Organized Labor in the Asia-Pacific Region: A Comparative Study of Trade Unions in Nine Countries*. Ithaca: ILR Press.

Begin, James. 1993. "Industrial Relations in Singapore." In Stephen Frenkel and Jeffrey Harrod, eds., *Industrialization and Labor Relations: Contemporary Research in Seven Countries*. Ithaca, NY: ILR Press.

Bello, Walden, and Roberto Verzola. 1993. *Revisioning Philippine Industrialization*. Freedom From Debt Coalition. Manila.

Bjorkman, M., L. Lauridsen, and M. Marcussen. 1988. "Types of Industrialization and Capital-Labour Relations in the Third World." In Robert Southall, ed., *Trade Unions and the New Industrialization of the Third World*. London: Zed Books.

Bowie, Alasdair. 1991. *Crossing the Industrial Divide: State, Society, and the Politics of Economic Transformation in Malaysia*. New York: Columbia University Press.

Chew, Soon Beng, and Rosalind Chew. 1993. "Impact of Development Strategy on Industrial Relations in Singapore." Paper presented at the Conference Industrial Relations and Human Resources in an Era of Global Markets: An Asia Pacific Perspective, Seoul (August 26).

Chiang, Tan Boon. 1988. "The Administration and Enforcement of Collective Agreements in Singapore." In ILO, *The Administration and Enforcement of Collective Agreements—A Survey of the Current Situation in ASEAN*. Bangkok: International Labor Organization.

Deyo, Frederick. 1989. *Beneath the Miracle: Labor Subordination in East Asian Development*. Berkeley: University of California Press.

Dhanraj, N., Paramjit Singh, Sarimah Moshidi, and Chan Kok Thim. 1992. Industrial Niches for Malaysia. Is Globalization the Next Frontier? MIER National Outlook Conference, Kuala Lampur (December 8-9).

ESP 2000: [Philippines] Electronics Sector Plan, Electronics Toward the Year 2000.

Freeman, Richard B. 1994. "Repressive Labor Relations and New Unionism in East Asia." *Proceedings of the 46th Annual Meetings of the Industrial Relations Research Association (Boston)*. Madison, WI: IRRA, pp. 231-38.

Grace, Elizabeth. 1990. *Short Circuiting Labor: Unionizing Electronic Workers in Malaysia*. Kuala Lampur: Insan.

Huff, W.G. 1987. "Patterns in the Economic Development of Singapore." *Journal of Developing Areas*, Vol. 21, No. 3 (April), pp. 305-25.

Jimenez, Ramon T. 1984. "The Practice of Industrial Relations in the Philippines: an Assessment." *Philippine Journal of Industrial Relations*, Vol. VI, Nos. 1-2, pp. 23-32.

Katz, Harry, Sarosh Kuruvilla, and Lowell Turner. 1993. "Trade Unions and Collective Bargaining." In *Impediments to Competitive Labor Markets: An Overview of Policy and Research Issues*. The World Bank, PHREE.

Kerr, Clark, John Dunlop, Frederick Harbison, and Charles Myers. 1964. *Industrialism and Industrial Man*. New York: Oxford University Press.

Kowalewski, David. 1986. "Transnational Corporations and Working Conditions in Asia." *Humanity and Society*, No. 10 (November), pp. 385-409.

_____. 1987. "Transnational Corporations and Unions in Asia." *Labor Studies Journal*, Winter, pp. 258-73.

Kuruvilla, Sarosh. 1993. "Industrialization Strategy, Industrial Relations and Workplace Practices in Malaysia." Paper presented at the Industrial Relations and Human Resources in an Era of Global Markets: A Pacific Perspective. Seoul (August 26, 1993).

_____. 1994. "Industrialization Strategies and Industrial Relations Policies in Malaysia and the Philippines: Implications for Comparative Industrial Relations Research and Theory." Paper presented at the Annual Meetings of the Industrial Relations Research Association, Boston (January 3-5).

_____. 1995a. "Industrialization Strategies and Industrial Relations Policies in Southeast Asia: Singapore, Malaysia, Philippines, and India." Working Paper, Institute for Collective Bargaining, Cornell University.

_____. 1995b. "Industrialization Strategies and Patterns of Workplace Industrial Relations and Human Resource Practices: Case Studies of Firms in Malaysia and the Philippines." Working paper, Center for Advanced Studies in Human Resource Management, Cornell University.

Kuruvilla, Sarosh, and Adam Pagnucco. Forthcoming. "NAFTA, AFTA, and Industrial Relations in ASEAN." In Harry C. Katz and Maria Cook, eds., NAFTA and North American Industrial Relations. Institute for Collective Bargaining, Cornell University.

Lai, P.Y. 1991. "Electronics and Information Industry." MIER 1991 National Outlook Conference. Kuala Lampur (December).

Macaraya, Bach, and Rene Ofreneo. 1992. "Structural Adjustment and Industrial Relations: The Philippine Experience." Paper presented at the Conference on Industrial Relations in Asia and East Africa. Sydney (September 5-7).

Ofreneo, Rene. 1993. "Changes in the Workplace." Intersect, Vol. 7, No. 4 (April-May).

_____. 1994. Labor and the Philippine Economy. Quezon City: School of Labor and Institute for Industrial Relations, University of the Philippines.

Ofreneo, Rene E., and Amelita M. King. 1986. "Labor Relations in the Marcos Era: Implications for the Aquino Government." In Labor's Vision of the Economic Recovery, Proceedings of the Roundtable Conference, Institute of Industrial Relations, University of the Philippines (July 7-8).

Onn, Fong Chan. 1989. "Wages and Labor Welfare in the Malaysian Electronics Industry." Labor and Society, Vol. 14, pp. 81-102.

Pang, Eng Fong. 1991. "Singapore." In Albert Blum, ed., International Handbook of Industrial Relations. Westport, Connecticut: Greenwood, pp. 481-98.

Penang Skills Development Center (PSDC). 1993. Training For Change: The Way to a Better Future. Penang: PSDC.

Philippine Department of Labor. 1993. 1992 Yearbook of Labor Statistics. Department of Labor and Employment. Manila, Philippines.

Pineda-Ofreneo, Rosalinda. 1985. Issues in the Philippines Electronics Industry: a Global Perspective. Quezon City: International Studies Institute of the Philippines, University of the Philippines.

Rajah, Rasiah. 1988. "Production in Transition Within the Semi-conductor Industry and its Impact on Penang." Journal of Malaysian Studies. Vol. 6, No. 2 (June), pp. 85-111.

_____. 1993. "Changing Organization of Work in Malaysia's Electronics Industry." International Labor Review.

Ramos, Elias T. 1990. Dualistic Unionism and Industrial Relations. Quezon City, Philippines: New Day Publishers.

Salih, Kamal, Mei-ling Young, and Rasiah Rajah. 1988. Transnational Capital and Local Conjecture. The Semiconductor Industry in Penang. Kuala Lampur: Malaysian Institute of Economic Research.

Sharma, Basu. 1985. Aspects of Industrial Relations in ASEAN. Singapore: Institute For Asian Studies.

Spinanger, Dean. 1986. *Industrialization Policies and Regional Economic Development in Malaysia.* Singapore: Oxford University Press.

Standing, Guy. 1991. *External Labor Flexibility in Malaysia.* World Employment Program Research Paper No. 59. Geneva: ILO.

Straits Times. 1993. "SNEF to Workers, Don't Expect Too Much." (November 19).

Torres, Carmela. 1993. "External Labor Flexibility: The Philippine Experience." Paper presented to the Tripartite Technical Committee Meeting on Structural Adjustment, Manila (October 8).

Villegas, Edberto M. 1988. *The Political Economy of Philippine Labor Laws.* Quezon City, Philippines: Foundation for Nationalist Studies, Inc.

Windell, James, and Guy Standing. 1992. "External Labor Flexibility in Filipino Industry." World Employment Program, Labor Market Analysis and Planning, Working Paper No. 59 (June).

CHAPTER 5

From Co-Governance to Ungovernability: The Reconfiguration of Polish Industrial Relations, 1989-1993

MARC WEINSTEIN
Case Western Reserve University

The central European revolutions of 1989 constitute a rare historical moment when the choices of strategic actors may leave an indelible legacy on the economic and political institutions of society. At this critical branching point, Ralf Dahrendorf (1990:40) has described the opportunity not as "a road from one system to another, but one into open space of infinite possible futures." Nowhere did the promise of labor participation in structuring this new world seem greater than in Poland where the Solidarity movement played an instrumental role in laying the foundations for the democratic transformation of the entire region. Yet since the collapse of Polish socialism, labor has been increasingly marginalized in Poland's economic and political transformation, and the Solidarity trade union movement has suffered a dramatic and quite possibly irreversible decline in authority.

The proximate causes for this reversal are easy to identify. After initially extending a "protective umbrella" over the government's economic reform program, Solidarity has been held responsible for a strategy that required its core constituents to make short-term economic sacrifices only to achieve a long-term position of relative economic and social decline. Economic austerity in the name of greater economic and social differentiation created a structural contradiction that undermined the organizational cohesion of the Solidarity movement and its ability to sustain support for the economic transformation program.

The dynamics of this process are not unique to Poland. Recent experiences in western Europe provide a number of cases in which trade union support for an unpopular incomes policy created pressures that made continued labor support for these policies impossible. In Great

Britain, trade union support for the Social Contract (1974-1979) began to erode three years after its initiation and finally collapsed under widespread plant-level rebellion against voluntary wage restraint (Flanagan, Soskice, and Ulman 1983). Likewise, the Italian *solidareita nazionale* (1977-79) was abandoned after just two years when labor recognized that the benefits gained through corporatist concertation did not offset the political cost for its support of a national incomes policy. These cases illustrate that organized labor's capacity to withstand the tensions intrinsic to neo-corporatist accommodation require monopoly rights to represent labor interests and the organizational capacity to enforce bargained agreements (Regini 1984). For bargained demand management to be more than just a fair-weather system, labor's incorporation must ultimately be built into multilevel institutional arrangements that not only facilitate organizational cohesion but also efficiency and productivity (Streeck 1984).

What makes the Polish case so intriguing is that while Solidarity endorsed the marketization program, it made little attempt to leverage this support into the multifaceted institutional changes needed to facilitate labor's integration in state policy formation or to enhance workers' collective rights in firms. Instead, the union leadership entrusted economic policy to neoliberal politicians whose economic program severely eroded the bargaining power and economic status of wage employees and diminished the organizational capacity of the union. At the same time, Solidarity leaders acceded to a number of statutory changes and managerial initiatives that have reduced stakeholder rights in privatized firms. The resulting decline in Solidarity's authority in the postsocialist period underscores how historically embedded institutions are, in and of themselves, insufficient to ensure the stable incorporation of labor. Rather, the experience of Solidarity illustrates that while institutions may define the range of choices available to strategic actors, the development of new industrial relations patterns are contingent on the interaction of actors' strategic choices and the institutional and economic environment in which those actors operate.

To understand this process, I explore the origins of Solidarity's initial policy choices in the critical period following the collapse of state socialism and describe how these strategic decisions created macro and firm-level outcomes that ultimately made further trade union support for the economic transformation program untenable. I begin by tracing the evolution of Solidarity's economic reform strategy from 1980 to 1989. This short history indicates that Solidarity's policy choices in the first years of the transformation were firmly grounded in a coherent interpretation of Poland's economic crisis. I then describe how these ideas were translated into macroeconomic and firm-level strategies that have had adverse outcomes for Solidarity's core constituents. Next, I turn to the impact of these policies on the further evolution of industrial relations in the postsocialist period. Initially, informal ties between the state and the Solidarity organization and societal consensus for sweeping change allowed the implementation of the economic reform program in an environment of relative industrial peace. Over time, however, the failure to create supporting institutional changes has contributed to a number of centrifugal tendencies in Solidarity that undermined the movement's ability to shape the economic transformation program. Finally, to appreciate the interaction of institutions and strategic choice, the experience of Solidarity in Poland is briefly contrasted with developments in eastern Germany and the Czech Republic whose labor movements have also had to face the dual challenges of marketization and privatization.

The Evolution of Solidarity Economic Reform Strategy

The Third Way, 1980-81

Solidarity did not always support a market-oriented economic reform program. On the contrary, in 1980-81 it promoted an alternative economic strategy that sought to build a "common front against exploitation, no matter what the slogans are used to disguise such exploitation" (*Tygodnik Solidarność* 1981a). Tourraine et al. (1983:50) noted that "the people of Poland did not want to become part of the capitalist world," but rather they sought to build a third way. This, in turn, led many to ask how the Left became so strong in Poland and how it became so influential in Solidarity (Ost 1991).

Though the Solidarity leadership was initially hesitant to become involved in government economic reform efforts, its program and organizing strategies reinforced workers' demands for greater economic equality in a system that, by the standards of market economies, was already highly egalitarian. Among the demands of striking workers in 1980 were flat-rate wage increases, equalization of family subsidies, the implementation of rationing instead of free-floating prices, the elimination of hard currency shops, and a massive shift towards social welfare spending. In its 1981 policy statement Solidarity did argue that people should be paid according to their work, but only within a system that fostered social equality:

We recognize the principle that one should be paid according to the quality, quantity, difficulty and risk of one's work ("to each according to his work"), and we will seek to level-off unjustified disproportions in that regard. *However, the principle of meeting the social minimum has precedence over the aforementioned principle* (Original emphasis) (*Tygodnik Solidarność* 1981a:1).

By the time Solidarity published this program, its leadership began to reconsider the strategy of not participating in economic policy formation. Fearing a popular backlash from its inevitable association with the country's economic collapse, Solidarity formulated an economic reform program that envisioned "a self-governing and democratic reform at every management level and a new socioeconomic system . . . [in which] the socialized enterprise should be the basic organizational unit of the economy" (*Tygodnik Solidarność* 1981b). Under this economic reform plan, Solidarity promoted the creation of employee councils with broad statutory powers that included the right to appoint managers and to co-govern enterprises.

On the eve of martial law in Poland, the Solidarity leadership remained committed to the self-management reform program. Though continuing economic decline inevitably diminished Solidarity's support among workers and helped dampen potential resistance to the martial law authorities, the egalitarian ethos of Solidarity endured. At the end of 1981, there was no indication that the Solidarity leadership was prepared to accept economic reforms that would lead to greater economic and social inequality. Rationing of goods (as opposed to price increases), flat-rate wage increases (as opposed to percentage wage increases), and pay according to one's needs (as opposed to pay according to one's work) all remained cornerstones of Solidarity's economic reform program.

The Ideological Transformation, 1982-89

The shift in opposition ideas about future economic and social reform in Poland evolved steadily throughout Solidarity's period of underground activity from 1982 to 1989. Shortly after the declaration of martial law, activists in the underground began an introspective critique of Solidarity's strategy in 1980-81 and its impotence in resisting martial law authorities. By the mid-1980s, the Polish right—"the political orientation afraid to speak its name"—asserted itself "with a self-confidence not seen since prewar days" (Stoltenberg 1992:281).

A recurring theme on the Polish Right was that socialism in Poland had created a collective mentality that destroyed the moral foundation of society (Walicki 1984; Kisielewski 1985; Wierzbicki 1985). Although opposition activists of all political shades acknowledged that the coercive power of the state was ultimately responsible for the repression of Solidarity, a growing minority in the opposition believed that Solidarity's leftist tendencies contributed to its demise. These activists argued that as stale and unconvincing as the socialist rhetoric of the party appeared, its mere dominance of postwar Poland permeated the Solidarity opposition. In this new interpretation, subtle and persistent indoctrination was responsible for Solidarity's errant political and economic strategy. This led to Solidarity placing excessive emphasis on mass action, democratic procedure, and egalitarian outcomes and insufficient trust in market economics and individual initiative. As a result, the Solidarity leadership was perceived to hold unrealistic assumptions about the ability to transform the political terrain of socialist Poland and were thus hindered in their ability to formulate a viable alternative economic reform program.

Just as the imposition of martial law demonstrated the political unreformability of the communist system, the deep economic crisis of the 1980s demonstrated once and for all the economic unreformability of state socialism. One irony of the 1980s was that while the government had outlawed the trade union, it had adopted key elements of Solidarity's 1981 economic reform program. This program was premised on the notion that market forces could be simulated and competition fostered if firms were provided sufficient levels of autonomy (Pysz 1987; Johnson 1991; Balcerowicz 1992). By introducing what came to be known as the three Ss—*samodzielność* (self-reliance), *samorzadowanie* (self-government), and *samofinansowanie* (self-financing)—the government hoped to rejuvenate the Polish economy without transforming status quo property relations.

This was not to be the case. Shielded from foreign competition, Polish firms used their oligopolistic position in the market to raise prices. Moreover, faced with soft budget constraints and negative interest rates, managers found it easy to acquiesce to wage demands. Without the legal mechanisms or the political will to force inefficient firms into bankruptcy, the state allowed many companies to incur large levels of debt that permitted their continued functioning even in the face of formal insolvency. In the end, the three Ss produced a spiraling inflation rather than the increased economic productivity and growth it had promised. The failure of the government's reform program provided additional impetus to the emerging consensus among Solidarity opposition leaders that state ownership of the means of production was at the core of Poland's chronic economic crisis. This loss of faith in the reformability of socialism was mirrored by a new infatuation with the power of markets. Contributing to this new creed was the success that market solutions provided to the organizational challenges facing opposition activists in the 1980s. Excluded from state sector employment, intellectuals and worker activists utilized Poland's increasingly liberal laws on private activity to form a number of worker collectives (Bielecki 1993). These collectives liberated activists from dependence on the state sector, and their economic success (often in large part a result of a continuous stream of contracts from the Catholic Church) further reinforced the value of free market activity and entrepreneurialism. Many activists turned their exclusion from state sector employment into a virtue by claiming their private sector endeavors separated them from any dependence on the state (Tusk 1993). The search for economic solutions even began to penetrate the logistical aspects of underground organizing efforts. A common sanction imposed on activists who distributed underground literature in the 1980s was the seizure of personal property. To protect activists from personal financial ruin, social insurance funds were created to compensate individuals whose assets had been seized by state authorities or who faced high fines for their underground work (Stoltenberg 1992).

The introspective analysis of Solidarity's failure and the new faith in private property and individual initiative combined to transform the world view of the opposition leadership. By the mid-1980s, liberal political discussion groups in Gdansk, Warsaw, and Krakow became increasingly influential in the Solidarity underground and were responsible for numerous underground publications and the dissemination of the writings of theorists such as Joseph Hayek and Milton Friedman. A number of underground publications devoted considerable space to a discussion of these works (Barycz 1984; Branecki 1985; Strzelecki 1985).

These groups forged important links with mainstream elements in the Solidarity movement as the ideals of worker control and egalitarianism came to be supplanted by those of the market. Specific examples of this ideological transformation are numerous as early as 1984. Jerzy Strzelecki, an adviser to Solidarity on self-management issues in 1981, became a leading exponent of property rights theory (Strzelecki 1984). Jadwiga Staniszkis, a sociologist considered left wing even by the standards of 1980-81, came to view private property as the key to Poland's economic and moral revival (Staniszkis 1987). Leszek Balcerowicz, Janusz Lewandowski, and Jan Szomburg, key theorists of worker self-management in 1981, developed an economic program based on the introduction of markets and the privatization of the economy (Lewandowski and Szomburg 1987). Thus, by 1988 even activists traditionally associated with mainstream Solidarity argued that Poland's economic and social decline was a crisis of the "system" and that private property and markets held the solution to the country's economic malaise (Geremek and Zakowski 1990). This ideological sea change was formally incorporated into Solidarity's program in April 1987, when a policy document signed by Walesa and others in the underground leadership adopted an economic strategy based on the privatization of the Polish economy (*NSZZ Solidarność* 1987).

The Economic Transformation Program

Sooner than opposition activists anticipated, a Solidarity-supported government would have the opportunity to implement the radical reform program formulated in the 1980s. After winning all but one of the 261 contested seats in the 1989 election, the Solidarity coalition had a mandate for fundamental change. Within weeks of assuming office at the end of August 1989, Prime Minister Tadeusz Mazowiecki quickly assembled an economic policy team committed to a decisive break with the socialist economy and to the rapid creation of an economy based on private ownership, free markets, and economic integration (Kuczynski 1992).

Whereas the First Solidarity Congress in 1981 had embraced the socialized firm as the centerpiece of economic reform strategy, the Second Solidarity Congress in 1990 endorsed

> the creation of a new economic system that should emulate the successful model of the developed countries, ensuring efficient production and rising living standards. . . . This process should lead us to a market economy which combines legally regulated capital, investment, and employment freedoms with trade union rights and elements of state-intervention in rectifying market imperfections (*NSZZ Solidarność* 1990:18).

Without fully understanding the details of the economic reform strategy, Solidarity trade union activists easily trusted their intellectual counterparts and allocated to them the task of economic reform. The ties that grew between these activists and neoliberal economic reformers during the underground period formed the foundation for vital shopfloor support in the initial phase of economic reform. Based largely on a strategy developed by Lewandowski, Szomburg, and Balcerowicz in 1988, this project involved two essential tasks: macroeconomic stabilization and the privatization of the economy.

Macroeconomic Strategy

The macroeconomic program implemented in 1989 was consistent with Solidarity's revised vision of economic reform developed during the underground period. Jeffrey Sachs (1993:44) notes:

> [Minister of Finance] Balcerowicz had been preparing for this opportunity for years, and had assembled a team of research economists around him who were prepared to help introduce and implement the reform measures. Balcerowicz held a vision of how Poland should proceed that was similar in concept to the program that Lipton and I had outlined for Solidarity in July [1989].

The details of the program, finalized with the help of Western advisors, followed a heterodox policy formulated by international financial institutions for the economic transformation of developing economies (Lipton and Sachs 1990; Bielecki 1992; Slay 1994). The primary difference between Poland's Structural Adjustment Program (SAP) and those for underdeveloped economies was that whereas the former programs typically predicated price and trade liberalization on progress in institutional reforms, the strategy in Poland was to overcome the inertia of existing structures by the shock of liberalization. To accomplish this first task, the money supply was sharply reduced. Subsidies to households and firms were largely eliminated, and the National Bank of Poland (NBP) tightened credit by establishing positive interest rates. Second, most price controls were eliminated, and those prices still regulated (energy, transport fees, rent, and medicine) were increased. Third, Poland's markets were opened to international trade to facilitate economic integration and to prevent Polish monopolies from obtaining excessive rents as a result of the price liberalization. Fourth, an excess wage tax (*popiwek*) was introduced to reduce upward pressure on wages. Under the terms of this law, a wage norm was established for each firm, and for every zloty that a firm's wage bill exceeded this norm, a 5 zloty tax was assessed. Poland's SAP had the broad support of the international financial community, and a one billion dollar IMF stabilization fund provided critical support for the NBP in its successful stabilization of the zloty.

When implemented in January 1990, the combination of these measures had an immediate and dramatic impact on the Polish economy. In the first months of the reform program, inflation was reduced to 5% a month, down from a 50% monthly rate in the last quarter of 1989. Zloty convertibility, combined with trade liberalization, contributed to a dramatic increase in foreign trade despite the collapse of the Soviet market. After dropping in 1990, foreign trade in 1991 increased 28% to $37.4 billion. Moreover, notwithstanding a sharp increase in the real exchange rate of the zloty, Poland had a trade surplus in 1990 and only a $200 million trade deficit in 1991 compared with a $1.8 billion deficit in 1989 (OECD 1992). At the same time, the elimination of subsidies helped balance the budget by 1991.

Despite these economic gains, the recession induced by the reform program was more severe than projected. From 1989 to 1991, industrial output declined 40% and real wages dropped nearly as much. Although a 90% drop in Soviet trade during this period partly explains the depth and duration of the Polish recession, the restrictive monetary policy alone could explain the dramatic drop in production (Cui 1992). Erring on the side of caution, Polish economic policy makers may have contributed to the severity of the recession by maintaining the restrictive monetary policy into the 1991 calendar year (Gomulka 1991). As a result of firm-level adjustments to the drop in production, employment dropped sharply. In 1990 total measured employment was roughly the same as it had been in the 1970s (OECD 1992).

Solidarity's traditional constituents suffered the greatest burden of this economic dislocation. Unemployment levels for college-educated workers leveled at 6.7% in July 1992, but skilled and unskilled blue-collar unemployment continued to rise and exceeded 20% for non-high-school-educated workers during the same period (*Glowny Urzad Statystyczny* 1993). In the first year of the reform program, real wages dropped more than 30%. Preliminary analysis of household income data indicated that wage dispersion increased dramatically in the first year of the economic reform program, and there was evidence that real wages dropped most precipitously among blue-collar workers (Radziukiewicz 1992).

Firm-level Strategies

Parallel with the adoption of a new economic reform strategy, Solidarity shifted its view of workplace democracy. Since the purpose of the economic transformation program was to create "real" owners who would have a material interest in realizing a profit from their assets, there was little point in creating the legal and economic conditions to allow employees effectively to preempt managerial prerogative regarding firm-level restructuring. There was widespread sentiment among shopfloor Solidarity activists that managers who owed their positions to the *nomenklatura* system of patronage should be removed. But there was equally strong sentiment that newly appointed managers in state-owned firms should have broad prerogative to restructure firms to prepare them for privatization (Chelminski, Czynczyk, and Sterniczuk 1993). In the words of one former worker council advocate: "No room can or should be allowed for democracy in an economic enterprise" (*Głos Szczeciński* 1991). Rather than viewing worker councils as important institutions in promoting enterprise reform, Solidarity economic reformers had come to see them as institutional relics necessitated by aberrant state ownership of the means of production. In this context, the promotion of employee control of privatized firms would undermine the basis of the economic transformation strategy.

Consistent with this new position, Solidarity never mobilized to expand worker councils to the privatized sector. More importantly, it consented to the "commercialization" procedure in which a firm's assets were transferred to the state treasury. This decision had important implications for firm governance and worker representation. In contrast to state-owned firms, which have worker councils with broad rights stipulated under the 1981 law on state-owned enterprises, commercialized and privatized firms are governed by the Polish Commercial Code of 1934, which gives shareholders the sole right to elect supervisory board representatives and has no provision for worker councils. Thus upon the commercialization or privatization of the firm, worker councils are replaced with supervisory boards whose sole legal mandate is to represent stockholder interests.

The impact of this revised view of stakeholder rights is revealed by a recent survey of state-owned, commercialized, and privatized firms (Weinstein 1994). In 55% of state-owned firms (n=31), top management held consultative meetings with worker council representatives at least once a month; in privatized firms comparable meetings were held with employee representatives in only one-third of the sampled firms (n=42). Moreover, whereas the topic of such meetings primarily concerned strategic issues in state-owned firms, in privatized firms they focused on wages and working conditions and thus were essentially an extension of the collective bargaining process. The extent of these differences was confirmed in a multivariate analysis that controlled for trade union density, employment levels, production strategy, and product markets. This analysis found that in state-owned firms management was 3.4 times more likely to discuss production issues and 2.2 times more likely to discuss firm finances with employee representatives than in comparable privatized firms.

At the same time, no statistically significant differences were found between state-owned firms (with worker councils) and commercialized firms (without worker councils). This suggests the key factor determining the extent of consultation was not the presence or absence of worker councils but was rather the presence or absence of private owners. In the view of trade unionists, workers, and many managers, as long as an enterprise remained "ownerless," employees had a responsibility to act as caretakers of the firm. However, once a firm was privatized, it was believed that governance should become the exclusive domain of owners and that trade unions should restrict themselves to the "normal" role of negotiating wages and working conditions. In a number of instances, Solidarity factory committees even disbanded once their firms were privatized, because it was not clear to local activists that a trade union was needed once a firm had a "real" owner.

Industrial Relations in the New Economic Order, 1989-92

The Protective Umbrella

Despite workers' adverse economic circumstances and diminished influence in firms, rank-and-file Solidarity members initially heeded their leadership's call to support the economic transformation program. Well before the introduction of the Structural Adjustment Program (SAP), the National Executive Committee of Solidarity publicly stated its support for market reforms. Within a week following the nomination of Tadeusz Mazowiecki as prime minister, Solidarity mobilized to support the introduction of the marketization program. In a public statement in which he called for a six-month strike moratorium, Lech Walesa asked Polish workers to "give the new Prime Minister time because great chances lie in him" and requested "all those who are raising wage demands not to undertake strikes in the present situation" (Tagliabue 1989:1). Railroad workers immediately suspended a two-week strike, and the federation of Metallurgical Trade Unions, affiliated with the Communist-supported All Poland Trade Union Confederation (OPZZ), echoed Walesa's appeal. The call for a strike moratorium was one pillar of what became known in Polish political parlance as the "protective umbrella"—a shield protecting the government from the social tension that was expected to result from economic reform and dislocation. To make the protective umbrella feasible Solidarity drew upon popular support for fundamental change, its moral authority, the legitimacy created by ad hoc union participation in policy formation, and its informal role as a mediator in state-owned enterprises.

The widespread recognition of the need for dramatic economic change was one of the most important factors stabilizing labor-management relations during this period (Adamski et al. 1991). In 1989 many workers did not perceive their interests to be in inherent conflict with those of other segments of society. In the early days of the transformation program, the experience of joint struggle produced the shopfloor support needed for the government's economic program, even when details of the program were not understood in their entirety. There was no schism between workers and intellectuals in Poland, in part because the Leninist system created the structural basis for cross-class alliances (Ost 1991). All citizens viewed themselves as wage laborers. Different social strata did not see themselves as having distinct, let alone opposing interests. Shopfloor activists easily trusted their intellectual counterparts to carry out economic reform. This trust in the newly elected leadership extended well beyond the union.

Whatever concerns local activists and rank-and-file workers may have had about the transformation program were also ameliorated by the continued high profile of Solidarity and, particularly, Lech Walesa in the reform process. Although Solidarity was committed to gradually easing away from political activities, long-time political activists had little intention of lessening their influence over policy formation and implementation. Moreover, by virtue of Walesa's role in Poland's democratization and his stature in Polish society, his every pronouncement carried weight in the ministries of the Mazowiecki government. As Solidarity extended the shield of its protective umbrella over the Mazowiecki government, rank-and-file members could view Walesa as wielding a shield protecting their interests.

Solidarity's political and moral authority was also enhanced by the easy flow of personnel and ideas between its national leadership and the ministries, parliament, and senate. Particularly in the first several months of the Mazowiecki government's tenure, the lines between union activists and state officials often became blurred. Nearly all of the 161 members of parliament and 99 senators elected on the Solidarity slate had strong ties to the former underground, and many held leadership positions in the national and regional structures of the trade union (Malarecka-Simbierowicz et al. 1990). There was also a strong union presence in the ministries of labor, health, and education. The ministries of Finance and Property Transformation were eventually to be staffed by individuals associated with liberal activists who traditionally had strong ties with Gdansk Solidarity leaders. Formal and regular government-union consultations were thus secondary to the informal network of relations among former underground leaders, and activists in the trade union wing of Solidarity could concentrate more on other union activities.

A final stabilizing force in Polish industrial relations during this period was the informal mediating role played by the regional structures of Solidarity and local activists (Dabrowski, Federowicz, and Levitas 1991). In the absence of suprafirm wage bargaining, Solidarity leaders played an instrumental role in mediating numerous local conflicts and limiting the wage demands of workers. Even in the early days of the economic reform program, employees of state enterprises faced severe economic hardship; disputes were inevitable. Wedged between management and workers in state firms, shopfloor Solidarity activists utilized their open door to managers, who often owed their positions to Solidarity-dominated worker councils, to convey and resolve worker grievances and diffuse potentially serious conflicts. When more serious disputes emerged between Solidarity factory committees and management or government ministries, national or regional Solidarity leaders mediated between the firm and government.

Nascent Industrial Relations Patterns under Stress

The factors supporting the protective umbrella proved fragile. One area of weakness lay in the tenuous links between Solidarity's national leadership, which supported the transformation program, and the thousands of Solidarity factory committees in state enterprises. The difficulty of enforcing organizational concentration was a legacy of the state's repression of Solidarity. The state had all but destroyed the union's presence in factories during its period of underground activity (Wujec 1984; Szczesna and Blumsztajn 1988; Stoltenberg 1992). The Round Table agreements leading to Solidarity's relegalization in 1989 were prompted by two strike waves in 1988. However, these strikes were initiated by young unaffiliated workers (Smolenski and Gielzynski 1989; Stoltenberg 1992). The ability of the underground leadership to parlay these strikes into a place at the round table negotiations was a tribute to the political calculation of the opposition leaders, but belied Solidarity's weak presence in Poland's industrial enterprises prior to 1989. A mass movement led to the legalization of Solidarity in 1980-81. Relegalization in 1989, however, was actively supported by only a relatively small group of workers and owed little to the organizational capacity of the underground opposition. Although thousands of Solidarity shopfloor committees sprang into activity after the union was relegalized in March 1989, they often had only limited support among rank-and-file workers.

Solidarity's ability to maintain industrial peace was also strained by the presence of other union organizations which undermined Solidarity's sectoral hegemony. The OPZZ, established by the Communist government in 1983 to replace the delegalized Solidarity trade union, displayed far greater staying power than the political party that created it. A continued irritant to the national Solidarity leadership, OPZZ owed its viability both to the independent initiative of local activists and to its increasingly populist platform which emerged even prior to the round table negotiations. During the 1988 strikes many local OPZZ activists supported rank-and-file wage demands. At the round table negotiations OPZZ insisted upon 100% wage indexation long after Solidarity and the Communist party had agreed to a lower wage indexation coefficient (PAP 1989). OPZZ would later be joined in its opposition to economic transformation by emergent branch interest sections within Solidarity and by numerous other independent unions.

A final and perhaps decisive threat to the fragile network stabilizing Polish industrial relations would be the *successful* marketization of the Polish economy which produced adverse labor market outcomes for key union constituents. Strong inter- and intraindustry wage norms were disrupted by the marketization of the Polish economy. Employees in the mining, shipbuilding, and steel industries typically enjoyed wage premiums related to an industrial policy that favored heavy industry. Centralized state wage policy favored blue-collar workers, and as a result many managers and white-collar professionals earned below market wages (Simon and Kanet 1981). The average monthly salary of company directors was only slightly more than twice that of blue-collar workers. In manufacturing and construction, college-educated engineers only earned between 30% and 40% more than their blue-collar counterparts. The base pay of physicians and dentists was less than that of many blue-collar occupations (GUS 1989). The introduction of a free floating price for labor and a new product market for professional services inevitably changed Poland's traditional income distribution, and those who had enjoyed above-market wages resisted departure from these norms. This would create especially difficult problems in collective bargaining, since reference to national wage norms had provided the basis for negotiations throughout the 1970s and 1980s.

War at the Top, Confusion Below

A divisive regional strike at the Polish State Railway (PKP) in May 1990 provided an important early warning sign that large segments of Solidarity's core constituents were growing weary of the economic transformation program and the Solidarity coalition that led it. Sensing this rapidly fading public support, Walesa declared a "permanent political war" to "shake" the government and accelerate the economic transition. In widely publicized back-to-back interviews five days after the start of the PKP strikes, Walesa accused his intellectual advisors of misleading him and "behaving like occupants," who wanted to "let society remain asleep" because "if it wakes up, it will eat us" (Engelberg, 1990:13).

Walesa's "war at the top" marked the start of enormous political turmoil within the Solidarity coalition and led to Walesa's win against his erstwhile ally Tadeusz Mazowiecki in the 1990 presidential election. Walesa's personal ambitions and his frustration with his inability to control the Mazowiecki government prompted his war at the top (Zubek 1992), but it also represented yet another ad hoc effort to extend Solidarity's protective umbrella over the economic reform program. For even as Walesa waged his personal campaign against the Mazowiecki government, he never withdrew his support for the basic direction of the economic reform program (Balcerowicz 1992). Rather, he argued that Mazowiecki had been too cautious in the implementation of the program which, he said, only prolonged economic hardship. Walesa asked for Solidarity's continued support for the acceleration of the marketization and privatization of the Polish economy, arguing that self-interested strikes would only delay this.

Yet, as Walesa drew upon his personal authority to bolster rank-and-file support for the marketization program, he did so at the cost of further weakening Solidarity's sectoral hegemony. Recognizing that he did not have the unequivocal support of leaders in the regional structure of the union for his campaign against the Mazowiecki government, Walesa resurrected the Network of Factory Committees (Sieć) of Poland's largest industrial enterprises, which had led the worker self-government movement in 1980-81. The enterprises represented by Sieć tended to enjoy the traditional privileges afforded to heavy industry in socialist Poland. The concern of the Solidarity National Council was that eventually this nonstatutory union organization, like the emergent Branch Committees, would press for the maintenance of traditional wage norms and state investments that were in conflict with the marketization program.

As the reemergence of *Siec'* disrupted Solidarity's sectoral hegemony, Walesa's war at the top also diminished the organizational concentration of union. By September 1990, the Solidarity national office in Gdansk had been transformed into a national election campaign headquarters. Trade union activists, already stretched by an earlier exodus of personnel to the Polish parliament, were now taxed even further as they were inevitably drawn into Walesa's presidential effort. For the thousands of factory committees attempting to cope with rising rank-and-file discontent, the presidential election could not have come at a more difficult time. In 1990, Solidarity factory committees were comprised mostly of activists who strongly supported the marketization program. During this same period, they had to contend with an increasingly dissatisfied workforce that was beginning to wonder just how many more sacrifices would be asked of them before they would see benefits from the Balcerowicz Plan. The ability of factory committees to work with managers, many of whom owed their positions to Solidarity-dominated works councils, was often undermined as rank-and-file workers became increasingly preoccupied with their falling real wages and looming layoffs.

Shortly after the presidential campaign, many of the pressures that had been building in Poland over the last year exploded into industrial unrest. The largest and most widely publicized strikes occurred at the state railways, in municipal transport authorities, and in the mining industry. These sectors shared three common features. First, all had been adversely affected by the government's decision to use September 1989 wage levels as the basis for determining the January pre-tax wage limits. Second, these three sectors were traditionally privileged monopolies that had effectively exerted strike pressure on the government in 1988. Finally, each continued to receive government subsidies and had their prices regulated by the state (Kloc 1992).

Less publicized but more disruptive to the protective umbrella were a series of uncoordinated strikes in small and medium-sized firms in the first months of 1991. Most of these strikes were prompted by wage demands and calls for the elimination of the excess wage tax. Even relatively moderate shopfloor activists in Poland found it difficult to understand the equity of state firms being subject to this tax at the same time that private sector firms were exempt from it. Equally disconcerting were numerous hunger strikes conducted by desperate workers in bankrupt firms. In some instances, these workers were the victims of outright privatization scams. In other cases, they were employees in state-owned firms with few prospects for survival in the newly marketized economy.

The Fragmentation of Solidarity

In this context, Solidarity had to formulate a new strategic direction without the leadership of Lech Walesa. The presidential campaign was an inauspicious start to this new era in Solidarity's history. In addition to strengthening nonstatutory union structures, the acrimonious election sowed discord in what had been a relatively cohesive national union. In the days immediately following the election, a number of longtime national Solidarity leaders were censored by their respective regional committees for not having supported Walesa's presidential campaign. Two months later at the Third National Solidarity Congress in February 1991, there were additional indications of a new alignment of forces in the national union that would make continued support for the protective umbrella problematic. Candidates strongly associated with the Gdansk leadership lost to a relative newcomer to the National Commission, Marian Krzaklewski, a union activist from Silesia. Krzaklewski's strength came from his position as liaison to the branch sections of the union. In turn, the branch structures gained new legitimacy at the Congress through the creation of thirteen industrial sections, each of which was now entitled to a place on the 52-member National Commission.

The extent to which the middle tier of the national union had become more militant was also evident at a conference of economic affairs, sponsored by the Solidarity National Commission in May 1991. What was intended to be a forum to develop a constructive modification to the government's economic program turned into a platform for attacking the economic transformation program. Expressing the views of many at the conference, Andrzej Slowik, leader of the large Lodz region complained: "Solidarity had supported the government and had been betrayed. The government is not paying any attention to its partner. Discussions with the Government lead nowhere. The reign of the present government will come to an end anyhow and we will be left without a base." His sentiments were echoed by Alojzy Pietrzyk, leader of the mining region of Katowice, who threatened: "If the government doesn't want to talk, we should leave it and talk man to man with the President" (*Zycie Warszawy* 1991:1).

In January 1992, the government once again announced an energy price increase. The Solidarity National Council held an emergency meeting to discuss the union's response in which two distinct factions emerged. The presidium of the National Council, the union's highest executive body, together with most representatives on the 26-member Solidarity trade union parliamentary caucus, counseled restraint and called for immediate negotiations with the government. Local representatives on the National Council argued that yet another round of negotiations would prove futile and instead called for an immediate general strike. Longtime Solidarity activists, most of whom had been active in Solidarity during its underground period, dominated the former group. Among the latter were a number of activists who had recently attained leadership positions in the regional structure of the union. Despite the increasingly militant mood among the National Council, moderates in the Solidarity leadership once again prevailed. But their efforts to balance growing discontent in the union with further negotiations were growing increasingly precarious.

The centrifugal forces tearing at the national union persisted into Solidarity's Fourth National Congress in June 1992. The lack of an alternative economic program contributed to a new populist tone in the union. This tendency could already be seen in 1991 when militants argued that the union's protective umbrella should not shield the government but the economic reform program. What was needed, they argued, was an *acceleration* of the reforms. In 1992 union militants replaced "acceleration" with the new theme of "decommunization." In this view, it was not the marketization and privatization program per se that was responsible for the hardships that Polish workers encountered, but rather the entrenched *nomenklatura* which hijacked the economic transformation. Union militants argued that communist managers, often in cahoots with foreign capital and corrupt politicians, had disenfranchised Polish citizens.

Thus despite the evident widespread discontent among trade unionists with the outcomes of the government's economic reform program, there was no substantive debate about labor-government relations, economic policy, or firm governance. Rather, this congress, like the one that followed it a year later, was dominated by talk of conspiracy and subterfuge as lists of supposed communist agents were circulated. Delegates ended the congress by passing a series of resolutions that "demanded an immediate process of decommunization in Poland be conducted in accordance with the law," rejection of "attempts at halting the process of disclosing UD and SB [communist security] agents," and demands that "they be eliminated from Poland's public life" (*Gazeta Wyborcza* 1992:1). Even by the standards of Polish political rhetoric, the level of demagoguery at the Fourth Congress was disturbing to many longtime Solidarity supporters. Tensions heightened the divide between new middle-level activists and those in the highest leadership positions in the union, who still hoped to mediate between the government and the growing number of disgruntled workers.

This populist tone reemerged at the Fifth Solidarity Congress in May 1993. The invective against supposed communist agents that had dominated the Fourth National Congress was now focused on the founding members of the union. Solidarity parliamentarians were roundly condemned by the congress for their support of the government. One of these, Bogdan Borusewicz—a historic figure for his role in organizing the Gdansk shipyards in August 1980—waited in vain for two hours at the congress podium as the delegates shouted him down. Lech Walesa canceled his scheduled speech at the congress after hearing declarations that inviting him is "like bringing a Trojan horse to the congress." A short time later Walesa lamented on national television that "My own and the present Solidarity's way depart" (*Gazeta Wyborcza* 1992:1).

As the middle and lower tiers of Solidarity became increasingly impatient with the economic reform program, the national leadership found it impossible to further extend the protective umbrella. A long-simmering public sector pay dispute finally prompted a frustrated Solidarity leadership to initiate a successful vote of no confidence in June 1993. In elections that followed, the parties emerging from the pre-1989 opposition suffered a resounding defeat, and the Solidarity trade union ticket did not receive the 5% threshold in the popular vote needed to enter the new parliament. Solidarity was not only alienated from its historic alliance with the intelligentsia but also was confronted with a reinvigorated "postcommunist" ruling coalition.

Lessons from Failed Labor Incorporation in Poland

In less than four years after the Mazowiecki government initiated the neoliberal economic transformation program, the costs of the program proved too high for the Solidarity trade union to bear. Though some have argued that the initial decline in real income has been more than offset by improved market conditions (Sachs 1993; Balcerowicz 1992), marketization has adversely affected the relative economic status of Solidarity's core constituents and disproportionately impacted sectors in which the union has traditionally been strong (Kloc 1992). Rising impatience with these outcomes finally led to internal conflicts within Solidarity that have ultimately diminished the influence of the movement.

The initial economic outcomes of marketization reduced support for the transformation program, but complementary institutional changes might have increased the stake of workers in the transformation program and subsequently sustained the organizational cohesiveness of the Solidarity movement. Yet rather than institutionalizing labor incorporation into state policy formation and building firm-level participative structures, the Solidarity leadership relied on informal labor concertation. The absence of more durable arrangements prevented the creation of incentives for workers to continue their support for the transformation of the program. Though one could view Solidarity's failure to build these supporting institutions as strategic miscalculation, it is important to remember that these decisions were consistent with the neoliberal ideas that predominated among the union leadership in 1989 and drove Solidarity's economic transformation strategy.

Despite the fragmentation of the Solidarity movement, the position of labor will continue to be a factor in Poland's political economy. Traditions of worker self-organization and the legacy of the Solidarity era are likely to ensure that Polish workers will continue to influence national economic policy and firm-level restructuring. For instance, concerns about economic distribution and enfranchisement have given Polish employees a greater economic stake in privatization than those enjoyed by stakeholders in other postsocialist countries (Earle, Frydman, and Rapaczynski 1994), and national tripartite consultation in Poland has evolved into broad-ranging discussions concerning economic and social issues (Thirkell, Scase, and Vickerstaff 1994). While these achievements are notable, Solidarity's failure to build multilevel institutions to complement its initial economic strategy has damaged its organizational cohesiveness and diminished its ability to affect national and firm-level outcomes.

Solidarity's Experience in Comparative Perspective

There have been differences in the implementation of marketization programs across central Europe, but highlighting these differences risks masking the important shared intellectual spirit of these projects. Policymakers in all these countries have emulated "the mores, methods, and models to help them catch up in ways congruent with their own highly selective historical memory and with the mythologized histories of the most advanced capitalist countries, particularly the free market paragons, Britain and the United States" (Amsden, Taylor, and Kochanowicz 1994:2). This raises a question concerning the relevance of national institutional differences in the evolution of industrial relations systems in postsocialist central Europe. To what extent have the hegemony of the Bretton Woods institutions—the World Bank and the International Monetary Fund—and their promotion of neoliberal economic policy precluded other paths of development? Alternatively, have the different historical legacies of socialism structured institutional outcomes in important and enduring ways in the postsocialist period? To address these questions, I will contrast Solidarity's strategic decision not to build new institutions with the relatively successful transfer of West German labor institutions to the eastern German states and to the Czechoslovak trade union movement's struggle to attain a voice for labor in the postsocialist period.

Germany

In the first months following the fall of the Berlin wall, the German trade union movement was hesitant concerning its expansion into the new eastern German states (Fichter 1994). There was a great deal of uncertainty about the extent of future economic integration and the potential benefits that western members would gain by organizing eastern workers. At the time, rapid economic and political unification did not appear inevitable, and as a result there was no consensus among leaders of the West German Trade Union Confederation (DGB) about the need to organize east German workers.

The victory of the Christian Democratic Union-led alliance in the 1990 all-German election prompted a change in strategy as the economic implications of an unorganized east German workforce became apparent. Drawing on its extensive resources, the DGB created the structures for a new union organization in the eastern states mirroring its pre-existing western institutions. This organizing effort, which rejected collaboration with the politically compromised East German Free Trade Union Confederation (FDGB), was largely successful. By the end of 1991 union membership in the east reached 4.2 million, and union density levels in the east exceeded union density in the western states (Turner forthcoming).

A large part of this success can be attributed to the transfer of the West German co-determination laws to the eastern states. This provided organized labor with an instant access point at the level of the workplace in the east (Wever 1995). DGB union members were elected to works council positions in large numbers, and many of these worker council representatives became key union activists. With a formal and protected status, new works councilors could effectively negotiate with management, build the union, and legitimate employee representation in eastern firms. This process was facilitated by the terms of the codetermination law, which authorized trade unions to train work councilors and required employers to give elected representatives time off for such training. German unions recognized the potential resource these new works councilors represented and invested heavily in their training.

Nonetheless, the outcomes of this institutional transfer were not guaranteed success. As in other postsocialist economies, a dramatic collapse of the economy was the dominant reality after 1989. Between November 1989 and early 1992, industrial output in Germany dropped to 30% of its former level and three million people lost their jobs (Dornbusch and Wolf 1994). Unofficial unemployment estimates were as high as 40%; many newly unemployed workers blamed the unions for failing to protect their jobs. In some cases works councilors formed alliances with managers against the unions, effectively competing against rival companies and plants faced with similarly daunting economic challenges (Wever 1995). In this context, the "Solidarity Pact" negotiations of 1992 and 1993 among business, labor, and government represented a reasonable extension of the postwar German social contract. In return for employers' promises of increased new investments, the trade unions indicated a willingness to restrain wage demand in both the east and west and agreed to support market-oriented development of the protected industrial core.

Persistent economic decline in 1993, however, prompted some German employers to reassess their position. In a move that threatened the Solidarity Pact and trade union advances in east Germany, the metal industry employers decided unilaterally to abrogate the terms of a previously negotiated three-year contract. Rather than accepting a face-saving compromise, the unions decided to resist the concessions demanded by employers. In the events that were to follow, the returns to the financial and human resources invested into union organization in the eastern states were realized. Employees in the eastern states mobilized in numbers that surprised even their union representatives to protect their earlier negotiated gains (Turner forthcoming).

In 1995 the eastern German landscape remained characterized by a range of labor-management "models." As in the west, differences in the tenor and outcomes of industrial relations could be attributed to industry characteristics, regional influences, union and works councils strategy, and of course, business strategy. However, the extension of the stable industrial relations institutions of the western part of the country to the new eastern states has by most accounts been squarely consolidated (Wever 1995; Turner forthcoming).

The Czech Republic

In contrast to Poland and Germany, Czechoslovakia had neither the tradition of an influential postwar trade union movement nor the institutional structures that might secure labor influence in the economic transformation program. Like the East German FDGB, the official Czechoslovak national trade union confederation, the Revolutionary Trade Union Movement (ROH) did not support the democracy movement. When the executive committee of the ROH refused to endorse the Czech Civic Forum and the Slovak Public Against Violence's call for a general strike on November 27, 1989, there was a mass defection from the ROH. An estimated 6,000 strike committees sprang up throughout the country to support the intellectual and student leaders of the "Velvet Revolution." (Pollert and Hradecka 1994).

Quickly responding to this mass support for the opposition, the ROH condemned the violent suppression of student protests, declared its independence from political parties, expelled a number of Communist hardliners from the ROH leadership, promised secret ballots in future ROH elections, and declared support for a second general strike. This late conversion failed to stem the mass defection from the ROH, and prior to the second strike, an estimated 70% of all union members joined strike committees affiliated with the Czech Association of Strike Committees or its Slovak counterpart, the Coordinating Committees of Working People (Kopanic 1994).

These two organizations subsequently met to form a unified Trade Union Coordinating Center and called on the government to recognize this new confederation as the sole representative of Czech and Slovak workers. The new organization also scheduled an All Union Congress to formalize the structure of the new trade union confederation and to elect a new leadership. Several weeks prior to the general congress, the Slovak ROH dissolved and subordinated itself to the new Trade Union Coordinating Center. The leadership of the Czech section of the ROH, hoping to salvage something from their discredited movement, allowed their organization to be subsumed by the new Czechoslovak Confederation of Trade Unions (CSKOS). This enabled a number of Communist-era officials to continue to retain positions in the new confederation, and in this way the new trade unions in Czechoslovakia arose both from and in opposition to the Communist ROH (Pollert and Hradecka 1994). In contrast to the highly centralized ROH, the CSKOS was organized as a loose confederation of unions. On a formal level, a key feature of union restructuring was the adoption of the ILO principle of pluralism, and in the spirited democratic environment of 1990 there was a proliferation of new unions and new union confederations. As an indication of its new alignment, the CSKOS withdrew from the Communist-dominated World Federation of Trade Unions based in Prague and joined the International Confederation of Free Trade Unions in Brussels. Though distrust of central authority and the subsequent splintering of Czechoslovak confederations somewhat diminished the organizational capacity of CSKOS, the new organization benefited from being able to inherit both the membership and material resources from the ROH.

These organizational changes contributed considerably to building the new labor movement, but at the same time the legacy of Czechoslovak socialism hurt the organizing efforts of the new confederation. The Czechoslovak rejection of socialism was accompanied by a rise of individualism and the rejection of notions such as working class solidarity. As in Poland, the Czechoslovak revolution was dominated economically and politically by neoclassical liberalism and, "the language of 'workers' struggle,' 'participation' and even 'social' (as in 'social dialogue') . . . [was] discredited as part of the ideological jargon of the former regime" (Pollert and Hradecka 1994:55). In this new environment, there was little opposition to the repeal of the 1988 State Enterprise Act which established worker councils in Czechoslovak enterprise. Few outside the leadership of the labor movement argued against the prevailing view that the State Enterprise Act with its participative provisions was a relic of socialism (Thirkell, Scase, and Vickerstaff 1994).

Despite lingering distrust of CSKOS and the general decline in social activism, the Czechoslovak labor movement has managed to institutionalize access to economic policy formation. In October 1990, the tripartite Council for Economic and Social Agreement (CESA) was created to permit labor, management, and government representatives to negotiate the terms of incomes and social welfare policies. This forum, whose work continued separately in the two republics after their division in 1993, has provided labor with continued input on a variety of economic issues. In 1993, 47 laws were negotiated through CESA; 60 laws were negotiated in 1994 (Mansfeldova 1995). Additionally, following tense negotiations and a strike alert in December 1990, Czechoslovak labor unions negotiated favorable changes in proposed labor law legislation. In the final draft of the 1990 law on collective bargaining, Czechoslovak workers were provided the right to self-organization, the right to strike, and the protection from dismissal during strikes.

Though the creation of CESA and the passage of the law on collective bargaining are important gains for labor, there remain substantial limits to the influence of the Czech labor movement. Topics discussed during CESA negotiations, for instance, are limited to a narrow range of issues that directly affect wages and working conditions. Neither Czech trade unions nor rank-and-file employees have demonstrated they have the power that might prompt the market-oriented Czech government to enter into negotiations on this issue (Thirkell, Scase, and Vickerstaff 1994). The weak position of labor and the relative strength of the state has generally meant that Czech privatization has been characterized by the absence of any formal preferences for insiders (Earle, Frydman, and Rapaczynski 1994).

On shopfloor issues as well, the influence of Czech trade unions appears not to be commensurate with either their high membership levels or their access to national labor policy through CESA. Most firms have collective bargaining agreements, but there is considerable individual negotiating over wages between front-line supervisors and employees (Pollert and Hradecka 1994). Moreover, the ease with which worker councils were eliminated demonstrates the ambivalence concerning employee participation in the current political environment. The lack of a strong presence in many enterprises and the absence of a well-articulated shopfloor policy may eventually undermine the limited influence Czech labor has gained on national policy issues.

Conclusion

In Poland the historically important role of labor in the democratization of the country placed Solidarity in the unusual position of being able to shape the institutional environment. However, for reasons that are both specific to the evolution of the Polish opposition and related to the support these policies received from international financial institutions, Solidarity endorsed a neoliberal economic reform strategy. Consistent with this decision, the Solidarity leadership was hesitant to leverage its authority into institutional arrangements that would undermine the state's ability to implement macroeconomic reform or the ability of private capital to introduce firm-level restructuring. Rather, Solidarity relied on informal structures to influence state policy and focused narrowly on issues of economic distribution. In the end, this strategy proved insufficiently robust to sustain either the integration of labor or continued support for the economic reform strategy.

The eastern states in Germany did not have a strong legacy of worker institutions but rather benefited from the transfer of West German codetermination laws, the DGB's decision to organize and integrate east German workers, and the collective action of east German workers. By contrast, workers in the Czech and Slovak Republics had to contend with the legacy of weak organization and a strong state. Given these constraints, one should not expect labor to be a dominant force in the postsocialist period. At the same time, the ability of Czechoslovak labor movements to influence labor law legislation and basic economic and social welfare guarantees illustrates the range of outcomes available within the constraints of national institutional configurations.

Patterns of labor-management relations in postsocialist central Europe will continue to evolve together with the economic and institutional environment in which they exist. Nonetheless, the initial relationships that have been observed are important, because they are likely to anchor future developments and because they provide a window to understand the origins and subsequent evolution of industrial relations patterns. Though these systems are still in an early stage of development, what emerges from these cases is the importance of institutional legacies *and* the choice of strategic actors in determining industrial relations outcomes.

Acknowledgment

I would like to thank Kirsten Wever, Lowell Turner, and Michael Fichter for their comments on an earlier draft of this chapter.

References

Adamski, Pawel et al. 1991. *Polacy '90: Dynamiki Konfliktu I Zmiana*. Warsaw.
Amsden, Alice, Jacek Kochanowicz, and Lance Taylor. 1994. *The Market Meets Its Match: Restructuring the Economies of Eastern Europe*. Cambridge: Harvard University Press.
Balcerowicz, Leszek. 1992. *800 Dni: Szok Kontrolowany*. Warsaw: Polska Oficyna Wydawnicza, BGW.

Barycz, Anna. 1984. "Refleksje nad Liberalizm." *Przeglad Polityczny*, no. 3, pp. 19-23.

Bielecki, Jan Krzysztof. 1992. "Problems of the Polish Transformation." *Communist Economies and Economic Transformation*, Vol. 4, no. 3, pp. 321-31.

_____. 1993. "Najpierw Jedno Ciasteczko, Potem Drugie." In Janina Paradowska and Jerzy Baczynski, eds., *Teczki Liberalów*. Poznan: Obserwator.

Branecki, Jedzej. 1985. "Hayek - Dogmatyk Wolnego Spoleczestwa." *Przeglad Polityczny*, no. 5, pp. 31-55.

Chelminski, Dariusz, Artur Czynczyk, and Stanislaw Sterniczuk. 1993. *Pierwsze Doświadczenia Prywatyzacji*. Warsaw: Centrum Prywatyzacji.

Cui, Zhiyuan. 1992. "Recessionary Bias of Polish Stabilization in 1990: Perspectives from the Economics of Incomplete Markets." In Roland Schonfeld, ed., *Transforming Economic Systems*. Munich: Sudosteuropa Gesellschaft.

Dabrowski, Janusz, Michal Federowicz, and Anthony Levitas. 1991. "Polish State Enterprises and the Properties of Performance: Stabilization, Marketization, Privatization." *Politics and Society*, Vol. 19, no. 4, pp. 403-37.

Dahrendorf, Ralf. 1990. *Reflections on the Revolution in Europe: In a Letter Intended to Have Been Sent to a Gentleman in Warsaw*. New York: Times Books.

Dornbusch, Rudiger, and Holger Wolf. 1994. "East Germany." In Oliver Blanchard, Kenneth Froot, and Jeffrey Sachs, eds., *The Transition in Europe*, Vol. 1. Chicago: University of Chicago Press.

Earle, John, Roman Frydman, and Andrzej Rapaczynski. 1993. "Introduction." In John Earle, Roman Frydman, and Andrzej Rapaczynski, eds., *Privatization in the Transition to a Market Economy*. New York: St. Martins Press.

Engelberg, Stephen. 1990. "Walesa Sets Out on Political War." *New York Times*, May 9, p. 13.

Fichter, Michael. 1994. "Revamping Union Structures: Does Eastern Germany Count?" In Timo Kauppinen and Virpi Koykka, eds., *Transformation of the Industrial Relations in Central and Eastern Europe*, IRRA 4th European Regional Congress (August 24-26). Helsinki, Finland: Finnish Labor Relations Assn.

Flanagan, Robert, David Soskice, and Lloyd Ulman. 1983. *Unionism, Economic Stabilization, and Incomes Policies: European Experience*. Washington, DC: The Brookings Institute.

Gazeta Wyborcza. June 12, 1992. p. 1.

_____. June, 1993, p. 1

Geremek, Bronislaw and Jacek Zakowski. 1990. *Geremek Opowiada, Żakowski Pyta*. Plejada: Warsaw.

Glos Szczecińska. 1991. "Rozmowa z Kuczynskim." *Glos Szczecińska*, March 19, p. 1.

Gomulka, Stanislaw. 1991. "The Causes of Recession Following Stabilization." *Comparative Economic Studies*, Vol. 33, no. 2, pp. 71-89.

GUS, *Rocznik Statystyczny*. 1989. Warsaw: Glowny Urzad Statystyczny.

Johnson, Simon. 1991. "Did Socialism Fail in Poland." *Comparative Economic Studies*, Vol. 33, no. 3, pp. 127-51.

Kisielewski, Stefan. 1985. "O falszywych slowach I falszywych nadziejach." *Aneks*, no. 36.

Kloc, Kazimierz. 1992. "Polish Labor in Transition (1990-1992)." *TELOS*, Vol. 92, pp. 139-48.

Kopanic, Michael Jr. 1994. "Czech and Slovak Federal Republic." In John Campbell, ed., *European Labor Unions*. Westport, CT: Greenwood Press.

Kuczynski, Waldemar. 1992. *Zwierzenia Zausznika*. Polska Oficyna Wydawnicza, BGW: Warsaw.

Lewandowski, Janusz, and Jan Szomburg. 1987. "Uwlaszczeni Wlasnosci Jako Fundament Reformy Gospodarczej." Paper presented at Conference of Transformation Proposals for the Polish Economy, SGPIS, Warsaw.

Lipton, David, and Jeffrey Sachs. 1990. "Creating a Market Economy in Eastern Europe: The Case of Poland." Brookings Papers on Economic Activity, no. 1, pp. 75-133.

Malarecka-Simbierowicz, Hanna, et al. 1990. *Nasi w Sejmie I w Senacie*. Warsaw: Oficyna Wydawnicza.

Mansfeldova, Zdenka. 1995. "Social Partnership in the Czech Republic." Paper presented at the V ICCEES World Congress, Warsaw, August 6, 1995.

NSZZ Solidarnosc. 1987. "NSZZ Solidarnosc o Gospodarce," *Kontakt*, nos. 63-64, pp. 57-8.

_____. 1990. *Documents of the Second Congress*. Belgium: Coordinating Office Abroad of NSZZ Solidarnosc.

OECD. 1992. *Industry in Policy: Structural Adjustment Issues and Policy Options*. Paris: OECD.

Ost, David. 1991. *Solidarity and the Politics of Anti-Politics*. Philadelphia: Temple University Press.

PAP. 1989. "Round Table Dispute over Wage Indexation," March 31.

Pizzorno, Alessandro. 1978. "Political Exchange and Collective Identity in Industrial Conflict." In Colin Couch and Allessandro Pizzorno, eds., *The Resurgence of Class Conflict in Western Europe since 1968*, London: Macmillan.

Pollert, Anna, and Irena Hradecka. 1994. "Privatisation in Transition: The Czech Experience." *Industrial Relations Journal*, Vol. 25, no. 1, pp. 52-63.

Pysz, Peter. 1987. "The Polish Economic Reform: Central Planning or Socialist Markets." In Peter Gey, Jiri Kosta, and Wolfgang Quaisser, eds., *Crisis and Reform in Socialist Economies*. Boulder, CO: Westview Press.

Radziukiewicz, Malgorzata. 1992. *Rozklady Dochodów i Struktura Spoleczno Demograficzna w Grupach Decylowych w Latach 1989-1990*. Warsaw: Glowny Urzad Statystyczny.

Regini, Marino. 1984. "The Conditions for Political Exchange: How Concertation Emerged and Collapsed in Italy and Great Britain." In John Goldthorpe, ed., *Order and Conflict in Contemporary Capitalism: Studies in the Political Economy of Western European Nations*. Oxford: Clarendon Press.

Sachs, Jeffrey. 1993. *Poland's Jump to a Market Economy*. Cambridge: MIT Press.

Simon, Maurice, and Roger Kanet, eds. 1981. *Background to Crisis: Policy and Politics in Gierek's Poland*. Boulder, CO: Westview Press.

Slay, Ben. 1994. *The Polish Economy: Crisis, Reform, and Transformations*, Princeton, NJ: Princeton University Press.

Smolenski, Pawel, and Wojciech Gielzynski. 1989. *A na Hucie Strajk/Gdansk, May '88*, London: Aneks Publishers.

Staniszkis, Jadwiga. 1987. "For a Theory of Socialism." *Labour Focus on Eastern Europe*, Vol. 9, no. 2, pp. 17-21.

Stoltenberg, Stephen. 1992. *An Underground Society: The Evolution of Poland's Solidarity, 1982-1989.* Unpublished Ph.D. Dissertation, University of California, Berkeley.

Streeck, Wolfgang. 1984. "Neo-Corporatist Industrial Relations and the Economic Crisis in West Germany." In John Goldthorpe, ed., *Order and Conflict in Contemporary Capitalism: Studies in the Political Economy of Western European Nations.* Oxford: Clarendon Press.

Strzelecki, Jerzy. 1984. "Teoria Praw Wlasnosci: Geneza, Podstawowe Pojęcia I Twierdzenia; Uwagi o Zastosownaiu do Analizy Gospodarki Socjalistycznej." Paper presented at Systems of Property Conference, SGPIS, Warsaw.

_____. 1985. "Wizja Fryderyka von Hayeka." *Przeglad Polityczny,* no. 5, pp. 56-8.

Szczesna, Joanna, and Seweryn Blumsztajn. 1988. "Que Reste-t-il de Solidarite? Enquete de la Nouvelle Alternative Survey en Pologne." *Nouvelle Alternative,* Winter, pp. 3-45.

Tagliabue, John. 1989. "To Buoy Premier, Solidarity Urges a Halt to Strikes." *New York Times,* August 21, p. 1.

Thirkell, John, Richard Scase, and Sarah Vickerstaff. 1994. "Labor Relations in Transition in Eastern Europe." *Industrial Relations Journal,* Vol. 25, no. 2, pp. 84-95.

Touraine, Alain et al. 1983. *Solidarity: The Analysis of a Social Movement: Poland 1980-81.* Cambridge: Cambridge University Press.

Turner, Lowell. Forthcoming. *Social Partnership in a Global Economy: Crisis and Reform in Unified Germany.* Book manuscript.

Tusk, Donald. 1993. "Krzyczelismy, Zeby Robic To Szybciej." In Janina Paradowska and Jerzy Baczynski, eds., *Teczki Liberalow.* Poznan: Observator.

Tygodnik Solidarność. 1981a. "Founding Principles." Trans. in Peter Raina 1985. *Poland 1981: Towards Social Renewal.* London: George Allen & Unwin.

_____. 1981b. Resolutions from the First Solidarity Congress. Trans. in Peter Raina. 1985. *Poland 1981: Towards Social Renewal.* London: George Allen & Unwin.

Wujec, Henryk. 1984. Rozmowa. *Tygodnik Mazowsze,* no. 102.

Walicki, Andrzej. 1984. "Mysli o sytuacji politycznej I moralno-psychologicznej w Polsce." *Aneks,* no. 30.

Weinstein, Mark. 1994. "Restructuring Interests in Post-Socialist Poland: The Power of Ideas in Macro and Micro Institutional Transformation." Paper presented at the American Association for Advancement of Slavic Studies, Philadelphia, PA (November).

Wever, Kirsten. 1995. *Negotiating Competitiveness: Employment Relations and Organizational Innovation in Germany and the United States.* Boston, MA: Harvard Business School Press.

Wierzbicki, Piotr. 1985. *Mysli Staroświeckiego Polaka.* London: Puls Publications.

Zubek, Vojtek. 1992. "The Rise and Fall of Rule by Poland's Best and Brightest." *Soviet Studies,* Vol. 44, no. 4, pp. 579-608.

Zycie Warszawy. 1991. Conference of *Komisja Krajowa* Solidarity. Trans. in Polish News Bulletin, May 9.

CONCLUSION

Markets, Strategies, and Institutions in Comparative Perspective

KIRSTEN S. WEVER
Radcliffe Public Policy Institute

If this had been another collection of country case studies, it would now be possible to map out the similarities and differences across the cases covered, possibly in a figure describing various IR-related issues by country. However, since this is a collection of different kinds of analyses with a variety of different focuses, the job of concluding this volume is not so simple. Nevertheless, in the very variety offered by the chapters in this volume, several themes emerge, most of which are at least implicitly, if not explicitly, clarified in the five substantive chapters. The chapters point up the need to analyze industrial relations developments in the context of a changing global economy—especially the context of the broader "competitiveness" pressures and debates that have taken center stage on national political and economic agendas. They illustrate the simultaneous pressures for decentralization and a realignment of the division of labor between central and local decision making and activities. They draw our attention to the continuing importance of existing institutions in shaping industrial relations outcomes *and* the increasingly important role also of actor strategies in shaping outcomes and influencing how institutions are used. Finally, the chapters underline the importance of including labor as a major negotiating partner if the benefits of economic growth and competitiveness are to be widely diffused across different socioeconomic groups and strata, *as well as* the continuing viability of a model of industrial competitiveness that excludes collective labor influence, whose benefits accrue to isolated segments of society and economy—not just in the developing world but in advanced industrial countries as well.

The first part of this concluding chapter will elaborate those themes, recalling the chapters as appropriate. The second part sketches out the implications of the six themes for how we think about industrial relations and for how the actors involved—and particularly organized, independent representatives of workers—develop and implement their strategies and policies. Three main conclusions follow. First, in order for the benefits of a competitive economy to be widely diffused, industrial relations and competitiveness issues must be consciously and substantively linked, strategically and institutionally, as well as vertically (across levels of analysis) and horizontally (across political and economic issue areas). Second, a strong labor movement by itself is not sufficient to ensure that such linkages be made—labor strength must be paralleled by particular kinds of labor strategies and politics. Third, organized labor is not necessarily involved at all in developing and implementing these linkages and, in the absence of appropriate strategies and institutions, may well be marginalized in the contemporary global economy.

In view of these conclusions, the only hope for labor—and ultimately for a model of competitiveness whose benefits are widely diffused throughout economy and society—is to develop strategies that insert labor interests and functions into these linkages and make the most of the institutional possibilities available in a given setting.

Six Themes

The chapters in this volume use a variety of approaches to the comparative subject matter. These differences in approach entail a focus on different independent and dependent variables and thus different outcomes. Richard Locke, in his broad sweep comparison of eleven OECD member countries, examines a balance of industrial relations, political-economic and human resources issues. The outcomes he focuses on are common patterns in employment practices, as well as marked differences with respect to the diffusion of employment relations innovations, employment security, and wage differentials—all of which are shaped by both institutions and actor strategies. Margaret Gardner's focus is narrower, concerning labor movement structures and strategies and the implications for labor's strength and adaptiveness. The chapter by John Paul MacDuffie has a dual focus on international management and HR practices, on the one hand, and plant- and company-level practices, on the other. The outcomes of interest to him have to do with the ways in which commonly adopted forms of work and production organization are implemented differently in different firms. Sarosh Kuruvilla, in his chapter on the Philippines and Malaysia, looks at the relationship between industrialization strategy (in the realm of political economy) and industrial relations, as well as the ways in which both sets of variables shape workplace HR practices. In the last substantive chapter Marc Weinstein provides a historical analysis of the strategic shifts in Solidarity and is concerned with the effects of these on the overall weakening of the labor movement in Poland.

Notwithstanding the manifest differences in approach and focus, taken together, these chapters suggest a series of interconnected propositions about the role of industrial relations in the broader political economy, the changing locus of the main "action" in industrial relations, and the influence of institutions and actor strategies on outcomes.

The Competitiveness Context

First, each of these chapters illustrates in one way or another the need to understand industrial and employment relations both as they influence firm, industry, and national competitiveness and as they are influenced by the specific competitiveness issues that are particularly salient in a given setting. In this sense, industrial relations must be analyzed in terms of political as well as economic "competitiveness context."

For example, as Kuruvilla shows, in Malaysia and the Philippines the link between industrial relations and competitiveness is straightforward and direct. The perceived needs of competitiveness (as achieved by particular industrialization strategies) more or less dictate the form and content of industrial relations. The two variables stand in simple causal relationship to each other. Workplace practices emerge as a function of both. Yet even in places like Australia and Germany, where labor movements exist as independent political and economic forces possessing widespread social legitimacy, labor increasingly needs to defend its actions in economic terms, even while continuing to tend to its political representative functions. Thus in Australia the ACTU's reconstruction strategy links increases in workplace flexibility (for management) with wage increases (for labor) and tries to achieve professionalized career paths (for labor) by relaxing job demarcations and broadening skills training (for management). In Germany the IG Metall's efforts to promote "group work" and to shorten the work week are aimed at providing employment stability (for labor) as well as increases in the flexibility of work practices (for management).

These chapters also make clear that companies, industries, and possibly even nations can be highly competitive without having especially democratic industrial relations or strategically influential labor movements. It is true that the competitiveness of German industry owes much to Germany's industrial relations system (Wever 1995; Turner 1991). However, numerous economies characterized by far less industrial democracy—the U.S., for instance—are also quite competitive by international economic standards. What is clear—and evident from both the German and American cases, as well as the others considered in this volume—is that there is little hope in the long term for an industrial relations system that cannot be made to fit a society's understanding (or at least that of policy makers) of what is competitive. This fit may entail extensive democratically institutionalized labor participation or a near total deregulation of labor standards and labor markets.

The Shifting Local/Central Division of Labor

The second theme that emerges from these chapters is that everywhere tendencies toward decentralization and deregulation coincide with the enduring role of certain centralized and centralizing functions and institutions. What emerges as especially important is not the degree to which a given setting is characterized by decentralization or centralization but rather the relationship between what happens at each of these levels. In other words, the focus needs to be on the division of labor, so to speak, between local and central actors, organizations, and institutions.

Thus, for example, Gardner points out the success of the Australian labor movement in promoting a shift to local flexibility but also the paradoxical weakening effect on the ACTU's ability to maintain central control over local policies and practices. Locke elaborates the increasingly important role of local institutions and strategies in shaping industrial relations outcomes at the local level but also shows the continuing at least potential importance of central institutions in mediating between pressures for cost-based and value-added approaches to competitiveness. In his analysis Weinstein links Solidarity's demise to its apparent near-abandonment of influence at the local level (e.g., workers councils), which then inevitably involved a loss of both political and economic influence in central forums as well. MacDuffie illustrates a measure of international convergence with regard to the implementation of lean production. Yet his chapter also demonstrates that company-based decisions about how new practices are implemented remain critically important in determining shopfloor outcomes.

The Continuing Importance of Institutions

The third theme is that the extent and nature of variations in outcome within a given country are influenced strongly by the nature of its
institutions. Among other things, some kinds of institutional structures
promote the diffusion of competitive practices, while others appear
actively to impede such diffusion.

Gardner illustrates, by virtue of the comparison between the U.S.
and Australian labor movements, how the relative paucity of centralizing
institutions in the U.S. is an important factor underlying the uneven
development of industrial relations and employment relations innovations. The importance of existing institutions and practices for diffusing
employment relations innovation is one of Locke's main conclusions.
Kuruvilla shows how in Malaysia centralized government efforts and
collaborative employer strategies to develop training resources are necessary to the improvement of local productivity. Weinstein illustrates
how centralizing institutions help account for the even diffusion of stable industrial relations practices in the eastern part of the new Germany,
while their absence helps explain very different outcomes in Poland.

The Relationship between Institutions and Actor Strategies

At the same time, actor strategies remain vitally important to shaping, if not determining, outcomes. The relationship between institutions
and strategies remains different in different settings but appears to be
changing in all settings. Thus the fourth theme is that this relationship
deserves to be at the center of industrial relations analyses.

In the Polish case it appears that the strategy of one of the main
actors—Solidarity—contributed to the reshaping of the institutions of
industrial relations in a way that ultimately weakened the union's overall
political and economic influence. In this case labor was powerful enough
to exert great influence on institutional outcomes, with the ironic result
that it thereby seems to have undermined its ability to continue to play
precisely this role. A very different case is that of New Zealand, where,
as Gardner illustrates, dramatic labor market deregulation likewise
undermined the influence of the labor movement at all levels—in this
case over the objections of labor. MacDuffie's cross-regional analysis
points to the continuing importance of company strategy—to some
extent independent of macro-level institutions (measured here by region
rather than by country)—in determining the shape of "lean production"
in a given setting and subsequent effects at the workplace. In all of these

cases there is no particular reason to believe that a given relationship between strategy and institutions is in any way frozen or static. Nor is there any reason to believe that one or the other is necessarily more important: Far from competing in a zero-sum game, particular institutions and actor strategies may either reinforce or undermine each other.

Diffused Competitiveness Requires Labor Involvement

With regard to the interrelations between structures and strategies, the fifth theme is more specific. In cases where the benefits of competitive firms and industries diffuse to be enjoyed by a broad-based spectrum of social actors and groups, labor is invariably included as an important negotiating partner in political-economic and industrial relations decision making above the micro (firm, plant, or workplace) level. Where labor is not an important actor in these dynamics, we find pockets of competitiveness coexisting alongside significantly less developed segments of the political economy.

For instance, income disparities in the U.S., where labor does not play a major role above the micro level, are extremely high by international standards. In Germany, where labor is one of the two main "social partners," income polarization is much lower. Similarly, Malaysia and the Philippines show distinctly higher levels of poverty and lower levels of wage increases in recent years than Singapore, where labor's role is somewhat greater. Institutions channel negotiations, and strategies (in this instance, labor strategies) give them meaningful content.

Segmented Competitiveness Is an Equally Likely Outcome

However, and this is the sixth theme, competitiveness with widely diffused benefits is not the only alternative. Many unevenly developed political economies with pockets of underdevelopment and low wages as well as high levels of income inequality seem quite stable, at least in the medium term.

Thus the development of the Polish economy proceeds apace at a rate roughly comparable to that of neighboring former east-bloc countries, notwithstanding the dramatic weakening of Solidarity and the increasing dominance of the Anglo-American free market model. Neither does the U.S. appear to be on the brink of any great socializing legislation. On the contrary, the contemporary political climate suggests precisely the opposite: a trend toward further shrinking of the federal government, cutting of social services and entitlements, and deregulation.

These developments occur in the face of frequent and dramatic signs of social tensions that twenty years ago would have indicated a need for more, not less, social democracy. In short, the requirements of competitiveness appear to be compatible both with labor-excluded and labor-included models of industrial growth and adjustment.

Implications for Labor and Industrial Relations

Three general conclusions are suggested. One concerns the importance of vertical and horizontal policy linkage. The second is the fact that union strength and adept labor strategy are not sufficient to ensure such linkages. And the third is the fact that this linkage can apparently be achieved without any labor involvement at all. These conclusions point to a familiar but increasingly urgent policy direction for labor which is briefly laid out at the end of this chapter.

First, key actors in advanced and developing countries alike are linking industrial relations structures and strategies into broader economic and social policies, as well as establishing linkages across the different levels (micro, meso, macro) at which production and industrial relations take place. These kinds of linkage are particularly evident in cases where the benefits of economic growth and competitiveness are widely diffused throughout the political economy.

For example, the horizontal and vertical linkages pursued by business and government in Malaysia appear to be significantly more developed than in the Philippines, while Singapore looks more "linked" again than Malaysia. In Singapore connections between labor issues, training and education, social policy, and economic development, from the micro to the macro level, appear to be conscious matters of policy; in Malaysia and particularly the Philippines these linkages are fewer and appear more reactive than strategic. Singapore's economy is somewhat more highly developed, with lower levels of income inequality and poverty than in Malaysia or the Philippines.

Consider also the contrast between Australia and the United States. In Australia the ACTU's "Australia Reconstructed" platform explicitly addressed the need to pursue a central strategic reorientation of labor's main goals. In tandem with this, however, the labor movement initiated significant measures for flexibilizing its role at the local level. Measures were promoted to broaden skills and encourage the development and professionalization of internal labor markets. Structural changes made it possible for local unions to engage in ongoing negotiations with employers about issues that have historically fallen in the centralized domain.

In short, the ACTU's strategy consciously linked the functions and strategies of labor vertically across levels. Horizontal linkage was also a central piece of the ACTU's strategy. The clearest example is the acknowledgement of the need to tie central wage determination mechanisms to measures of workplace flexibility. In other words, the economics of industrial relations were linked directly to the politics of work. These linking strategies appear to be at least in part responsible for the relatively wide diffusion of workplace innovations referred to by Gardner in her comparative analysis of Australia, New Zealand, and the United States.

Gardner notes that the diffusion of workplace innovations in the United States appears to be considerably more spotty than in Australia (though differences in measurement techniques applied in the two countries makes comparison difficult). There has indeed been a very uneven diffusion of employment relations innovations in the United States, with continuing high levels of income inequality and poverty and large regional pockets of relative underdevelopment. The competitiveness of the U.S. economy—undisputable in international perspective—benefits certain socioeconomic segments significantly, while leaving others untouched (or worse off than they would otherwise be).

Moreover, there is a connection between this lack of diffusion in the U.S., on the one hand, and the relatively fragmented and decentralized nature of American worker representation, on the other. There is no equivalent to the powerful and strategically adept ACTU in the United States. Union rivalries in the U.S. are far more widespread and politically damaging than in Australia. Local unions continue to guard jealously their prerogatives with regard to reaching (or rejecting) agreements with local managers about workplace reorganization. The lack of political power at the national level makes it difficult for labor to draw the horizontal (political-economic) policy links the ACTU was able to draw as part of its reconstruction strategy.

The second general conclusion is that labor's strength and adept strategy are not sufficient to ensure these kinds of linkages. In Poland, where Solidarity was both unusually powerful and possessed impressive strategic capacities, labor has increasingly backed away from involvement in most of the forums in which it once seemed poised to play important roles. To the extent that Solidarity is still involved, its involvement is—at least relative to the circumstances of 1990—unlinked across levels or across issues. Once active in debates about national economic strategy and in workplace restructuring initiatives, Solidarity's influence is weak in both areas today, while its roles in these two arenas do not appear to be consciously linked. The contrast to developments in eastern Germany is instructive. Here, due to the important role of the western unions and to employers' familiarity with the advantages of the "negotiated" model of competitiveness, things look quite different. While in the new eastern German states labor is still less powerful and influential than in the western part of the country, its role is unmistakable and clearly embedded in the competitiveness of the eastern economy. Unions and works councils (often in collaboration with local and regional governments and businesses but also often quite on their own or in opposition) have developed strategies linking everything from job definitions and training mechanisms to local and regional economic development projects, retraining companies, and social and educational policies (see Wever 1995; Turner 1995; and Knuth 1995).

The contrast between eastern Germany and Poland is striking. Yet labor's relative success in eastern Germany and its relative decline in Poland can hardly be attributed to differences in union power or strategic aptitudes. While these variables are important, they do not appear to be determinant in regard to the dynamic of linkages. Rather, for these cases, contrasting institutional frameworks and union/employer decisions appear decisive.

Thirdly, labor is not necessarily involved at all as a unified actor at the intersection of employment relations and industrial growth and adjustment. It seems plausible, and certainly it would be nice if, over the long run, successful vertical and horizontal policy linkage required the incorporation of labor's interests. Certainly no other institution can articulate workers' employment relations needs and interests as effectively as good independent worker representation. In the short term, however, it is clear that economic growth and competitiveness are quite possible without such representation.

The fact that linked policies supporting significant economic growth and development do not require any significant labor involvement is illustrated by the cases of Malaysia and the Philippines. In Malaysia political circumstances have made possible a shift to second-phase export-oriented growth. This, in turn, has necessitated increasing linkages across levels (e.g., to develop training programs that can provide the workforce necessary for competitive successes) and across political and economic domains (for instance, linking industrial policies with education policies). In the Philippine economy this transition has been slower in coming, and there continues to be less linkage of both sorts, as well as a less competitive and more unevenly developed economy. The difference is most obvious in the area of training, which is considerably less developed than in Malaysia. But in both countries the repression of labor is striking, although in the Philippines it appears to be even greater by several measures than in Malaysia. The prevalence in Southeast Asia (as, indeed, elsewhere in the world) of management-dominated unions, the fragmented nature of the union movements, and the continued illegality of strikes in most core industries serve as reminders that powerful and independent worker representation does not inevitably accompany economic growth and competitiveness.

It seems likely that we will see an eventual shift in policies to accommodate or at least quiet the large population of poor and un- or underemployed who continue to be excluded from the benefits of growth. Those countries in Southeast Asia that have moved on to more advanced stages of development have all done so with some improvement in labor standards and loosening of restrictions on unions. But there is no reason to believe that a country could not go on for a long time—as the U.S. is apparently doing—faring quite well economically (albeit with pockets of extreme underdevelopment as well as widespread and growing income polarization) without a strong labor movement.

Conclusion

Worker representative organizations, institutions, and movements must find ways to insinuate themselves into the vertical and horizontal linkages between policies and negotiations—to perform linking functions that make organized labor useful, if not necessary, to business and government decision makers interested primarily in economic growth. The shape of labor's linking strategy in practice will vary significantly across settings. Politics and circumstances may require of labor only that it play a significant role in one of these linking functions in order to create enough leverage to diffuse the benefits of growth and competitiveness. However, in some cases much more will be needed.

Oddly enough, although the approach to comparative industrial relations implied by this analysis is new, these policy implications are not. The kinds of linking functions that labor has played in a variety of countries in the past illustrate the kinds of strategies called for today. For several postwar decades, the German works councils' value to management had mostly (though not exclusively) to do with their taking over and standardizing basic human resource management functions and quieting discontented workers. The German unions' contribution to the interests of German capital had a great deal to do with forcing employers to centralize collective bargaining, thus taking labor costs out of competition among employers, pushing companies to develop non-cost-based competitive advantages in international markets (Streeck 1992).

A central American union role in the New Deal system of industrial relations was to regulate the shopfloor, thus—in ways quite similar to the roles played by works councils in Germany—leaving management free to focus on other, more strategic and directly production-oriented matters (Katz 1985). Australian unions have maintained relevance and organizational integrity in a difficult period of industrial restructuring by actively promoting decentralized workplace flexibility from central union headquarters.

The idea that organized labor needs to perform a useful socioeconomic function—beyond the politically desirable function of representing the workplace interests of employees—is also old. What has been less apparent in the past is exactly where organized labor must seek its new roles. As noted above, the increasing diversity of local IR politics and outcomes means there can be no simple strategic formula equally applicable across the board. But the chapters in this volume lend enough further evidence to what we know about comparative industrial relations and political economy to narrow the locus of effective labor movement strategy to the points of linkage that are, first, most important to the functioning of the political economy and, second, most accessible to labor's influence. What labor needs is complementary and mutually reinforcing influence at national and local levels.

What can be done in a given setting will be shaped by labor's organizational and political power and influenced by institutional possibilities and constraints. But not to try to do something along these lines is to conspire in the continuing weakening of labor representation and workplace democracy in supposedly democratic societies.

References

Katz, Harry. 1985. *Shifting Gears Changing Labor Relations in the U.S. Automobile Industry*, Cambridge: MIT Press.

Knuth, Matthias. 1995. "Active Labor Market Policy as Currency for Negotiating Dramatic Change: The Role of Employment and Training Companies in the Process of Outplacement from Treuhand Establishments." In Lowell Turner, ed., *The Political Economy of Germany: Reform and Resurgence or Another Model in Decline?* Manuscript in progress.